"*[Frederick Turner] is an anomaly in the literary world, an elegant writer whose range is so immense that critics cannot pigeonhole him. Indeed, his interests span America, which he never tires of exploring. Jazz and baseball, wild mustangs and planned communities, John Muir and Leslie Marmon Silko—he writes about a bewildering variety of subjects, all with a grace and depth rare in contemporary American letters.*"

—*Christopher Merrill,* El Palacio

"*There are people around—Evan Connell, John McPhee, Peter Matthiessen—who can pick up just about any subject, give it some reflection, and there-upon crank out a dazzling and novel essay, opening whole new avenues to explore. They fascinate me, these Original Thinkers, and it is always a treat to discover another of the band. Frederick Turner's* Of Chiles, Cacti, and Fighting Cocks ... *ranges all over the American West, from Native Americans to saguaros to the Basques to Billy the Kid to cowboys. Each essay is well turned and basted with Turner's elegant prose.*"

—American Geographical Society

"*A **thoughtful** montage of western experience. This book is a lesson in consciousness.*"

—Outside Magazine

# of chiles, cacti, and fighting cocks

notes on the AMERICAN west

Frederick Turner

of chiles, cacti, and fighting cocks

notes on the AMERICAN west

Third Edition

Frederick Turner

Fulcrum Publishing
Golden, Colorado

Library of Congress Cataloging-in-Publication Data
Turner, Frederick W., 1937-
 Of chiles, cacti, and fighting cocks : notes on the American West / Frederick Turner.— 3rd ed.
     p. cm.
 ISBN 1-55591-486-1 (pbk. : alk. paper)
 1. Indians of North America—West (U.S.)—History. 2. Legends—West (U.S.) 3. West (U.S.)—History. 4. West (U.S.)—Description and travel. I. Title.
 F591.T934 2004
 978—dc22

                                              2004012368

ISBN 1-55591-486-1

Printed in the United States of America
0 9 8 7 6 5 4 3 2 1

Design: Jack Lenzo
Cover image: © Wendy Shattil and Bob Rozinski

Fulcrum Publishing
16100 Table Mountain Parkway, Suite 300
Golden, Colorado 80403
(800) 992-2908 • (303) 277-1623
www.fulcrum-books.com

For Alexandra, Jessica,
Charles, Lauren, and Aaron

Contents

Introduction

In Tucson, years ago, I was at a dinner party with Dave Foreman, of
Earth First! fame. Dave was a full-blown radical activist and a genuine
hero or anti-hero of the environmental movement, depending on your
point of view. Real act-it-out radicals make me uneasy. They take risks,
and they're impatient. Maybe it's a schoolyard thing—maybe I think
they're tougher than I am. Maybe I'm right.

So I was uneasy with Dave Foreman. But soon we were talking
about a book called *Beyond Geography*, by a man named Frederick
Turner. It was a secret, sacred text that had turned each of our heads
a decade before, when we were each doing a lot of reading, trying to
understand reasons behind the transformations taking place out in our
American West, our mutual homeland.

Beyond Geography is among other things a look at the ways cultures
have cut themselves off from nature; over the last ten thousand years
we've come to treat nature as fundamentally other than ourselves,
another kind of thing, to be used, manipulated, and even exploited,
without moral qualms. This is a disastrous idea—nature lives everywhere inside us, under our skins, in our blood and in our brains.
Destroying nature, we destroy ourselves.

The health of natural processes is thus always of moral concern.
Despite that fact, the notion that nature exists in order to be heedlessly
used by humans is central in the story the most powerful of world cultures use to define themselves and the ways they act out their ambitions.

These notions have been widely discussed in recent years, in part
because of *Beyond Geography*. But they weren't much in the air during
the early 1980s. This man, Frederick Turner, and this book, helped me
define my thinking, and, thus, myself.

Dave Foreman and I talked about what a thing it would be to have
written a book like that. We wished Fred Turner was with us, so we
could pour him a drink. Later on I though our emotions were like those
of Holden Caulfield in *The Catcher in the Rye* as he dreams about reading

a terrific book and being able to call the writer on the telephone and talk about the book. I wanted to be able to talk to this fellow Frederick Turner.

Fortunately, just in time to feed my hunger, Turner had been traveling around the West, then going home to Santa Fe and writing a set of essays about what he found. We have them here, in *Of Chiles, Cacti, and Fighting Cocks: Notes on the American West*, first published in 1990 and reissued with three new essays in this third edition. He wrote about the attraction of the West to anyone who lived in the other America where he grew up, the East. "Western heroes, and even outlaws, seemed manly, robust, in touch with the great outdoors. And this was a world that we ignorantly aspired to, a world of sun, space, wind."

"The old, compelling images of horse, horseman, cattle, guns, and unimproved space still exert a power that can be startling to one who comes to the region from outside." The West, Fred Turner writes, is for outsiders "truly a country of the mind."

The West is these days mostly filled to overflowing. But it's still seen as a vast emptiness, a dreamland for the taking, and as such draws stockbrokers from Chicago who practice their trade by wireless means and then go out fly-fishing. It draws the disenfranchised from Poland and Mexico and Laos, from countries all around the world, individuals and populations inspired by visions of freedom and economic opportunity. The open lands, even as they continue to be logged and mined and grazed unto death, still symbolize possibilities of a kind that don't much exist elsewhere these days.

What was the West really, when it wasn't all dressed up in costumes from a mythic past? Turner tells us of Clark Gable, in *The Misfits* (1961), chasing free-range mustangs. Turner says "What once seemed an innocent, if mortal, way to make a buck has now been transmogrified into a vicious and inhumane business in which the cowboy is a kind of ignorant serf to the faceless men from the city."

"Now in this fading desert half-light the gathered weight of four centuries of New World history had come to rest on his shoulders: everything's changed. 'It's like roping a dream now,' he says." (Gable died in Reno, of a worn-out heart, shortly after delivering that line.)

I grew up in those times, in a horseback world with men who ran down mustangs and sold them to be slaughtered for chicken feed. Rangeland freedoms died as they went about that work.

How did the processes turn? Fred Turner gets down to details and cases. He fits Billy the Kid, saguaro cactus and Basques, cockfighting and Custer, and cooking with hot chiles into a story of Western happenstance and consequence that helps us understand who Westerners have been and might become in an ever more overpopulated and commoditized world community.

Over recent decades the West had undergone a reevaluation of traditions and thinking. An iconoclastic school of "new" Western historians has evolved. Dozens of first-rate essayists, poets, and fiction writers, now into the second generation, have emerged, among them Hispanics, Native Americans, and Asians, cowhands, and even a one-time college professor who grew up in Chicago, this fellow Frederick Turner. All his work, certainly these notes on the American West, in *Of Chiles, Cacti, and Fighting Cocks*, has been a profoundly useful part of that reevaluation. Better yet, Fred Turner's books are a pleasure to sit down with. I lost myself in this one again, third time through, all night long.

William Kittredge
Author of *Owning It All* and *Hole in the Sky*

Encountering a Real West

Growing up east of the Mississippi in the years before Sputnik, we had the West all around us. I don't mean the physical, corporeal West, nor do I even mean the "historical West," if by that we understand the West of brute fact. I mean the West of the imagination. The earliest popular songs I can remember were those about the West. My older brother and I sang along to "Don't Fence Me In" and shared its yearning sentiment, though our landscape was that of the crisscrossing wires, tall buildings, and rectilinear boundaries of south Chicago. Where we lived there was nothing *but* fences: even the tiniest lawns had their ankle-high hoops of wire warning you and your dog to keep off. No matter. If anything, these realities made the sentiment and the locale of that song all the more appealing. We sang, too, "Pistol Packin' Mama," and while I don't recall that the locale of that piece-packing woman was ever specified, it sounded as if it came out of Texas—for us, the quintessential Western state. When we sang, "The stars at night / Are big and bright," then supplied the four quick, Spanish-tinged handclaps that preceded "Deep in the heart of Texas," we saw an immense sky, a cowboy on his horse, a tall cactus with candelabra arms.

These songs came to us over the airways. So did the thrice-weekly adventures of Tom Mix and his wonder horse, Tony. Before we could hear the thrilling sounds of the *William Tell Overture* announcing the Lone Ranger, we had to endure market reports on soy beans and hogs, and while these were mundane intrusions into an imagined world that could have no truck with such earthy items, at the same time they transported us some ways toward sun-soaked plains and six-guns. When the Lone Ranger came on we were ready. We followed his exploits in comic books as well; also those of Roy Rogers and Gene Autry, whose horse, Champion, had miniature pistols adorning his bit. The first movie I ever saw was *Desperadoes*, a Technicolor Western my grandfather took me to, and I can still visualize man's head being smashed through the parti-colored glass of a saloon window. For years my idea of the sublime

1

was not that of Longinus: it was instead a darkened movie house, and on its screen the sun glancing off the bluing of a horseman's rifle barrel. Saturday afternoons we often broke off our neighborhood games of outlaws and sheriffs to go to the movies, where we saw serials featuring Gene, Roy, and Johnny Mack Brown. Sundays, my brother and I raced downstairs to look at Fred Harmon's Red Ryder strip in the *Sun Times*.

To be sure, there were competing images. Back in the first part of the 1940s there were our fighting men, and we were hardly immune to the daily accounts of their heroism. Once, under their spell, we decided we'd get G.I. haircuts. But soon at night we listened to more than our radio programs: we listened for the sound of our hair growing, because we had discovered that what was sauce for one sort of game was grit for another. Cowpunchers and lawmen, we knew well, didn't have G.I. cuts. Navy Don Winslow in the Sunday funnies was not, finally, as compelling as Red Ryder, nor was the heroism of Private Roger Young quite equal to one good man and his horse against the evil that stalked a dusty Western town.

Farther out in the imaginative landscape were hermaphroditic figures like the Phantom, the Shadow, the Green Hornet, Batman, Superman, and the Vigilante, and while these heroes were by no means inconsequential, you could hardly feel a deep identification with them or their landscapes. Their very mystiques were for us their failings. They intrigued but did not compel any lasting allegiance.

Hard-boiled private eyes offered some competition, too, and every boy in our neighborhood could have told you what had happened in the latest radio episodes of Boston Blackie, the Fat Man, the Thin Man, and Bulldog Drummond. But it was considerably harder to impersonate these natty, wise-cracking guys in their snap-brim hats than simply to don our gunbelts and become backyard centaurs, closing the eye of the mind to the urban realities amid which we galloped.

The other side of the dicks were the gangsters, a very real part of our Chicago landscape, and while we hardly dared impersonate Capone, Dillinger, and Bugs Moran in our games, still they had a certain sinister weight to which we were helplessly drawn. In the Western movies of that time the heroes were the guys in the white hats. Not in Chicago. There the bad guys wore the white hats and white-on-white ties, and their style—if not too closely examined—had its attractions. I would like to be able to write that we were finally unable to play much at gangsters because we were morally repulsed by what gangsters actually did, but in view of the fact that a fair number of my childhood play-mates went on to become hoods, if not quite gangsters, this probably wasn't the root reason. It was simply the fact that gangsters seemed unhealthy (Capone, after all, died of syphilis—how much more unhealthy could you get?), whereas Western heroes, and even outlaws, seemed manly, robust, in touch with the great outdoors. And it was this great world that we ignorantly aspired to, a world of sun, space, wind.

In those days Western Avenue in Chicago still pretty much meant what its name said: it was the city's western boundary. Beyond in unin-corporated territory the houses were fewer, the spaces and sky wider, and ten blocks out you saw cows, pastures, and fencing. On holidays, searching for a West within reach, we rode our bikes out there, maybe a half-dozen of us, each armed with a Red Ryder Daisy air rifle to shoot at almost everything: billboards, fence posts, the green glass conductors of power lines, even each other. In our Earp/Clanton shoot-outs, the rule of safety was that you couldn't aim above the belt, but in the heat of bat-tle the rule was occasionally violated, and I bear a scar below the corner of one eye that is the badge of one such engagement.

So things might have gone on for my brother and me, with the West a gradually fading phenomenon as we moved gingerly into the steamy jungle of adolescence. But then one day a great change was announced to us in a ukase that was the parental style. We were to be sent away to school that fall of 1951—to the effete East. But before that we were to take a family trip into the Great West. We were going to Wyoming. I knew about Wyoming, had read Mary O'Hara's books about it, but I had to look at a map to see where it was. Finding it, snugged in between the spreads of Colorado and Montana, I could hardly believe after all the years of gaudy imaginings I was actually to go *there*. A sudden sense of the immense distances that intervened drained the assumed cowboy bravado out of my shoes, rendering me timid, my mind fact-bound.

Travel then was much less common than now, to say nothing of permanent removes. A child's unvoiced expectation was that he would pretty much stay put, as my father had. He lived eight blocks from the house he'd been born in, and I think most of us in the neighborhood

3

believed we would lead all of our immortal lives right where we were. We talked a lot about the West, but I doubt any of us really expected to visit there, let alone live there. We were like the kids in Willa Cather's early story "The Enchanted Bluff." They are shown lying out in summer's heat on the banks of the Republican River in a southern Nebraska village, talking, as Cather herself once did, of the Enchanted Bluff in New Mexico. None has ever seen the bluff, but each swears to make that trip someday. None does, as the story turns out. And so it was with us. The West was for us truly a country of the mind, "and so eternal." Now this: the prospect of a real Wyoming.

Looking at a map of the states showing the railroad lines of that time, I see we must have gone out through Des Moines, Omaha, Grand Island, Casper, Lovell, and so into Cody, Wyoming, end of the line. But I remember none of the way stations, only my delight in the sensations of train travel: the hissing clouds of departure from a cavernous station that was either La Salle Street or Union, dinner in the diner with its snowy tablecloths and napkins, the heavy scarred surfaces of the table service, the starched whites and smiling black faces of the waiters who moved so surely along the aisles of the lurching, clicking car. On one of those nights of passage I awakened in my berth, pinched the metal control knobs of the window shade, and ran it up to look out into the black and fleeting night. What, I wonder now, could I have expected to see?

Whatever it was, it could hardly have been equal to what in fact I did see when we swung down from the train in Cody and I found myself in the geographical West. When in my late twenties I first looked on Paris, my heart sprang out toward the splendid city like a bird, and I am not sure it has ever quite come back. But that was nothing to what I felt in that morning moment when I stood with my family on the worn bricks of the station platform and looked across the tracks to the little town founded by Buffalo Bill himself. I saw men going abut their business under the brims of Stetsons while here and there a horse stamped in the street. And then, on all sides of town, glimmering purple and red and still flecked in their creases with last winter's snow, the Shoshone Mountains. Heretofore my idea of a dangerous height was the meander of that hill behind a nearby school where we sledded winter afternoons, or the ominously named Devil's Hill where Dad had broken his leg in a youthful sledding accident. But in this moment and forever after my

sense of scale was wrenched into a greater amplitude, and unwittingly
I became a fellow to those explorers of the previous century whose eyes
had first gazed on the stretches of the American West and who never
afterward were able to refocus them on the smaller and tamer vistas of
the known.

There was, too, the Irma Hotel, where we put up for the night,
it like the town itself a bequest of that legendary dreamer, Buffalo Bill
Cody. In its crowded, buzzing barroom was a magnificent expanse
of cherrywood furniture—shelving, inset mirrors, and forty feet of
counter—that had been a gift to Bill from Queen Victoria. To get to
where I now saw it, it was said, the piece had come by steamer, railroad,
and buckboard. The mere sight of it had provoked Bill's wife in her late
years to institute a suit against the Queen for alienation of affections.
Later that evening as we sat in front of suitably out-sized portions of
beef and potatoes, an old woman gabbling over her food at a nearby
table was pointed out to us as Buffalo Bill's girlfriend—no great
distinction, as I was years later to learn.

That fall, when my brother and I went to school in Connecticut, I
did my best to represent myself as a Westerner. I didn't have the right
gear for this, having been outfitted instead at Rogers Peet in New
York—tweeds, white bucks, button-down shirts, rep ties; I had only a
rawhide thong, which I wore on my belt, and a silver dollar—meager
effects, after all. But I did have a certain amount of inventiveness, in
part the bequest of my years of Western dreaming, which I now applied
to my situation in the Berkshires, stretching my three Wyoming weeks
into an unspecified number of years of riding, roping, and wrangling.
To my indifferent classmates I insinuated a deep familiarity with mountains (*real* mountains, I would have them understand), rushing streams,
mesas, benches, saddles, all manner of horsey tack. *My* eyes, I implied,
could not quite focus on this prim and huddled New England landscape
before me. And maybe they really couldn't, for I had in truth "seen the
elephant," and the Berkshires, for all their hardwood glory, seemed
somehow predictable, a variant of the known. I am not going to say that
this dislocation of vision was the reason why, a year later, it was gently
suggested by the school's headmaster that I might be happier elsewhere.
Other personal factors, like sloth and lack of discipline, seem more
germane to my abysmal performance there. But still I hold out some

small reserve of opinion that the Great West had something to do with my inability to adjust to New England.

• • •

What we actually did in those three weeks at Valley Ranch outside Cody was tame enough, and yet it was real, too. The ranch was run by Larry Larom and his wife, and though I suppose I will have to admit it was what is still called a "dude ranch," the Laroms themselves were the genuine item. They were Westerners, but they were Westerners who had learned that their market lay east of the Mississippi. Years after that summer I made a return visit to Valley Ranch and there found the widowed Mrs. Larom living as a guest on premises over which she and her husband had once reigned. The ranch was still in operation, but I thought it wore a slightly down-at-heels look, and of course Mrs. Larom felt things were not what they used to be. She spoke with nostalgic fondness of the seasonal recruiting trips she and Larry Larom would make through Chicago and Philadelphia, New York and Boston, how they would put up at the Palmer House or the St. Regis. "I'll tell you," she said with a worn smile, "we used to go *first class*."

And that was the way they ran Valley Ranch. The daily routine there was carefully calibrated to what folks who bore names like Pillsbury, Pabst, and Du Pont could be expected to tolerate. It was, I now see, a skillful blend of fantasy and practical comfort, of the Western ranch and the Eastern country club, with the latter in sufficient disguise to assist the illusion of the former.

Days began at the jangle of the cast-iron triangle announcing breakfast: steak, eggs, flapjacks, homefries, hot biscuits, just as if you'd worked up a hearty appetite on the morning wrangle. A decent interval was allowed between the end of the last sitting and the gather down at the corrals. There Ott, a crusty old cowboy moving heavily behind an enormous paunch that threatened the lower pearl snaps of his denim shirt, would drawl off the names of the riding parties and assign a trail guide to each: "Johnny'll take Group B up to the Bench. Trail lunch. Back at two." Your party and guide assigned, destination appointed, you waited for your horse to be cornered in the corral. When at last it appeared before you, it was bridled and saddled, and you swung up into the well-oiled leather and waited while a ranch hand adjusted your stirrups. All safely mounted, your group moved off into the shining air, splashing through the creek that crossed the wide trail east of the ranch and then, as the trail narrowed into the slopes, falling into a file that lasted much of the rest of the ride, the horses slow, undulant, farting, as they settled into the grade. For a couple of hours you moved slowly upward, stopping once to rest, perhaps where the trail crossed the South Fork of the Shoshone. By the time you reached the Bench, your butt bones were sore from jolting hours in the saddle, your thighs quivery from tensing where the trail had briefly turned downward and your horse had eased into a shambling trot. You were ready for that "trail lunch." You swung stiffly down and walked about the short grass on legs peculiarly light and seeming to have had little previous acquaintance with the earth.

This was not the only strange thing up there. The air had at once both a visible purity and an essence. You were up so high you could see the blue and taste it, while all around were the mountains—great, silent presences with a fixed gaze that caused your breath to catch in your throat. In Chicago as elsewhere east of the Mississippi, the grand, subliminal attraction of the West had always been its imagined potential to lift you out of yourself, maybe even to snatch your soul from you and return it reconditioned. Back there in childhood's cap-gun days we surely weren't up to verbalizing this attraction, but it was there nonetheless, and I think even the most prosaic pretend gunslinger among us moved and played to its obscure promise. Thus, in a sense, what I looked out on from the Bench during those noontime hours was anticipated. Still, its reality, the abiding and almost casual power of it, could never have been expected. And in that way also I had become a kind of honorary fellow to Boone, Jim Bridger, Hugh Glass, and the rest of those explorers and mountain men who had been forever changed in the seat of the soul by their encounters with the West's vast and luminous spaces.

Customarily you had about four hours of afternoon to recover from the rigors of the ride. Many of the adults seemed to need them, but we were young. We sat around our cabin, reading or playing cards, waiting for the punctual arrival of the afternoon thundershower, which could be seen far off on its appointed approach, moving swiftly toward us through a "V" in the mountains at the eastern edge of Yellowstone Park. When it had come—dropping its quick, heavy burden, strafing the ranch buildings with bullets of rain or hail—and gone, the sun would roll out on the puddles and the suddenly spangled roofs and eaves, and then we might find a couple of other kids and take a short ride along the valley's flats on horses that hadn't been out yet that day. Out of sight of the corrals and Ott, their brooding guardian, we would race down the hard-packed trails of the flats, whooping at our horses in approved cowboy fashion, slashing alternate sides of their necks with the reins' ends, just like in the movies. If we lathered them, as we sometimes did, we took care to cool them and to wipe away telltale streaks of gray from their necks and withers.

Before dinner we strolled down to the rambling mess hall to sit in the voluminous leather chairs and sofas and leaf through the slick magazines that lay on the tables: *Life, Time, Fortune, Holiday, Red Book, Field and Stream*. F. Scott Fitzgerald writes that his character Jay Gatsby knew when to quit when he furnished his outrageous mansion: he didn't bother to cut the pages of the expensive sets of books with which he stocked his library. The Laroms knew when to quit, too, and didn't stock their sitting room with copies of those pulp Western magazines then found on the racks of American drugstores. I, for one, missed them.

After dinner we were entertained by a band made up of the college kids who were spending their summer out there as potato peelers, pot scrubbers, waiters, busboys, and carpenters. That summer a number of them seemed to be from Yale, including a rollicking two-fisted piano player, Delaney Glenn, whose rendition of a somewhat obscure song titled "You Dirty Lady" unfailingly produced clamorous calls for an encore.

So the simple days passed amid such natural splendor as could not fail to stir the heart of even the most pampered among us, and if this adventure was (as it may now appear) the thinnest simulacrum of the real West—the West of blizzards and droughts, of snakebite, of calving in the late snowstorms of spring, of cowboys old at forty—I can only report that it seemed real to me, certainly far more real than that fictive fare upon which I'd fed on Chicago's south side. And in fact I did learn a few small skills of the region, however much these might already have become culturally obsolete by the time I learned them.

I learned to enter a coral of milling, bunching horses and without fear wade through them to my mount. I learned to corner him, bridle him, and lead him out, docile enough now that he knew the game was up. I learned how to saddle a horse, how to wait until he'd expelled that deceitful lungful he'd taken in while you were cinching him up. Johnny, a bandy-legged cowboy whose mythical stature was only slightly diminished by my awareness one morning that he was terrifically hung over, taught me the rudiments of roping. Out of a junior-sized length of rope Johnny fashioned me a slip noose, then patiently demonstrated the motions of swinging and throwing, so that for hours I could practice roping a fence post. I also tasted just a bit of range life as it might once have been, when my sister and I went out on the morning wrangle. In the blue half-light we took our breakfast with the hands, bolting our too-hot Cream of Wheat for fear of being late to the corral. Then we were off after the remuda, our horses' breaths hanging white against the rising sun. And how proud we two were to come back with the wranglers, driving the herd across the stream and on into the corrals while the dudes straggled up from their cozy beds to the ringing of the breakfast triangle! The memory of all this earnest play has lasted me a sizeable portion of my allotted span, and so profound is the nexus it makes with the national fantasy of the West that I have no doubt I will go on thinking about those few Wyoming days until I can remember nothing else of this human life. At which point I may dream silently of becoming a horse, as I did in early childhood while under the spell of the horse-book authors, Will James, Marguerite Henry, Mary O'Hara, and Walter Farley.

• • •

If there were anything idiosyncratic in the foregoing history, it wouldn't be worth the writing. But in fact there is not. For the better part of the past two hundred years the West has been a striking and seductive phenomenon in the American imagination, and no one will ever be able to compute how many boys and men have been as taken as I was by the West, both as fantasy and as fact. If the West has been a more compelling phenomenon for males (those eternal escape artists) than it has been for women, and if the image of the West remains predominantly masculine, there have always been girls and women who have felt the lure as well, who responded to some of the same promises implicit in a sunset on an unscarred skyline. Gretel Ehrlich's work or that of Annick Smith reminds us of this, and numerous illustrations drawn from our daily life tell us in other ways of the undiminished attraction the West exerts on so many of both genders.

Today, for instance, there are in our Western states astonishingly authentic reenactments of the mountain men rendezvous of the first part of the nineteeth century. Here grown men, many of them carrying responsibilities of one weight or another, are found publicly reverting to the games and dreams of childhood. They gather together in greasy buckskins, fur caps, and moccasins to shoot off black-powder firearms, lie, drink, fornicate (if they can), and gallop horses. Once, in mufti, I attended such an event in Santa Fe. The old boys were there in force, dripping fringe, bowie knives, replica Hawken and Sharps rifles, power horns, and beads. They hefted bottles of what was said to be Taos Lightning, laughed hugely, slugged each other's shoulders. The air was thick with exploded powder, broiling beast, testosterone, and liquor. All that was missing from a scene that might have been painted by Alfred Jacob Miller in the 1830s were the Indian "squaws," and there were enough interested-looking women in the audience to suggest that even this historical deficiency might be remedied.

Let us say the mountain men rendezvous are rare and special events and that even rarer would be a event like the mammoth trail drive that commemorated the Montana centennial. Still, we have the rodeos, quick-draw contests, re-creations of outlaw shootouts, Pony Express runs, chuckwagon suppers, and annual "Frontier Days" celebrations of dozens of Western communities. More ordinary, but no less revealing, are the still-flourishing dude ranches that dot the West just as they did in my youth. These are now so common a feature of the national life that they no longer draw particular attention, except insofar as they symbolize a sort of privilege. And still more ordinary and pervasive are the cowboy hats, jeans, wide belts, and boots that are standard items of clothing from Des Moines to Reno and fashion statements in New York and Los Angeles. Rifles racked up on the rear windows of pickups are a common sight in Western states, even though often the weapons may serve no more functional a purpose today than the cowboy hat, which originally was designed to protect its wearer from rain, sun, or driving snow out on the range.

In these as in unnumbered other ways it is clear that the American

West lives on in the national imagination—and nowhere is this more obvious than in the West itself. Here the old, compelling images of horse, horseman, cattle, guns, and unimproved space still exert a power that can be startling to one who comes to the region from elsewhere. Oddly chthonic, despite their wide and windy origins, they live on in the minds and habits of those inhabiting a region that in many respects bears little resemblance to that which originally gave the images birth. Oh, the Shoshone Mountains are still there, all right, and the spaciousness of the West still makes its grand statement to the traveler as to the resident. But Dallas and Denver, Sun City, air inversion, and water wars are now more conspicuous features of the American West than mountains and horses, and the webbing of superhighways has compacted the immutable distances themselves, even in this age of stratospheric gas prices. The persistence of the old images in the very rush of change is what imparts so strange and exciting a tone and temper to contemporary Western life. Practically speaking, the West's colorful past has little enough to do with its current realities and even less to do with the region's future realities and problems. Emotionally speaking, however, that past has *everything* to do with today, and with the West's tomorrow as well. Where I live in New Mexico not very long ago it was possible to sit in your pickup with your .30-.30 behind your head, watching a cowboy movie at a drive-in that is surrounded by high-rise tourist hotels and fast-food restaurants. No one around you seemed concerned to sort out the realities in this extraordinary tableau. It was simply The Way Things Are, to use Rolfe Humpries's felicitous translation of *De Rerum Natura*.

It may be that other parts of the country are just as deeply involved with their past: the South, for instance, with the brooding shadow of its gracious, white-columned antebellum past; or New England with the Puritans and the high achievements of Emerson, Thoreau, Hawthorne, and Longfellow. The past lives in these places, all right: I have seen it flash from the face of a ninety-year-old Creole lady, illuminating the dim dampness of her ancestral home in New Orleans's Garden District. But only in theWest is its presence so actively felt that it filters the quality and style of an average day.

In the land of the wide skies, sharply etched mesas, and herds of grazing horses you can see, if you look, the dull mauve of air pollution when the wind is right—or when you are nearing Albuquerque or

Denver or Phoenix. Elsewhere you can read the signs of the West's exorbitant demands on its finite supplies of groundwater: land subsidence, sheered well casings, and the steady salinization of soils. These, too, are parts of the West as well as portents of its future.

And yet. And yet there are the rodeos, barbecues, cockfights, and chili cook-offs. When I attend these celebrations of what the West might once have been, I am reminded of what it still wants to be. And at such moments I am back in the Chicago of my youth, hearing again the "hoofbeats of the great horse, Silver." And I have lots of company.

Life on the Line:
Along the 100ᵗʰ Meridian

There is an invisible line that cuts right through the heart of America. On the maps it's designated as the 100th Meridian, and more than a century ago John Wesley Powell, the one-armed major who explored the Colorado when it was still a raging river, warned those planning the nation's westward expansion that the 100th was where things changed. The old Euro-American settlement grid couldn't be imposed on the lands west of the 100th, Powell reported. They were too tough, too dry. At the 100th a new kind of thinking and new patterns of settlement had to take over, ones more closely attuned to the lands and their climate. But Congress was in a bullying, expansionist mood and wouldn't listen. Neither would the land speculators, the boomers, the drifters, and the hardworking aspirants who believed their pot of gold lay waiting for them at the line—or maybe just beyond it. In the decades following Powell's report the emigrants hurled themselves against the line, settled it, then moved on into the Great Plains, thereby apparently proving the major a false prophet. But was he?

The line enters the U.S. near Dunseith, North Dakota, follows Main Street out of Rugby (the continent's geographical center), and passes through the hamlets of Arena, Tuttle, Driscoll, and Hague. In South Dakota it runs east of the impounded sprawl of the Missouri and through the Lakota reservations of Cheyenne River, Lower Brulé, and Rosebud before crossing the Niobrara on the edge of Nebraska's Sandhills. Ainsworth, Anselmo, Arnold, Arapahoe—you have to love these Nebraska place-names and so many others along the way: there's an unpremeditated poetry in them that rises up from the obdurate land and the outsized hopes and follies and unchronicled sacrifices it has inspired over the brief generations of white occupancy.

On its way into Kansas the 100th crosses the Platte, which to sojourners and settlers seemed a "mile wide and an inch deep." It runs east of the brawling old cow town of Dodge City, now slaughterhouse to the nation, then follows the north-south jut of Oklahoma and Texas into

13

the leathery stretches of west Texas. Then comes the beautiful lilt of the Hill Country northwest of San Antonio, then cactus and scrub down to the border at Laredo.

It's about fourteen hundred miles from the wheat fields and silos of North Dakota to the riverfront streets of Laredo, if you could travel it in a straight line—which you can't. In any case, you wouldn't want to travel the heartland that way. "You never learn nothing on a main road," an old goat herder told me in Bloom, Kansas. And, of course, he's dead right.

The 100th is, to be sure, an imaginary line, a convenience of geographers and navigators, but once you're out along it, you find it becomes an increasingly felt and visible reality—as Powell wished to point out in his 1878 report to Congress. You discover that he was right in stating that it is where some things end and others begin, especially if, like the history of American settlement itself, you come to it from the east. That way you can't miss the changes in vegetation and soils, in settlement patterns and weather, in skies and horizons. Out here you feel the Native American presence in ways you haven't before: reservations, place-names, artifacts—the arrowheads and age-stiffened buckskin clothing displayed everywhere from local museums to gas stations. On the long roads at night you find the lights of settlements thinning out and more and more black spaces in between, and for the first time you're gripped by the simple yet mysterious *extent* of America, an extent you could get lost in. In daylight you miss what you'd been taking for granted for days now—that dense, verdant prosperity of the Midwest with its fecund soils fashioned by the great, grinding glaciers. But the glaciers stopped their work east of the 100th, and didn't build the soils of the Great Plains. The weather changes out here, too, for by the time the westerlies reach here they've been wrung out by the Rockies, and so what you get, what you feel walking a section-line road, is a dry and wearing wind. It blows across fields of wheat, milo, corn, and alfalfa; across acres of grazing cattle and pens of hogs; through the cotton fields of southwestern Oklahoma and Texas; through rangeland nibbled to dirt by goats. At last in south Texas the relentless assault of wind and sun will permit little to grow except monstrous clumps of cactus capable of standing up to any kind of weather in Michigan or Michoacán.

It isn't tourist country. It isn't smiling country, either, despite its wide skies and sun. Rotarians were the first to insist that the smile was the official national expression, long before Reagan. It's never felt right to me and certainly doesn't along the 100th. But the 100th is quintessentially American. America, wrote the poet Archibald MacLeish with brilliant compression, "is West and the wind blowing." West begins along this line, and in a sense that can't quite be qualified by the actualities of our history; here you feel that you've arrived at the heart of what we are. In all my travels over forty years to the far reaches of this country I've nowhere felt that so constantly, so profoundly, as I did along the 100th: not in old Boston with its North Church and the slanting tombstones of the first patriots; not at the mouth of the Mississippi where the country's main artery empties itself into the Gulf in a broad, brown swath; not on California's astonishing northern coast where ancient redwoods march right down to Pacific waves. All these places are deeply American, of course. But if I were to advise a foreign visitor who wanted a vivid understanding of who we really are—and who we think we are—I wouldn't route him first to Boston or Houma, Louisiana, or Arcata, California. I'd send him down the 100th—and he might end up knowing more about us than we do ourselves. For along this line he would encounter the stark and sometimes shocking realties that lie behind some of our most cherished national myths: the American Dream, the Jeffersonian ideal of the Yeoman Farmer, and the limitless Promise of the West. Here these myths we have lived by lie in shattered heaps, their shards palpable and visible in one warped hamlet after another; in the sullen restaurants where the few, elderly customers pick glumly at their suppers; along the empty section-line roads laid out in defiance of Powell's view that settlement needed to follow the contours and configurations of the landscape. Everywhere under the broad sky there's an aura of failed hopes so that after a while the outsider comes to feel he's traveling in the wake of some huge, unchronicled disaster where the few survivors are struggling on into an uncertain future, stripped of their characteristic American optimism—but not of their native courage.

One October at the end of the last century, I set out along the 100th, north to south. I walked the bluffs above the Missouri where Lewis and Clark wintered with the Mandans. I talked with bartenders and businessmen in villages where the last spark is winking out. In a locker-room in Nebraska I listened to a football coach's pep talk during the homecoming game. In a squad car I rode the darkening streets of a Kansas slaughter-house town where, when the wind is right, you can smell arterial blood. I watched an eight-ball pool tourney in Oklahoma and heard Cheyenne singers mourn their dead at the Washita Battlefield. I sat in on a high school sociology class and a south Texas goat auction. At the end of a long road I watched with the Border Patrol as fugitive figures from the Mexican bank of the Rio Grande waited for their chance to slip across and become a part of all this.

• • •

Mid-October, Rugby, North Dakota

The Old Folks at Home
Hard Times Getting Harder
Sid's Place and a Brief History of Defeat

At two in the afternoon the sun finally cleared the fog and low-hanging cloud bank and lit up the landmarks of the town proud to be known as the "Geographical Center of North America": dome of county courthouse, huddled shops along Main Street, senior citizens' center, stubbled fields visible at either end of the central intersection, grain storage tanks. Rugby is not only dead center; it's also the prototype of the Great Plains town.

Two days earlier I'd left my Santa Fe home for Minot in a Cessna 182 with pilot Ken Mock. Turning east into the rising sun and then northeastward, we watched the Rocky Mountain landscape flatten into wrinkles, then folds, until in the afternoon we sailed above the broad fields of the Great Plains and their green circles made by center-pivot irrigators. Ahead lay the solid purple-gray cloud bank of bad weather, and Mock said we'd have to settle for Bismarck, not Minot.

The bad weather came scrolling down from Canada, enveloped Bismarck, and stayed on. The Cessna stayed on the tarmac at Bismarck ("Where the Sky Meets the Prairie"), and I took to the back roads in a rental car. Under gunmetal skies and in a bitter wind that smelled of winter I explored the nearby Lewis and Clark sites of Fort Clark and the Knife River villages, and then one morning drove north toward Rugby. At ten o'clock it was so dim trucks ran with their headlights on.

There were flocks of wild turkeys nodding across the harvested fields, and on the radio a singer told her new cowboy lover that she didn't know nothing 'bout rodeo, "but I can put you back in the saddle, baby, and stand you up tall."

In Carrington, just south of Rugby, I stopped at a café to eavesdrop over coffee. The Chieftain featured a giant wooden Indian out front and inside an impressive display of arrowheads, most of them no doubt turned up out of the surrounding fields by the bright blade of Progress that had broken the aboriginal land.

Except in its larger towns and centers like Bismarck the Great Plains is becoming a region of those too old to move on. Senator Tom Daschle of neighboring South Dakota had recently introduced a bill designed to help counties and towns just like this one cope with the steady loss of their young and promising. "More and more," Daschle's bill read, "young people are being forced to leave the towns they grew up in for better jobs in urban areas." The local weekly I picked up at the Chieftain provided various confirmations of this trend with its front-page story about an AARP forum, its photos of elderly members of the American Legion Post 30 Auxiliary, its notices of golden wedding anniversaries and senior meals. So too did the looks of those gathered along the café's Formica counter—old men in flannel shirts and visored caps who were kidding the waitresses and arguing about the protein content of various strands of wheat, subsidies versus the costs of shipping and storage, and the shocking collapse of the Asian markets. Rumors of massive federal assistance to hard-hit area farmers had yet to prove true (though late that year the feds did come through with a record $5.9 billion in aid), and there was a shared sense among these men that Washington was preoccupied with other matters. Well, *their* struggles with crops, the market, and the weather were evidently over, and you couldn't miss the air of relief in their leisurely conversation and postures.

Up at the John Deere dealership in Rugby, though, the struggle was very much on the mind of Clem Schiele, especially the market. Currently, he told me, it cost a farmer about twice as much to raise a bushel of wheat as he could hope to get for it on the market. Beyond his office windows the company's lot was filled with the monster rigs of modern agriculture, but the implement business, along with just about everything else related to farming, was "way off." (Indeed, the same weekly I scanned in the Chieftain reported that farm machinery sales were down twenty percent for the year.)

"It used to be this phone would be ringing all day long," Schiele said, tapping it with a forefinger. "Now you see it isn't. Instead of prospects coming in here to see you, you have to go out to see them." He had to make just such a call this afternoon, but in the meantime was glad enough to talk.

Schiele's father, just retired at seventy-eight from a lifetime of grain farming, thought the agricultural economy had never been worse, not even in the notorious thirties. "We're going to see another mass exodus this year," his son predicted, "though some will try to hang on." And the others? "Well, some go to work as truckers, welders, implement repairmen, or at the hospital. Some hire out to larger farmers. Some go back to school to try to pick up a new skill. A lot are trying to diversify, but not everybody can make the transition. Some are getting into raising exotic animals—buffalo, emus, and so forth."

Out in the lot, dwarfed by the rigs' metallic immensities, Schiele showed me around the latest combine with its thirty-foot header used to harvest sunflowers, an increasingly popular crop for the oil. The whole thing cost $111,000. How, I wondered, could anyone except a corporation afford this in so depressed an economy? "Well, usually there'll be a trade-in," he explained. "That'd be the down payment, and the rest'd be financed at, say, six percent for five years."

I asked if he was worried about his own job, and he shrugged his shoulders under his heavy jacket. "I think we all are," he said at last. He had three kids in school here, and his wife had a good job at the bank. He looked away at the fields stretching southward. "I have a background in radio, and I've done some play-by-play. I could fall back on that. If I had to." In the pause that followed, the wind, sweeping across the treeless plains, whined in the raised arms of the combine. "We don't want to move," he said finally.

At the Pierce County Courthouse I had some trouble finding a pulse but finally stepped into a room off one of its empty, echoing corridors and interrupted a small conference. Three women and a man sat over Styrofoam cups, talking quietly. I'd been trying to find someone who could tell me whether Pierce County was losing population, I explained, but couldn't find anyone who seemed to know. They looked silently at each other, and then one of the women spoke. "Probably are."

She was right. Pierce, I later learned, had lost almost ten percent since the last census, and there were others along the 100th in North Dakota that had lost even more, according to Census Bureau stats: Logan County, for instance, had lost fifteen percent and Sheridan almost seventeen. But I didn't really need these stats, nor even the fact that in recent local elections up here twelve contests had been decided by coin flips because so few were left to cast ballots. More eloquent were the blackened windows of the abandoned farmhouses, tangles of rusted machinery, vacant schools, auction notices, closed-up villages. And these spectral voices, I was to learn over subsequent weeks, would be joined by others all the way down to Laredo. Sometimes at night, standing outside my motel room in Pierre or Childress or Uvalde, after a long day on long roads, I could almost hear these voices joined in a mighty dirge. How could the rest of America not hear it?

In Tuttle, just outside Bismarck, I stopped at Sid's Place where Sid and I were the only ones in the dim, yellowed room with its brittle strings of flypaper hanging over bottles of booze that didn't look as if anyone had lifted them in an age.

"This (Tuttle) used to be a pretty thriving place," Sid told me. "Used to be three restaurants, a bowling alley, two grocery stores, an implements dealer. Hard times, getting harder. Some more will likely quit this fall." Like Clem Schiele, he spoke of the local efforts to survive by diversifying into canola oil and pinto beans, forsaking the hard wheat of their forefathers.

Later, when I'd left the bar and was bent over the hood of my rental car, scribbling notes, I saw Sid coming towards me, walking right down the middle of the main street. When he came up he smiled and cocked his head quizzically. "Say," he said, "you aren't related to *Ted* Turner, are you? You look kinda like him."

"Sid," I said, "if I was related to Ted Turner, what would I be doing in Tuttle?" That made him laugh. I glanced at my notebook, pretending to read notes from our conversation in his bar. "But I do have you down here on the record, Sid," I said: "Sid says, 'Fuck 'em all!'"

"Oh, Lord!" Sid laughed again. "Don't write that!"

• • •

Valentine, Nebraska

Homecoming Parade on the Rosebud
Homecoming off the Rez
Of Mastodons and Football

I called Bill Quigley from the Rosebud Reservation in Mission, South Dakota, where I was visiting with Victor Douville at the tribal college. I'd asked Quigley if he could get me into the locker room before tonight's homecoming game between Valentine and West Holt, and now he was telling me he'd arranged it. That done, Douville and I resumed our conversation.

We'd known each other for some years, and in his office cluttered with papers, books, and tribal artifacts we ranged freely over topics like the role of the native language in tribal survival, the Lakotas' continuing battle to regain title to their sacred Black Hills, to Bill Clinton's troubles in the Monica matter. Along with others on the tribal council, Douville thought Clinton might have been edging up to "something really big, some executive order," that would help the Lakotas in their Black Hills negotiations. Now that seemed a very remote possibility, and Douville's hopes had shifted to ex-Senator Bill Bradley, who was friendly to the Lakotas and was seen as a presidential possibility.

Afterwards, I took Douville's suggestion and went from the campus to Mission's main street to watch the homecoming parade in a gelid drizzle. The kids looked frozen in their costumes and slickers, though the homecoming king and queen tried bravely to smile, riding through the bruising air in an open aqua blue '55 Chevy convertible. The paper decorations of the floats had become sad, sodden rags, and the letters of a sign memorializing a recently murdered schoolgirl named Richy Robideaux ran down the purple cardboard like a mother's tears. This, too, was America, I was thinking, watching a band of Lakota boys sit their ponies with superb élan. But what a world away it seemed from hundreds of other homecomings on the eastern side of the 100th.

Inside the Rosebud Casino the tribe operates on the South Dakota/Nebraska border the atmosphere was even more dreary than the parade. Douville had told me the casino provided critically necessary revenue for the tribe and that the cooperation between Indian and white employees there had been a boost to interracial understanding. Still, the sight of these elderly white farm couples glumly shoving slugs into the machines while all around lights blinked and bells and whistles sounded was something Dante might have imagined after an off bottle of Tuscan red. After a lifetime of relentless daily toil, was *this* the payoff? If so, it seemed a grisly joke. My last glimpse of this terminal place took in a video screen on which the rolling graphic read: "JACKPOT POWER-BALL. 20 MILLION—DAKOTA CASH $68,000—WILD CARD 745—GAMBLING PROBLEMS 1-800-781-HELP."

Down in Valentine Bill Quigley told me things at the casino were usually livelier than the scene I'd reported, especially on weekend nights. With his brother Jim, Quigley practiced law in Valentine, and we had a mutual friend in the writer and bon vivant Jim Harrison. We stood talking outside the Valentine Badgers' locker room, watching as the parking lot filled with cars and pickups. In these parts, Quigley explained, far from centers where so many other diversions were available, high school football took on dimensions hard for outsiders to imagine. Even the tiniest hamlets fielded teams, though these might have to be the brutally demanding eight-man versions. And, of course, throughout the state the Nebraska Cornhuskers were the secular religion. For them anything less than an unbeaten season and a bowl bid were regarded as disasters equivalent to a cyclone or a crop failure—maybe worse.

When we entered the locker room, the young, first-year coach, Mark Hagge, had turned from his blackboard diagrams to face his squad. A wide-body Omaha native who'd played under the famous Tom Osborne at Nebraska, Hagge had his Badgers at 4–2 as they strapped it up to face the West Holt Huskies. ("That's a bit east of the 100th," Quigley teased me.)

"Special teams win football games!" Hagge bellowed, the chords in his huge neck standing out. "I want to run one back tonight! On offense: blocking, blocking. It's as simple as that. I want you to hit them in the chops from the first play and keep hitting them until it's over. Defense, I want fifty-one (pointing to his star linebacker) to be all over thirty-one (the opposing fullback). I want you to change his number so he's wearing fifty-one at the end of the game, okay?" Hagge paused, letting a dramatic silence shawl down over the room with its half-dressed young men, strewn clothing and equipment, assistant coaches huddled near the door. Then in softer tones he told them that no matter what happened tonight, they'd already done something significant.

"Valentine," he reminded them, "hasn't played a seventh game [of a season] that's really meant something in a good while, and this one does. If we win tonight, we go to the play-offs. You're going to go on from football into life, but what you do out there tonight will stay with you. They can never take it away from you—it'll be yours forever. And you know, fellas, when you shoot for the stars, sometimes you hit one. Sometimes you hit one."

The Badgers aimed high—but missed. West Holt whipped them, 16–0, and as if Nature wished to hide the spectacle, by game's end the fog was so thick you couldn't see the field's far side where the Huskies' reserves stood exchanging high fives. The party at Jim Quigley's afterwards was thus turned into a wake. Coach Hagge sat stunned at the dining room table, surrounded by friendly faces, his bottle of Miller's untouched. They tried to comfort him: the Huskies were too big; his quarterback was afraid of getting hit and so threw too soon; he'd already made a big improvement on the record of his predecessor, no matter how the final game came out. But nothing worked until someone said the Badger players needed to work harder in the weight room during the summer, that what they hadn't done in there in July and August had come back to haunt them tonight against West Holt. They just weren't physically ready. That brought the coach out of his shock. He slammed the table with his meaty palm, then took his first swallow of beer.

"Well, they will be!" he hollered. "If they don't want to hit the weights in the summer, they don't want to play for me!"

While an analysis of individual players followed, Jim Quigley took me into his living room with its big, glowing fireplace to show me his collection of Indian artifacts and fossil materials, collected through years of fishing the nearby Snake River ("the best goddamned trout fishing stream in North America!") with his brother. The Lakota arrowheads and spear points were severely beautiful, but more impressive were several large fragments of mastodon tusks. These were heavy, dense things, striated and glistening with the polish of millennia, and when you held one in your hands it was as if suddenly the old globe itself were exerting some minute fraction of its force, tugging at the bone and insisting on its primal right of ownership. In that moment, holding the fragment, you saw right through the fiction of this portion of America—or any portion of it, really—as a New World. It was a world already immensely ancient when Coronado trooped through these very red-grassed stretches, searching for cities of gold; when Eric the Red landed in Greenland; when the first hunters followed the mastodons and other big game over the high wastes of the northern land bridge and then wandered south into sunlight. Now the excited talk from the other room died away, and even my host faded out for a moment, and there was only this tusk with the firelight glinting along its ponderous curve.

When Bill Quigley drove me back to my motel Anne Quigley, his handsome, vivacious wife, spoke up from the darkness of the backseat. She had trouble, she said, taking high school football so seriously. "They talk about it like it's the whole world," she said. "It isn't. And some of these kids just can't do that strength training in the summer: they're rural kids who live way out there, and they can't get in here for that." Clearly, she had a point, and her husband said so. As for me, a passing stranger, the arrowheads and the tusk fragments made it easy enough to feel that high school football wasn't the whole world, only a flood-lit, chalk-marked sliver of it.

• • •

Garden City, Kansas

Smoke and Names on the Land
The Goat Man of Bloom
Back to School
A Squad Car Tour of the New Garden
On the Killing-House Floor

When the ceiling finally lifted up in North Dakota Ken Mock brought the Cessna down to North Platte, and so once again I got that wonderful, airborne vantage as we lifted over the Platte River Valley and its soft green folds and streamside groves, heading south into the flat stretches of Kansas.

23

More bad weather caught us there, and so in another rental I took to the roads, exploring the countryside around Dodge City. Southwest of Dodge on Kansas 56 huge billows of smudgy smoke stood out above land flat as a tabletop, reminding me of Catlin's painting of a prairie fire when the Indians and the game ran before the awesome sweep of what the natives called the "red buffalo." At Montezuma where Mock and I had hamburgers and coffee we learned they were burning the chaff of corn and milo before putting in winter wheat. At Montezuma and Copeland and Sublette the grain elevators bulked darkly against the brief afternoon sun, and golden piles of the scientifically engineered surplus lay next to them under bulging tarps and spilling out onto the margin of the road. When a truck heading for the nearest elevator came abreast of our car the gust of its passage rocked us, and scatters of grain strafed our windshield. At Satanta, "Home of the Fighting Indians," the streets were named "Comanche," "Kaw," and so forth, and the town librarian told me that every year the community named an honorary chief and princess. But not everybody, she added, was exactly thrilled by all this homage to the vanished tribes, and some had been positively disgusted that when the town was incorporated in 1912 it had been named after the Kiowa chief Satanta. "He was a drunk and a murderer," she said of the great patriot who killed himself rather than endure imprisonment at Leavenworth. "Of course, we murdered Indians, too, as far as that goes." As she told me this I wasn't seeing her, her pleasant, well-meaning face and the meager book stacks behind her. I was seeing Satanta, his fierce, close-set eyes, the desperate patriotism the white photographer had captured.

South of Dodge we stumbled into one of the many ghost towns you encounter along the 100th—dusty, emptied testaments to Major Powell's prophetic warnings. Nothing we could see moved in Bloom except a flap of metal roofing torn off the auditorium by a long ago tornado—that and small flocks of goats penned here and there on both sides of the main drag. Presently, a shambling figure under a black cowboy hat approached us at one of the pens. When the goats saw the man they came bleating and crowding to him, and he scooped up some spears of hay and handed them to the nodding, jostling heads with their peculiar no-color eyes. Yes, they were all his, he told us, and much else that was left of Bloom.

"This here is actually the third Bloom," Ray told us, taking his eyes from the goats to glance around the tumbled-down barns, stranded machinery, snarls of wire, and the few inhabited homes whose vital signs were upright TV antennas. "The other ones got burned down by drunk cowboys. I live over there, and I own the building down there that used to be the bank."

Before he began raising goats Ray ran a shop here, making specialty tools for farm equipment companies, something he'd gotten into by accident. Quite a bit of his life, apparently, had a random quality to it, including how he happened to end up in Bloom. He wasn't from anywhere near here, he said; this was simply where he'd run out of money on his travels. "I'm a Blanket-Ass [Indian], in case you haven't figured that out yet," he added with a twinkle in his eye. "Chippewa."

The goat business was pretty good these days, he said over his shoulder, moving into the pen where the animals thronged around his waist, butting for position. Much better than cattle or hogs, which were losing propositions. He trucked them for sale as far as San Angelo, Texas, and got ninety-two cents a pound. He cuffed the goats playfully and told us their names: "This 'un's Snowball. That big ole fella's Elmer. This 'un I got for nothin' 'cause they said she was blind. Well, it took me two days to get her seeing again. Two weeks, why, she could see real good. Bacteria was all it was." When I asked if he himself ate goat, he scoffed and said the meat was "way too expensive." Quite a few people in the region seemed to have developed a real taste for it, including the Vietnamese. But he wouldn't sell to them.

"You know how they kill 'em [the goats]? Beat 'em to death with a stick. They claim it makes the meat more tender. I wouldn't want that happening to any of mine."

He took us down to his old tool shop, now used to store feed. Then he turned slowly and spread his hand outward over the jumbled, beaten village. "It's hard to live in this old town," he said reflectively, twirling the end of his long, greasy moustache. "You wouldn't think it, but it is. Bunch of obnoxious people here. Can't keep out of other people's business, and I'm just the fellow they need. But it don't bother me none. I tell 'em just where they can put it: where the sun don't shine."

On our way back to Dodge following Ray's directions along dirt roads I asked Ken Mock if he thought there could be a Mrs. Ray. He glanced over at me, then out the window at the flowing fields. "Maybe we already met her," he said.

The Vietnamese Ray wouldn't sell to were indeed in force in Dodge and neighboring Garden City. Along with others from Southeast Asia, South America, and Mexico they'd come here to work in the slaughterhouses the packers have built in the heart of cattle country. Along the streets of Dodge and Garden City you saw some of the enormous changes the slaughterhouses and their workers have brought to this part of the heartland: Asian community centers, Mexican grocery stores, Vietnamese restaurants. You could smell the change, too, for when the wind is right the molten scent of blood and organs has replaced the old familiar odor of sugar beets.

At Garden City High they didn't have room now for all the new kids and were planning a second high school—surely one of the very few places along the 100th where lack of space is a problem—and the signs in the halls were in English, Spanish, and Vietnamese. A longtime teacher there, Rocky Welton, said, yes, it was very different from the old days when the population of school and town was homogeneous, but he thought the community had made a handsome adjustment. When I sat in on his sociology class I got a sense of how pervasive the changes were. There were the Asian and Hispanic faces of his students and the urban clothing styles brought here by TV and film. But there was more. After Welton asked a Caucasian girl to define the term "interaction," he prompted her with a follow-up: what had she said to her mother this morning before leaving for school?

"I said, 'Goodnight, Mom,'" the girl answered. Welton looked puzzled for a moment. "She was coming off the night shift," the girl explained.

I thought Welton worked his pupils pretty hard through the period, even requiring them to do a bit of writing, which they weren't happy about. Afterwards, we chatted in the emptied classroom. He was originally from Arkansas but had moved to Kansas more than forty years before, "and I've been here ever since. My wife and I just love it. You can see everywhere. In Arkansas, you can't see around the next bend." He stroked his close-cropped gray hair. "Here, everything's open, and you can see for *miiiles* in any direction. The skies are so wide—just grass and sky. And wonderful sunsets. I took another job east of the 100th

Meridian once (a smile here), and nine months was all it took. We left for here the day school ended."

That evening at the Garden City Police Department I met with officer Harold Millirons to ride with him for the early part of his shift. When I found him he was checking a shotgun out of the equipment room to carry with him in his cruiser. It wasn't that he had any particular expectation of needing it tonight, he said with a small smile; it was simply S.O.P. An officer never knew what might happen on any given night, and this was as true of the old Garden City as of the new. "Maybe you've heard about a case we had here years ago," he said. "A guy wrote a book about it, and now they're doing a remake of the movie—*In Cold Blood*? We have some of the evidence on display just down here." He directed me down the hall to a display case. I knew the case, of course, and stared through the glass at the boots whose tread marks in the blood of the Clutter family led police to the killer Perry Smith and his partner. The boots looked small and as innocent as if some kid had outgrown them and left them behind on his journey out into the broad world.

Millirons was too young to have remembered that case of forty years ago, but he was certainly old enough to understand the changes that had taken place since Iowa Beef Processors opened their plant in 1980. Before that, he said, burglaries were rare events and folks routinely left their doors unlocked. Domestic violence was almost unknown (and surely almost never reported), while gangs were the plot devices of TV and movies. Now there were thirteen known gangs in and around Garden: Asian ones, Latino, white, even a girl gang. Also, local chapters of the national outfits, the Crips and the Bloods. As he finished telling me this Millirons pulled his cruiser around the back of a darkened restaurant. At the back door to Mi Officina a weather-blackened wreath lay in tribute to the owner, found dead of multiple stab wounds a few days earlier. The murder was most likely gang related, Millirons said. (So it proved on subsequent investigation.)

Away from the lights of its main arteries I thought Garden looked as safe and snug as it must have when Harold Millirons had been a boy, and in some areas it was, he said. "But since the plants came in there's been a big increase in domestic violence, particularly among the Latinos. The Asians tend to take care of their own problems themselves. I think it's because they don't trust us to take people away and bring them back.

They haven't gotten used to the services we provide." He didn't wish to be misunderstood here, though: this wasn't the Wild West, nor was the G.C.P.D. any Fort Apache. The plants had certainly brought a "lot of good things here. The economy's way up, construction, and so on. We see the good things, and like I say, there are a lot of them." He wheeled the cruiser into a U-Pump-It convenience store and waved to a man just coming out. "But from our point of view [law enforcement], we have to see the problems, too, and there are a lot of them."

Rocky Welton's talk about the plants and Millirons's, too, made me eager to have a look inside one of them, though I'd been forewarned this would be very difficult—for a writer almost impossible. "You'll never get in there," a local businessman had told me by phone. "They don't want people to see the conditions because, frankly, it's slave labor and very dangerous. For Christ's sake, don't quote me! Years ago, when the companies were moving in here, they said they were going to hire all the young guys from around here. Didn't happen. The young guys took a look at what was required in there and said, 'No, thanks.' Their parents probably would have done it. The Asians will, and bless their hearts, when they get enough put by, why, they move on."

He was just about right about access to the plants. On the outskirts of Garden and Dodge I drove around in the trailer barracks where the workers lived, and the parking lots gave me a sense of the scale of operations where as many as eight thousand cows a day can be slaughtered at the IBP plant alone. I had some background in commercial slaughtering from my Chicago boyhood when I'd seen the way it was done at the old stockyards. Nothing, though—*nothing*—can truly prepare you for the sensory assault of actually entering one of these facilities. With the afternoon shift I walked through security at ConAgra's Monfort plant, the only white face in the gang, and into something that must be called "infernal": the ferocious din of slaughter, fabrication, and packaging; the floors that are slippery with animal grease no amount of hosing can cut; and a smell as piercing and palpable as smoke. Everything in you shrinks from the encounter, and so I was almost happy when my ignorant blunderings about the ramps caught the attention of management and I was escorted to the personnel office where Gary Goodwin politely told me I had to leave.

"We've been the subject of a lot of negative reporting by the media," he said. "People understand that when they buy hamburger in the supermarket it comes from cows. But the slaughtering of cows, the skinning of them, the gutting, and so forth—it repulses them. They're not ready for that. It's very tough work. It's dangerous, noisy, the smell is terrible. Our workers take between a week and ten days before they even begin to adjust and can eat in the cafeteria. So, you can imagine what a problem a person like yourself would have going through our facility in just an hour. It's too much to take in and understand. I'm sorry." He smiled that regret and said, "Tell me a little about your project, won't you? Sounds interesting."

• • •

Late November, Cheyenne, Oklahoma

Eight-Ball in Oklahoma
Cheyenne Mourners

It was 7:30 in what few at the Boyett Club would have called "evening." The place was packed and the jukebox up so loud you could feel the bass notes through your boot soles. A Clarence Carter number, "Strokin'," was getting repeated plays. To a twangy accompaniment Carter revealed that he'd been making love to his woman when she said to him, "Clarence Carter, don't you stroke it so fast / And if my stuff ain't tight enough / You can stroke it up my—*twangg*!"

I was in town for a Cheyenne tribal ceremony the next day, and though the walls of the Boyett Club were decorated with photos of bonneted chieftains of times past, I saw no Indians in here, and it was hard to imagine they'd be welcome. The clientele was exclusively white: monstrous men in jeans, cowboy hats, and T-shirts stretched over eighteen-inch biceps and proportionate bellies. A few had consorts but not many. The bartenders were women, though, squeezed into jeans and tank tops, two of them drinking right along with their customers.

The occasion was an eight-ball pool tourney scheduled to begin shortly. The players were already at warm-up games on the hard-used tables, and the playing style was immediately evident. On the break, you hit the cue ball so hard the balls jumped up from the table and fell back

29

down with an exclamatory *clack*. When you had a clear shot at your
stripe or solid, you didn't aim simply to sink that sucker: you aimed to
ram it home so hard you shook the table. I saw only two contestants
who displayed what you might think of as "touch": a hefty woman who
moved and played with an almost incongruous lightness and an older
man who played hatless, his hair wispy and fragile-looking under the
intense lights, and who handled his stick almost tenderly.

I wanted to see how these two would come out against their powerhouse opponents, but more than an hour later the master of ceremonies
was still calling out the pairings and the bets as if at a cattle auction.
"Bud and Dave!" he hollered. "Bud and Dave! Thirty dollars. How
about thirty-two? Got thirty-two there. Got fifty there." Dave stood
next to me at the bar, a stocky man in mud-spattered hunting fatigues
who was getting determinedly hammered but still put five dollars on
himself to beat Bud. It seemed more a matter of self-respect than sporting judgment. "Ohhh, I ain't gonna win nothing'," he announced to no
one in particular, and I myself would have taken that bet. But I could
see it was going to be a very long evening at the club and I wanted to be
up early for the ceremonies. I wished Dave well, but he was too busy
making blunt advances to one of the barmaids. I didn't like his chances
there, either.

The ceremonies were in memoriam to the Cheyennes who'd fallen
at the Washita, November 28, 1868. The site itself was no more than a
mile from the Boyett Club, and at dawn I drove out there to try to re-
create in my mind something of that bitter dawn 130 years ago when
Custer and his Seventh Cavalry surprised the village of the noted peace
chief Black Kettle, the soldiers' mounts thundering across the snow-cov-
ered flats and the band playing "Garry Owen" until the spittle froze in
the tubing of their shining instruments. Nobody knows how many
Cheyennes—warriors, women, children—fell with Chief Black Kettle.
Custer claimed 103, a figure some think inflated by the boy-general's
customary exaggerated style. But the Indians' losses were heavy, including all of their winter provisions and the 875 ponies Custer ordered shot.
William Tecumseh Sherman, in charge of the army's Plains campaign,
had wanted either to kill or utterly impoverish the tribes, and here on
the Washita his man had done both.

At this early hour there was no one at the site, only some Indian offerings of ribbons and feathers hanging limply in the windless, foggy air. I walked down onto the flats where the village had stood, the scrubby trees along the river's meander dead black and interlaced, the tawny grasses tugging at my trousers as if they wanted to hold me here, to whisper, Stop. Here.

I paused above the riverbanks beneath which, waist high in the icy swirl, the Cheyennes' warriors had fought a rearguard action to protect their fleeing families. Later, while the soldiers went about the methodical business of destroying everything in the village, a survivor said she could hear the gunshot ponies dragging themselves through the grasses above her, moaning like humans.

Later that morning a group of Cheyenne elders gathered at the nearby Coyote Hills Ranch. The sun came out and the wind picked up, whipping the flames of a campfire about, flapping the ends of a red robe worn by the head singer. Probably no one in the crowd of watching whites knew Cheyenne, but afterwards Lawrence Hart, executive director of the Cheyenne cultural center in Clinton, provided a gloss. They'd sung for the fallen at the Washita, he told us, and then they'd sung some of the songs of the Cheyennes' military societies. "And we have certainly included songs for the soldiers who lost their lives here."

At the banquet that followed at the ranch I sat next to Hart, eating buffalo stew and listening to an elderly white woman play "America the Beautiful" and "Home on the Range" on an upright piano. When she finished, Lorena Savage Males sat down next to us and told Hart her father had once owned the store in nearby Hammon where the Cheyennes traded. "I know," Hart replied, his dark, handsome face creased in a smile. "My parents used to take me there to get my school shoes."

"And you know," Mrs. Males went on, recalling her girlhood spent during the teens of this century, "we had the only telephone for miles around. The Indians would come in to use it and get so excited when they heard talking on the other end they'd just stand up on tippy-toe and shout into the receiver."

• • •

31

Of Chiles, Cacti, and Fighting Cocks

Early December, Laredo, Texas

Dust Bowl Memories and the Dust Bowl That's Coming
The Laredo Hustle
With the Border Patrol

There may be lonelier, more desiccated stretches of America than that
between Cheyenne and Laredo. The roads north of Nixon, Nevada,
through the Black Rock Desert to Harper, Oregon, come to mind. But
zigzagging down the 100th through Erick, Oklahoma, and Hollis;
through Quanah, Texas, and Crowell and Paint Rock and Roosevelt will
satisfy anyone with a taste for solitude, wind, loss, and desert scrub.
Cheyenne and the country west and south was the epicenter of the Dust
Bowl, and all of the Cheyenne-to-Laredo stretch has been subject to
periodic drought. Looking at the dust aloft in the constant wind, reading the reports of drought, listening to the preacher at the Church of
Christ in Quanah talk of the hardness of earthly life—all this kept
throwing my mind back to my conversation with Lorena Savage Males
about the Dust Bowl. She'd lived through what she called "those terrible, terrible years" and had spoken so movingly of the greatness of heart
it had taken to survive them. "The Okies that went to California, they
were *great* people," she said with force, "and so were the ones that
stayed here. Who else could have lived through it?" In the depths of it,
she told me, the hallways of the school where she'd taught music were
drifted in dust. "And you would have thought the teachers and students
were playing Cops and Robbers—they had handkerchiefs over their
mouths and noses. My husband was president of the bank, and he got so
depressed by conditions that some days he would just come home and
get into bed."

More greatness of heart may be required of those few who remain
on the land. The year was as dry as the worst of the "Dirty Thirties"
according to officials, and every one of Texas's 254 counties had been
declared a federal disaster area—this just two years after another
drought brought severe hardship to the same region. In Abilene, Texas,
I spent a morning with Wayne Davis who supervised a training program there for aspiring oilfield roughnecks. The water wells in neighboring San Angelo, he said, had gone dry this past summer, "and if we

32

don't get rain this winter, we'll have to go to water rationing by May."
Davis's immediate problem was the depressed price of oil that since
April had cost the industry about 50,000 jobs nationwide.

But the real problem, the intractable one, was water and always had
been. Large portions of the 100th lie atop the Ogallala aquifer—southernmost South Dakota, almost all of Nebraska, the Oklahoma
Panhandle, and the Texas Panhandle down as far as the Abilene area—a
vast storehouse of fossil water that farmers, ranchers, and communities
have been sucking on for much of this century. Before its discovery and
before settlers figured out how to tap into it they had practiced small-
scale dry-land farming, and they hand-dug wells hundreds of feet deep.
Or else they laboriously rolled huge water barrels half a mile or more
from the nearest source to their homesteads. But with the appearance
on the land of the gasoline-powered pump, the gasoline truck, and the
tractor in the years before the Great War the mechanics of big-time
hydraulic agriculture were all in place. In 1906 a farm historian had
echoed Major Powell's warnings when he observed that the expanse
between the 98th Meridian and the Rockies was deep in tragedy. But
then the gas-powered pump apparently changed all that. But only
apparently, for a few years later, in the midst of the Dust Bowl, FDR's
Public Works Administration was echoing Powell anew when it
reported that extensive areas of the Great Plains "must be classed as
unsuited to sustained cultivated crops, and should therefore never have
been plowed."

But plowed they were and more extensively and intensively than
ever once the drought cycle of the Dirty Thirties ended. Now another
one appears to be in process, and the Ogallala is going fast. Some say it
will last another thirty years—less than that if conservation methods
aren't enacted. Wayne Davis recalled his experiences up near Garden
City. He'd been there on a job in the 1950s, he said, and had been back
there last year. "And I was talking with a fella who told me the water
table has dropped eighty-one feet in the last seventeen years." He spit
snuff juice into a cup he kept on his desk and tilted back in his swivel
chair. "In thirty years this'll be a Dust Bowl again. We have the oil, but
we don't have the water." I spoke with him of my growing sense of traveling in the wake of disaster, of all the collapsed, boarded-up towns I'd
seen along the way, and he nodded. He'd come from such a place himself

33

and knew what had so long been in the making: the heart of the heartland was shockingly depopulated and likely to become even more so.
"The hundred-acre farm is now a hobby," he said. "You've got to be
almost *huge* to make it. The rest move to town, they move to places like
Abilene. Or they commute. In the evenings they buy their groceries for
less than they can from that one little store that's left in their hometown.
They put gas in their truck for less than what that one gas station left is
selling it for. And then they drive sixty miles back to their little town.
But even the big operators are facing trouble because that Ogallala is
being rapidly depleted, and it cannot be replenished except very, very
slowly. The time will come when the price of gas will be half of what
water will be."

In most countries on earth fourteen hundred miles in any direction
can take in a lot of differences. On my journey down the 100th I'd had
plenty of time to make the adjustment from the stolidities of North
Dakota and the hard angles of its light and culture to the desert landscape and Spanish tinge of Laredo–Nuevo Laredo. What was a bit more
difficult to comprehend were the differing responses to economic adver-
sity from north to south. No place I saw along the way looked really
flush in the midst of this period of sustained national prosperity, and
plenty of places looked hard hit, even devastated. But in retrospect there
now seemed to me a kind of bafflement up north, a resentment that the
historic, grand hopes hadn't been realized. Sometimes I got the feeling
up there that people were looking around for someone to blame—
Washington, hoggish middlemen, the Japanese. Their politics tended to
be conservative, a fact amply demonstrated again in the off-year elections. When I'd asked Bill Quigley in Valentine if there were *any*
Democrats in that vicinity he quoted me the local response, "Yes, but we
spray for 'em."

But I felt no such resentment or xenophobia down on the border.
What I felt was *hustle*, as if down here there were no great expectations
and never had been, NAFTA or no. You just got up in the morning and
began to hit it, doing the best you could. I wondered whether the
American Dream had ever been planted here, whether it couldn't take
root, as so many other things couldn't. Across the river in Mexico a mysteriously steeped psychological cocktail of Spanish Catholicism, Indian
stoicism, and climate had induced a fatalism that was proof against the

centuries of exploitation and hopeless poverty. You couldn't travel many days down here without coming to understand that there wasn't any such thing as "The Mexican Dream." The closest thing to it, and wider than the river, was the dream of El Norte.

The riverfront streets of Laredo looked and felt precisely like those of other border towns I'd seen: Brownsville/Matamoros, El Paso/Juarez, San Diego/Tijuana. There were the same bars, Laundromats, and stores in whose windows you found a literally stunning salad of stuff: watches, clocks, knives, purses, pouches, sandals, giant wooden pencils, caps, barrettes, gardening gloves, whistles, pocket flashlights, and now also laser pointers. Every day and well into the night there was an almost motionless gridlock in these streets, the trapped exhaust hanging blue between the buildings. On the Convent Street Bridge the pedestrian flow at night was south to the Mexican side, and at that end of the bridge there were knots of young men and boys looking north, always north. When their eyes swept over you it was with an appraising, comprehensive glance that instantly marked you as friend, foe, opportunity, or nullity. How many of the watchers, I had to wonder, knew very much about the reality of the lands I'd been traveling? Or were they thinking instead of Dallas or Chicago?

Most of those hoping to enter, legally or not, wouldn't be pointing for those hopeless little hamlets I'd been passing through on my way down the 100th, Danny Garza told me; they'd be pointing for larger centers where they'd heard there was work—just like so many of the young people Senator Daschle's bill mentioned. Garza was a ten-year veteran of the Border Patrol who'd agreed to take me along on his nightly rounds. While I waited for him at headquarters I looked through the patrol's photo albums showing recent drug busts and the places the druggers concealed their cargo: behind car radios, beneath the beds of pickups, in sealed-off partitions of gas tanks, in rocker panels. The faces of the apprehended looked neither frightened nor shocked. Instead, they looked resigned, as though they were thinking, "Oh well, it was worth the risk."

And for the successful it really was, Garza said later. "If they can make it through, they can be set for life," he said as we turned down Pico Road toward the river. This was prime drug-smuggling habitat rather than a crossing point for what Garza called "aliens." The two groups tended to maintain a distance and to recognize each other's territories. High above the river's turbid crawl we got out of the white-painted wagon and stood talking on the bluffs. Three hundred yards away another wagon of what's known as "La Migra" was parked on a promontory. "We try to be a visible deterrent," Garza explained, nodding at the neighboring unit, "but we're spread pretty thin. Between here and Eagle Pass there are only two units. We have the [buried] sensors and the dogs, so we pick up some that way." It seemed pretty hopeless to me, and when we headed back down the road and then swung north of the city I said so. He didn't see it that way—or if he did, he wasn't admitting it tonight to his passenger. Drugs and aliens got through, sure, and there was the endemic corruption you had to deal with on the border, but the force did its best, and surely its best was far better than surrender. Currently, Garza added, the force was bracing for a flood of desperate refugees from Hurricane Mitch. "They should be showing up in spring," he said with what I took as professional resignation.

At the end of a narrow, deeply-rutted road running between immense clusters of prickly pear we came to an area known to La Migra as the "Hog Patch," a popular crossing point for aliens. It was now the blue-gray twilight of the year's end, but below on the river's Mexican side five figures were easily visible. When we got out of the wagon they ducked behind some boulders. Garza flicked his flashlight in their direction, then pointed out to me the approximate locations of the electronic sensors buried below in the willow flats. There were enough of them spaced about that it would be pretty difficult for a man to avoid tripping one, he thought. The lightest footfall, even that of a dog, could do it. The signal then registered back at headquarters. Still, that didn't appear to discourage the aliens, even though the folklore of the border told them that crossers at the Hog Patch were routinely apprehended and sent back. The ones we could see now were simply waiting for us to leave and for night to fall.

But it wouldn't be full dark this night, for as we stood looking across space and history a huge melon of a moon lifted through the feathers of the mesquite trees and made black silhouettes of the cactus clumps. With a certain boldness two of the figures came out from behind the boulders and strolled to the river's edge. A cigarette flared. Neither Garza nor I could distinguish the faces over there. They were just forms, and so were we. I could hear Garza's calm breathing next to me—just another night. And at that moment it occurred to me that it was certainly possible that the hearts of the watchers and the watched, law enforcement and its would-be evaders, were beating in unison on opposite sides of a river once nameless in what was then a New World without meridians and their barriers, their promises. And what were the American dreams we now breathed together in this, our common darkness?

Purple Kid

In the late summer of 1947, on my way to becoming a little outlaw myself, I stole a paperback copy of Walter Noble Burns's *The Saga of Billy the Kid* from the drugstore at the corner of 107th Street and Hale in Chicago. In the alley just off the Rock Island tracks I opened its brittle-backed pages—and was disappointed: there were no pictures, and I had wanted so much to see the Kid's face, his guns, and horse. So shortly thereafter I put this apparently fraudulent work on the secret bookshelf in my closet, where it reposed next to a salaciously titled book by Sigmund Freud that had disappointed for the same reason.

Three years later—again it was summer—I took Burns's book out from its guilty obscurity and read that famous flat first sentence: "John Chisum knew cows." Now, more than a half century later, I can still see that page, those words, and the shaded summer light that fell across my bed as I read the opening chapter. It was putatively factual in intent, and yet it was painted brightly enough to give the wary reader, easily bored by cowhide history, a hint and promise of gaudier colors ahead and of designs larger than history. Like John Chisum forking over a debt he owed the Kid, Burns delivered fully on his promissory note, and for the rest of that summer I *was* the Kid as Burns had made me so vividly see him.

Of course, there is much writing in Burns's *Saga* calculated to gratify and amaze the literary sensibilities of an adolescent boy—considerable stretches where the painting is purple. Subsequent acquaintance with the ever-expanding bibliography on Billy the Kid and on the Lincoln County War has made it clear to me that Burns both enlarged and simplified. Yet nothing I am aware of that has been published in the intervening decades seems as intuitively true and right on these subjects as Burns's book on the Kid and his war. Michael Ondaatje's *The Collected Works of Billy the Kid*, Bob Dylan's compositions for the film *Pat Garrett and Billy the Kid*, and Larry McMurtry's *Anything for Billy* bear closest comparison, but all owe much to Burns and would be impossible without him. Robert Utley, the distinguished historian of the American

West and author of books on the Lincoln County War and on the Kid, once told me he regarded Burns's *Saga* as the second most influential book ever written on the Kid. "Garrett's is the most influential," Utley said, "because without it Burns wouldn't have had anything to work with."

From a cause-and-effect point of view, this may be so. Would Burns—or anyone else outside of New Mexico—have known anything about this marginal and obscure hired gun if Garrett, his slayer, had not cooperated in the ghosted account of his brief life, all to build Billy into a giant so that he, the slayer, would therefore be the giant-killer? Probably not. Probably Billy Bonney, a.k.a. Kid Antrim or Billy Kid, would have faded into the sere brownness of local lore until, with the passings of the primary tale-tellers, Kid Antrim would have been lost, surviving only as a name in the fragmentary documentation of an old vendetta.

But then, ask this: what if Burns had not written his purple-hued book? Garrett's ghosted and self-serving account is, after all, too slender a reed to bear the weight of legend. For that, something more was needed. Just a year before publication of *The Saga of Billy the Kid* in 1926, the Western writer Harvey Fergusson had rhetorically wondered in H. L. Mencken's *American Mercury* whether anyone remembered Billy the Kid. By 1927, however, the Kid was firmly reestablished in the American imagination: *Saga* was a Book-of-the-Month Club selection and a best-seller, and even readers who could not identify on a map of the states the locale of the Kid's crimes were nonetheless convinced of the authenticity of Burns's portrait of the doomed, handsome boy killer.

Burns was hardly breaking new ground with his 1926 book. By that time the legends of the Lincoln County War and of its most famous participant had had more than forty years to gather life and force, and the Kid had been celebrated in dime novels as well as in more apparently sober treatments by Garrett, Charles Siringo, and Emerson Hough. But his legend was by then showing signs of shrinking back to the purely local.

Its rescuer came to the legend as a veteran, itinerant newspaper man. Burns had knocked around a good deal, had made a whaling voyage out of San Francisco to the South Pacific, had been to the Arctic Circle, and had served in the Spanish-American War. For the better part of forty years he had been on the staffs of Western newspapers— Louisville, St. Louis, Kansas City, Denver, San Francisco, Chicago. He would subsequently go on to write entertainingly of the famed frontier town of Tombstone and of Joaquín Murrieta, California's Hispanic Robin Hood. Yet in the same way that the Kid owes Burns so largely for his posthumous fame, so Burns himself owes his subject. For without his controversial Billy book, Burns would doubtless share a fate oddly kindred to the Kid's: remembered, if at all, as a purveyor of legends of regional interest only. But there was the Kid, and Burns spent the best of a genuine if limited talent in conjuring up from the dusty and neglected past the ghost of a killer, evoking the drama of his hero's split second on the human stage.

To be sure, Burns's Kid *is* a killer, a clear-eyed, quick-fingered shootist with zero at the bone (to borrow from Emily Dickinson). He kills without remorse and without undue regard for the code of honor that says even outlaws must fight fair. But Burns's Kid is also the heroic victim of a tragic drama, pulled unwillingly and unwittingly into a vendetta between two factions fighting for economic control of the southern territory of New Mexico. And this vendetta itself is seen as the last act in the frontier history of New Mexico and the Southwest as a whole. "His destructive and seemingly futile career," Burns writes, "served a constructive purpose: it drove home the lesson that New Mexico's prosperity could be built only upon the basis of stability and peace."

Billy Bonney, Burns tells us, had no interest in any of these larger matters. He was, after all, only a boy. He was "a boy when the tale begins, a boy when it ends; a boy born to battle and vendetta, ... to tragic victory and tragic defeat, and who took it all with a smile." Fate, Burns says, set the stage for the drama of the Kid's life. "Opposite him played Death. It was the drama of Death and the Boy." But for a while the Boy eludes Death, escaping miraculously when there was but one chance in a million. "He laughed at Death. Death was a joke. He waved Death a jaunty good-bye and was off to new adventures." But in the darkness of Pete Maxwell's house in Fort Sumner, Death came for him again, and just at the moment when escape seemed possible. "The boy had had his hour. It was Death's turn. And so the curtain." I ought to know better by now, but Burns's tableau still gets to me—and long after I myself was a kid.

Part of what makes this book so effective is that Burns was working in harmony with the force and flow of local opinion in Kid country. This

really was the way many New Mexicans viewed Billy the Kid, though
Robert Utley cautions that Burns's book was so immediately influential
that even those who participated in the events of the Kid's days subsequently found themselves remembering things the way Burns had said
they happened. Burns apparently never viewed himself as a professional
historian, charged with the solemn responsibility to weigh evidence and
sort out probabilities from the welter of conflicting testimony. He was a
journalist, though, and he knew a story. What he stumbled across in
New Mexico was all that and more: it was a genuine, living folk legend,
complete with its doomed hero, its dramatic oppositions, its tragic
betrayal (Garrett's of the Kid, his quondam friend), its numerous for-
mulaic tales, and variations of these. Talking with Lincoln County old-
timers who vividly remembered the war and who carried still their
wounds and passions; sitting through leisurely afternoons on the benches
of the plaza in Santa Fe with old men puffing handbuilt cigarettes;
spending evenings before the fires of the tiny adobes spread along the
green floor of the Bonito Valley, Burns heard something that had escaped
the notice of his literary predecessors. It was the perishable breath of
oral tradition, and he caught its content, tones, and cadences. Drop in,
he invited his readers, to some little adobe home in Puerto de Luna.

> Or in Santa Rosa. Or on the Hondo. Or anywhere between the
> Ratons and Seven Rivers. Perhaps the Mexican housewife will
> serve you with frijoles and tortillas and coffee with goat's milk.
> If you are wise in the ways of Mexicans, you will tear off a
> fragment of tortilla and, cupping it between your fingers, use it
> as a spoon to eat your frijoles that are red with chili pepper and
> swimming in soup rich with fat bacon grease. But between
> mouthfuls of these beans of the gods—and you will be ready to
> swear they are that, else you are no connoisseur in beans—don't
> forget to make some casual reference to Billy the Kid. Then
> watch the face of your hostess. At mention of the magic name,
> she will smile softly and dreamlight will come into her eyes.
> "Billee the Keed? Ah, you have hear of heem? He was one
> gran' boy, señor. All Mexican pepul his friend."

Later, when some hotly questioned his method and the constructions
it led him to, Burns defended himself, saying that what he had been
after in *Saga* would never be found in documents. Writing from
Chicago in his late years, he told a sympathetic inquirer that an "official
record is at best only a sketchy outline of a cause and you must depend
for details, especially if you wish to get some color into your story, upon
extraneous sources."

• • •

There was another "extraneous source" besides the old-timers that
Burns drew on in *Saga*, a powerfully authoritative one, and this was the
landscape of the Kid's outlaw domain, from Santa Fe in the north to
Fort Sumner in the east, to Lincoln and Roswell in the south. Making a
pilgrimage there was for me both revelation and delight, for in doing so
I found Burns's ultimate vindication: despite its many factual errors, *The
Saga of Billy the Kid* is *imaginatively* right, and only the most stubborn
momus would refuse to grant this in traveling the lonesome, narrow
roads down to Lincoln. There are stretches here that are just about
what they were in Burns's time—or the Kid's, for that matter. Between
Encino and Duran there is nothing but the land itself, unimproved,
unreclaimed, its long, undulating reaches a battle-tested brown with
dots of green—junipers and piñons, bunchgrass and several varieties of
cactus. Where the land is barest, dust devils send red cones upward for a
moment. There is no water in summer, and the dry washes look like the
split veins of a huge anatomy. In the wind, hovering hawks glide close
to the surface or allow themselves to be taken effortlessly upward, and
to the unpracticed eye the tumbleweed in the distances also looks like
birds—brown, dense, windborne.

At Duran the land begins to change, and heading south into sunlight you raise the Jicarilla Mountains dead ahead, the nearest displaying
their own unique colors, the next range deep purple, and the farthest the
best blue in a French palette. Where the Jicarillas become the Capitans
there is a sign for White Oaks, and nine miles deeper in you come upon
the splayed husk of a town that contains no kernel. If, as Burns wrote
and Hough before him, the town was "cradled" by two mountain
ranges, time demands a change in metaphor, for White Oaks has now

43

slipped from sleep into the longer stillness of decay, the valley floor littered with the chalky bones of adobes, some of them barely visible above the waving tops of grasses. And where the mind's eye reconstructs the center of the town, a tall, gaunt hulk keeps sentinel over nothing. Was it in front of this building that the long-limbed Garrett stood, reflectively picking his teeth after a good meal, his deputy, John Poe, beside him, when the winded Mexican rider galloped in with the news that El Chivato had killed his two jailers and escaped? And where is the Dedrick brothers' livery stable, where the Kid hid out before riding northeast to Fort Sumner and death? Without guides such as Burns had, these ruins are hieroglyphic.

The road out of White Oaks to Lincoln keeps company with the Capitans now, at the head of which is Capitan Peak. Burns described the peak as the only headstone of Morton and Baker, gunmen of the Murphy-Dolan faction in the war and executed by the Kid and his posse at Agua Negra between Roswell and Lincoln. A farmer selling the cold cherry cider that is a staple of this fruitful little valley has never heard of Agua Negra, and so for him and his questioner, Morton and Baker, murderers themselves, lie somewhere at the eastern foot of the peak, undiscovered, undiscoverable.

Lincoln is huddled within the Capitans on the north and the Capitan foothills on the south, the latter rising steeply from the back of town—and you think as you see the way they overhang the single street how perfectly situated those snipers would have been during the five-day battle that marked the turning point in the war. Here, then, is that street with its lazy bend, at its western end the old Murphy-Dolan store, later the county courthouse, then a school, and at last a museum. Its twin staircases are gone now, leaving the front porch without access except from within. But you can still stand where the Kid stood at the porch's eastern edge and muse on the homicidal rage, the bottomless revenge that filled him that sunny April day when he pumped the last chamber of Olinger's shotgun into the deputy's already lifeless body, smashed the stock against the railing, and hurled the remains down at the corpse while the townspeople watched from the shadows of their homes and stores.

In his reconstruction of the Kid's remarkable escape, Burns chose to follow a version that has Billy wrest Deputy Bell's pistol from him, then shoot him when Bell tries to flee. While there is no doubt the Kid shot the fleeing Bell before he killed Olinger, the prosaic truth seems to be that he shot Bell with a pistol that had been hidden for him in the jail's outhouse. This detail notwithstanding, there beneath you in the shade of the old building's corner is a marble tablet that marks the spot where Olinger looked up into death when the Kid made his casual, fatal salutation: "Hello, Bob."

The lower floor of the building contains photos and documents relating to the Kid and the war in which he came to murderous prominence, and from a coffined glass case the face of the Kid's companion bravo, Tom O'Folliard, stares out, frozen in youthfulness by the winking eye of the camera. Some itinerant photographer had invaded the pictureless, imageless West with his big, cumbersome box and plates, for here are the shadows of cowboys, Indians, and settlers, most of their names now lost, detached from these faded impressions. And here are other men the Kid once rode with: Charlie Bowdre, dressed to kill with his cartridge belt, revolver, and rifle, his handsome, fiery wife, Manuelita, beside him; Fred Wayte; and Hendry Brown, who tried to go straight and couldn't. Dolan; Murphy; the McSweens; Poe and Pat Garrett: the principal actors in what Burns has made so many readers see as a tragic drama.

And, of course, the Kid, the single tintype of him fuzzily revealing a narrow-shouldered, weak-jawed boy, slovenly in his bulky range clothes, posed in front of old Beaver Smith's saloon at Fort Sumner one dateless day, doubtless under circumstances much like those that caught O'Folliard. And you wonder what that photographer thought, lining up his sights on this subject who seems distinguished only by his youth. Burns drew a far more flattering portrait of the hero than this photo shows; indeed, the critic Burton Rascoe was once moved by this discrepancy to comment that the real Kid bore all the outward appearances of a cretin. No matter. Burns had the weight of local support for his picture of the Kid as nice-looking, with a clean, fair face only mildly disfigured by buck teeth. Old Man Foor, Burns's guide to the graves at Fort Sumner, said these teeth made the Kid look like he was smiling when he wasn't—a fatal delusion.

In a far corner, as if in hiding from the stare of the photographed Kid, is a full-color portrait of Billy as tourists (perhaps guided obscurely by Burns) would have him: blue-eyed, apple-cheeked, under a wide gray sombrero, looking like a cross between Tom Mix and Johnny Mack Brown. It is one of the few false touches in the museum.

Upstairs is the large courtroom, bright, high-ceilinged, in the north-west corner of which the Kid was confined. A faded outline in white along the wide-planked floors gives the original dimensions of the cell that eventually gave way to expanded judicial needs, a single mark of triumph here for law over outlawry. And here is Billy the Kid's window, from which he gazed upon the tiny world of Lincoln. The pasture is there where Burns described it, and sparrows and robins still clamor among the bushes along its borders.

There are two holes in the wall at the foot of the stairs leading down from the prison room. Legend and Burns, its recorder, tell us that these are the exit marks of those shots the Kid fired at Deputy Bell. Generations of school kids, trooping upstairs on sentences of their own when this was the schoolhouse, have greatly enlarged whatever was there so that now the holes might have been made by cannonballs. Just to the left of these stairs a door opens out onto the back pasture, and out of it Bell stumbled blindly into the spring sun, a mortal hole bored through him, back to front.

Balancing the Murphy-Dolan store at the opposite end of town, the counterweight to the feud, is the Tunstall-McSween store, as big though not so high as its rival. Its shutters still carry their protective metal inserts between thick wooden slabs, and within, the high shelves still bear relics of the merchandise once dispensed to this farming and ranch-ing community, simple items answering fundamental needs: tack, rope, lamp chimneys, buckshot, feed, coffee, tea. The ledger books, neatly ruled and entried, show the outlays of plowline and lumber to the Oteros and Bacas and Salazars who planted and reaped along these green Bonito bottoms and who lie now in the stubble-spiked cemetery east of town, crosses and markers worn and tilted in a wind that moves the iron turnstile at the gate in a creaky dirge that few attend.

The store's original owners, both victims of the war, lie out behind the building. When Burns was doing his collecting in the mid-1920s, Tunstall and McSween lay markerless beneath a smoldering pile of rubbish. There are two neat granite markers now, and the rubbish pile has been moved a few yards to the east. Burns says that the lawyer Chapman, murdered by Dolan, Jesse Evans, and Bill Campbell, lies alongside Tunstall and McSween; if so, he still awaits commemoration.

Just up the street from the store is the supposed site of the McSween house, burned to the ground in the climax of the five-day battle that effectively ended the war. I was there on a scorching July day in 1986 when an archaeological team began excavations hoping to uncover telltale fragments of the house in which the Murphy-Dolan forces cornered McSween and his hired guns led by the Kid. Gary Miller, director of the Lincoln County Heritage Trust, a sponsor of the dig, stood with me in a room of the Fresquez house, which had been built on the site. Workers had pried away its flooring and were already several feet down in the cocoa-colored, friable soil. He told me that as part of the dig the Trust had engaged the services of a psychic from Santa Fe who had surveyed the site and predicted that searchers would find pieces of Mrs. McSween's piano, a skeleton, and some firearms. In his reconstruction of the battle, Burns has Mrs. McSween playing the piano while her home goes up in smoke and enemy bullets crash through the windows, a piece of fiction the widowed woman bitterly resented when she read it years later. I told Miller that Burns had admitted to this outright invention and then asked him his opinion of the book. "I regard it," he said carefully, his eyes on the sweating diggers just beneath us, "as an entertaining novel with a lot of holes in it. But it for sure was the first book to try to tell the story from beginning to end, and he did interview a lot of people who were there at the time. I guess you'd have to say it was that book that really started the whole thing [the legend, the notoriety of the town, and its annual Billy the Kid pageant] rolling."

And the Kid? He laughed shortly. "Well, the historians' view of him keeps changing. There's just not that much historical documentation of him, which, of course, is why he's always fun to write about: you can pretty much peg him any way you want to. It's kind of like the issue of what he really looked like. You've seen the photo they usually print of him—the one where he's holding the rifle? Well, we have the original tintype, and when you look at that and enhance it, you come up with a different image of him, not at all the moron he looks like in the standard reproductions." Maybe, I said, Burns was more right than Burton Rascoe in describing the Kid as a good-looking boy. Miller raised his eyebrows and said maybe he was.

Beneath the scaffolding that had been laid across the excavation, the patient picking and sifting continued. It was possible, Miller was saying, that they were digging in the wrong spot, but among the many speculations and mysteries that surround the Kid and the war there was no doubting that we were at that moment on the very site of tragedy, where men had died with their boots on. The Kid and a few of his compatriots had escaped out the kitchen door of the house to the Bonito; McSween, however, stubborn to the end, had refused to surrender or run and had been gunned down here. After which the Murphy-Dolan men had heaped blazing timbers from the house on his corpse.

• • •

Minor Good Thomas was a voluble, articulate little woman who had been a resident of Lincoln for well over half a century. I found her in the dim Tunstall store, where she kept track of the tourists who wandered through the silent, musty rooms and answered their questions if they had any. I found in putting a question to her that she was not at all reluctant to speak out on Burns, the Kid, or the war. "That book," she said emphatically, "belongs on the fiction shelf, and that's just where a good many librarians put it now. It was really based on Garrett's book, and that book itself wasn't written by Garrett but by Ash Upton, and *he* was a terrible alcoholic. So how accurate could it [*Saga*] be?" Her eyes snapped behind the lenses of her glasses. "Burns portrayed Billy the Kid as a Robin Hood. Well, he wasn't that by any means. But he wasn't a moron, either, as some have said. And he wasn't a back-stabber. Remember, we mustn't judge those people by our own standards. This was *territory* then. *Most* of the people out here were just one jump ahead of the law. There were buffalo soldiers stationed here, lots of quarrelsome Irish, outlaws, rustlers. It was a rough time and place, and Billy the Kid was just one of the rougher ones."

How much, I asked her, of the interest in the Kid had been sparked by *Saga*? "Oh, a great deal. A very great deal. But you know"—and here she regarded me closely—"there is a lot more history to Lincoln County than Billy the Kid or that book written about him. There is a great deal of Indian history here and a great deal of cattlemen history, too. But all anybody wants to hear about is 'Billy-the-Kid,' 'Billy-the-Kid.'" She sang it with a contemptuous lilt.

That was certainly all I wanted to hear about on this afternoon, and as soon as I gracefully could I chucked my responsibility to learn more about these other dimensions of Lincoln County history and wandered out onto the shaded porch, happy as a truant schoolboy.

It is just possible that this now-quiet town is still divided along the old factional lines, the Tunstall-McSween followers tending to live eastward around that store, the Murphy-Dolan people to the west. And that beyond this—and as if to reinforce the division—those around the eastern store seem partial to *The Saga of Billy the Kid*, while those at the other end of town are much more aware of the liberties the writer took with history. Such at least is suggested by talks I once had with two remarkable women.

Rafaelita Pryor lived on the eastern edge in one of the neat adobes, shadowed and bird-sung, that line the street. She was the granddaughter of Saturnino Baca, founder of Lincoln County, and on the other side of her family she was a Salazar, the county's other great family name. Rafaelita's brother married Yginio Salazar's daughter, that same Yginio who, by playing dead for hours among the actual corpses, survived the flaming end of the five-day battle and lived on to become a major informant of Burns's. It's all in that book, Rafaelita told me, and she went on to say that she herself heard the story from Yginio years after he had talked with Burns. Like Yginio and Burns, she thought well of the Kid. "Yginio really liked him," she said. "Most people did. He was very nice to old people, poor people. But"—she wagged an admonitory finger—"you'd better not cross him." In illustration of which characterization she offered an anecdote about her uncle Bonifacio, witness to the assassination of Sheriff Brady and his deputy by the Kid and his men, who shot from the cover of the Tunstall-McSween store. Bonifacio was called to testify at the Kid's trial at Mesilla and did so. Some time after the Kid's escape from Lincoln, Bonifacio met him on the road to San Patricio. " 'You know,' said the Kid, 'I'd kill you right here if you'd lied at my trial.' Didn't make any difference to him which way the lie had gone. Just that it was a lie. *That's* the kind of man the Kid was!"

But on the other edge of town, a broken one-story adobe lies in a grave of high grass, the green of the fields beyond visible through its naked roof beams. This was the home of Sheriff George W. ("Dad") Peppin, successor to the murdered Brady, unflatteringly described by

Burns as the willing tool of the Murphy-Dolan faction. Next to the ruin is the tidy homestead of Peppin's granddaughter, Belle Wilson. A strong-framed woman even in her old age, large sunbonnet shading a direct, lined face, she answered my opening question about Burns's book: "Yes, I've read that book, and I don't mind telling you I don't think much of it." This was by way of an invitation, and she welcomed me in.

So that I would not misunderstand her, she wanted to make clear a distinction: that book was very enjoyable, "but he has a good many things in there that didn't happen and couldn't have happened." The heart of the objection was historical: Burns took liberties with the truth, she told me, and got most of his information from the Coe family, especially Frank Coe. Naturally, his book would be biased, because both Coe brothers rode with the Tunstall-McSween forces and did their share of rustling and killing. "At least we know Frank did. The only comment I can remember my mother ever making about the Coes was that they weren't neighborly people. Just not the kind you'd want around you."

She wanted to set me straight on John Chisum, too, since Burns had so many good things to say about him. She told me that around here, "we know that Chisum had as much to do with this as anyone. But since that Burns book nobody says these things. But Billy the Kid always blamed Chisum for much of the trouble he got into. So you see, although that book was very enjoyable to read, very entertaining, it isn't the full story of it, but only one side." That, she concluded, is the trouble with history. But then, in the best left-handed compliment Burns's book may ever get, she said, "If it wasn't for that book, there wouldn't be all this: that book started it all," her hand sweeping outward in a gesture that included all of Lincoln, its festivals, museums, the entire legend itself, and what it has meant to New Mexico—indeed, to the entire Southwest. That may well be the trouble with the way Burns has given us this history. But by the same token Belle Wilson has told the whole truth about *The Saga of Billy the Kid* and the long purple shadow it continues to cast.

The Life of Dry Spaces

Some years ago the *New York Times Book Review* ran an illustration accompanying a review of James A. Michener's *Texas*. The drawing showed a giant saguaro cactus in the form of a candelabra, its arms shaped into pencil points. The idea here was clear and effective: this was a big novel about a big, tough place—the American West. Subsequently there appeared in the pages of the same publication a letter from a Texas historian, patiently pointing out that the saguaro doesn't grow in Texas and wondering whether this botanical error wasn't really another example of that Northeastern provincialism about which Texas writers have sometimes complained.

The professional historian is often a killjoy, and I happen to know that this one does not confine himself to pointing out to New Yorkers their vulgar errors: he has, for instance, dared to give public lectures to Texans in which he says it's likely that Davey Crockett didn't die heroically at the Alamo but instead was captured alive and executed. In any case, the *Times Book Review* was not instructed by the historian's quibble. Indeed, it committed the same error again when, in a review of Texas writer William Humphrey's collected stories, it ran a drawing of a human figure dangling from the spine of a saguaro.

So the saguaro doesn't grow in Texas but is instead confined to a small area of Arizona and northern Sonora, Mexico. Big deal. Readers doubtless got the point of both illustrations, which were after all cartoons, not realism. Texas is a cactus-covered place, isn't it? And of all cacti, surely the most readily recognized is the saguaro. It would be a lot harder to hang an idea or a human from the low, squat pod of a prickly pear cactus, numerous varieties of which do grow in Texas—and almost everywhere else in the lower forty-eight states. Besides, from the vantage of Manhattan or Westport, Connecticut, the difference between Texas and Arizona (where the saguaro truly does grow) is small, as the oft-reproduced Saul Steinberg illustration reminds us: there, Manhattan's west side looms far larger than the whole of the American

51

West, which is only vaguely, sketchily depicted.

The saguaro *is* a convenient image to hang things from, and as the *Times*'s illustrations make plain, in America the saguaro is the generic cactus that stands for the life of all those lands "out there" in the West. It stands for sun, for space. It suggests, too, a parching and pervasive dryness, cacti being popularly supposed to be exclusively inhabitants of the desert. There is a psychological, perhaps even vaguely spiritual, dimension to this image as well, for the saguaro stands for a certain tough quality we attribute to Western life, a regional ability to handsomely endure even the severest hardships of a harsh environment. Standing sentinel in the forbidding desert wastes, the saguaro constitutes a grand, green answer to our oldest question, What are Life's chances against Death?

• • •

Inevitably in the American mind's eye the saguaro's image is colored in with sun and shadow, and this is as it should be, for there really is a hell of a lot of sun in the saguaro's domain and throughout the West. Western weather patterns consistently operate against the formation of large, long-hanging cloud blankets, and there is much less vegetative cover and airborne water vapor than east of the Mississippi. Out here when the sun shines, much of its force is felt on the land. Several years back scientists determined that, for example, Yuma, Arizona, received ninety-three percent of its possible sunshine while in that same year Norfolk, Virginia, with its denser vegetation and higher humidity, received but thirty-one percent. Thus Western plants like the saguaro have had to adapt to this relentless solar assault with a variety of ingenious stratagems.

Cacti, for instance, which probably began as woody shrubs in subtropical regions of Mexico, "learned" that in the American West leaves were an expensive luxury because they caught too much sun. On the newly formed pods of prickly pears you can still see ephemeral leaves, but these soon disappear: spines are what are left of leaves, a beneficial development, since spines significantly reduce the amount of a cactus's surface exposure. Cacti also developed a tough, waxy skin that helps protect them from the sun, and if you are brave and dexterous enough to peel away the skin of a prickly pear, you'll discover just how tough that protective casing is. It is about the consistency of a leather sole, though of course not nearly so thick. Beneath it the prickly pear seems as soft and vulnerable as a Bartlett.

As with sun, there is a great deal of space out here, a fact that has teased the American imagination at least since Lewis and Clark, and for which the towering, freestanding saguaro is, again, so apt an image. Looking at the national map, you're struck by the progressively larger size of the states as you scan westward. By contrast, the map looks crowded east of the Mississippi, as if the way the country took shape here were a weird prefiguration of the traffic jam. And the farther west you go, the more space there is—more space to traverse, more space between natural features like mountains, buttes, rivers, trees.

The saguaro is no exception to the region's generous spacing. Ground-level photographs of saguaros make it appear as if they stood close together in dense groves, but aerial views reveal a definite, if irregular, pattern of spacing. The plants, like Daniel Boone, need elbow room so they can minimize the peer competition for water and soil nutrients. In a stand of saguaros outside of Tucson, I confirmed this for myself by pacing off the distances between one giant and another. Standing on their ground, it indeed looked to me as if I were in a grove, yet when I did my primitive pedal calculations I found that in no case was the distance between the plants less than eleven paces or more than twenty-six.

And like their region, they are *big*. Here again, photographs are deceiving, for no two-dimensional shot can adequately capture the sheer majestic amplitude of these cacti. For that sense you must simply stand close up under one and crane your neck skyward. Next, take a hike around it. After carefully inspecting the ground, lie down at its base and dream upward. Then you will be willing to agree that the saguaro is the fit representative of the great West, a region that easily contains within it mountain ranges as vast as the Bitterroot, the Cascade, the Sierra; canyons like the Black on the Gunnison and the Grand; fauna like the buffalo, the grizzly, and the steelhead; and flora like the sequoia and this great green giant that now soars above you, poking its needle towers into the sun.

This is America's biggest cactus, overtopped in all the world only by its Mexican relative, the cardón. Built around an infrastructure of vertical

53

woody ribs, a mature plant can reach as high as fifty, even sixty feet and weigh as much as ten tons. In the *Guinness Book of World Records* a saguaro located near Cave Creek, Arizona, has for years been listed as the "world's tallest," at seventy-eight feet. But Frank Casanova, a retired Forest Service ranger, says the alleged height is a "bunch of baloney." Casanova, like the Texas historian a lover of truth, measured the Cave Creek giant after it had fallen to its death and found it to be only fifty-seven feet tall. Yet this will not be the last outsized lie the West will generate, for the magnitude of Western space encourages a corresponding largeness of verbal conception.

That so huge a plant could prosper in a region popularly supposed to be utterly parched must be a significant part of what recommends the saguaro to the national imagination. It is as if the very existence of this cactus constituted a tremendously successful answer to the challenge of an environment set against such glowing expressions of life. In fact, the West is very dry, and its plant life often seems low and stunted when compared to the lush flora of the East and South. But it is not so dry as some other parts of the earth, nor can our Western deserts bear strict comparison with the Sahara or the Kalahari. A desert specialist I talked with in Tucson said that when visitors from such places see the "desert" at Tucson, they laugh at its comparative lushness.

Still, the West and its deserts do their xeric best. More than a century ago John Wesley Powell established what has remained a de facto definition of the region when he proposed that lands where the average rainfall is less than twenty inches be treated as a unit. All these lands lie west of our 100th Meridian, a line that halves the Dakotas and Nebraska and cuts down through Texas just west of Abilene. Within this area the Chihuahuan, Great Basin, Mohave, and Sonoran deserts are drier still: there the average annual rainfall is ten inches or less. Death Valley in the Mohave Desert averages a minuscule 1.63 inches; Tucson, on the edge of the Sonoran Desert, is blessed with 11.2. Saharan desert dwellers might scoff, but these figures do not exactly answer to the standard notions of paradise.

There are, however, creatures and plants that find even the West's most arid stretches paradisiacal: the fringe-toed lizard that swims in the sand; the kangaroo rat that lives on a totally dry diet, extracting its water from the plant life it consumes; the javelina, wild pig of the Southwest, that happily disregards the prickly pear's spiny defenses and gobbles the whole plant, fruit, pod, spines, and all. And the lordly saguaro, towering over all and expressing in its serene longevity—a century and more— the adaptive qualities of life in these dry spaces.

Unlike the kangaroo rat, the saguaro needs rainwater to function. Considering the plant's huge tonnage, a lot of water is involved here: as much as eighty percent of the plant is water, a fact you comprehend only when you come across the prostrate, long-dead hulk of one of these giants. In death the plant is nothing but a dozen or so strips of mummified wood. The green, watery life of it is utterly gone, and behind are left only what stark, stalky remains the searing dryness permits. Without water the saguaro could not carry on the vital process of photosynthesis (which it commences in daylight but concludes only in the safe coolness of the desert night), and its cells, robbed of their medium of mainte- nance and transport, would collapse in on themselves.

What rainwater there is comes in buckets, quickly emptied: the desert storms drop deluges in their brief and infrequent visitations, then are gone, and the sun streams down unimpeded out of the now-cloudless blue. The baking earth steams a short while, and the water runs off the hardpan soil, only a fraction of it seeping downward. The saguaro's root system, however, is wonderfully adapted to precisely these conditions, for it lies just beneath the surface in a large disc that might measure one hundred feet in diameter. So situated, saguaros can catch the water of the brief storms before it is lost.

When the roots trap the water, it is sucked up into the plant's body, which during these rare rainy episodes expands measurably like the stretched pleats of an accordion to accommodate the welcome new supply. Then the plant, holding in suspension its great columnar reservoir, is ready to tough out a spell of drought that might be several months or more in duration. A saguaro is capable, in fact, of living off its stored water supply for as long as two years if need be, during which time its accordion structure steadily contracts around its draining supply, its pleats becoming more pronounced as it abides the strenuous conditions of its habitat.

Despite these varied adaptive mechanisms, and despite its great size and long life expectancy, the saguaro is an incongruously vulnerable organism. In the protracted years of its infancy it needs a nurse. At this stage it is too tender to bear the direct rays of the desert sun and requires the shade of another plant, typically a palo verde tree, a mesquite, or an ironwood. Such nurse trees the desert's ecosystem obligingly provides, because desert birds like the white-winged dove eat the seeds of the mature saguaro and, finding them indigestible, excrete them at the bases of the trees wherein they roost. So it happens that a saguaro seed germinates within the protective shadow of the tree and spends its tender years there. And so it happens that in saguaroland you often come across the lordly cactus spiring straight up from the encircling arms of the palo verde, the mesquite, or ironwood that in the long ago spread its vital shadow over the nursling. It is a curiously affecting sight.

But the germination of the seed is by no means a common phenomenon. In the course of a lifetime a mature saguaro might produce forty million seeds, but out of that massive reproductive effort only a scant half-dozen or so will germinate and survive into maturity. "When you see a mature saguaro," says Tony Burgess, a desert specialist with the U.S. Geological Survey in Tucson, "you're looking at an extremely rare event." You can, of course, readily assent to that simply by looking at the size of these plants. But when you learn something of their chances of reaching such a size, then your appreciation of their rarity takes on a dimension of awe, for here in spires and spines is the very mystery of Life and its survival.

That must have been at least part of what Tony Burgess meant when he said that he lived "surrounded by mystery." It was a summer afternoon, and we were sitting in his office. "Look out that window," he said to me. I could see the arms of a saguaro and the tips of several cholla cacti and, beyond, the burning blue of the desert sky. "Talk of survival," Burgess said. "Tell me how any of those plants really work. Oh, it's true we've learned a lot about cacti in this century, but really we know very little."

We have learned, though, that other factors figure in the rarity of the mature saguaro, like winds and lightning. Because its root system is so well adapted to the conditions of desert living, the saguaro is vulnerable to the high-powered desert winds that come whipping along at ground level and can set the tall plant into a dangerous swaying motion. If this condition persists, the shallow root system may be ripped loose, toppling the plant. The plant is also prey to the thousands of lightning strikes that hit the Sonoran Desert in summer: several years ago fifteen thousand strikes were recorded in a single day in the Tucson area. Here, as with the desert winds, it is the saguaro's majestic height that makes it so conspicuous a target, rather like the monarch of some tribe who is long nurtured and guarded by his people so that in the fullness of his puissance they may ritually sacrifice him.

And then there is man. However much we may admire the saguaro as fact and as symbol, there is also that obscure impulse within us that sometimes drives us to enact an obscure vengeance against plants or animals whose grand size attracts our attention. We all know of the vandalism perpetrated against giant sequoias, the ruthless extermination of the elephant. Naturalist and author John Hay told once of seeing people on a New England beach torture a stranded whale by tossing lighted cigarettes into its blowhole. So in Arizona the destruction of the giant saguaro by roadside vandals wielding tire irons, baseball bats, and shotguns has been an unhappy fact.

Saguaro rustling is also a practice of this region. If the rustlers can uproot a saguaro undetected and then fake the state cards certifying that the plant has been legally taken out of its original habitat, they can sell it for a very substantial price to an individual or a nursery. Current state law prohibits and punishes such behavior, and there are laws on the books, too, protecting the saguaro against the planned depredations of real estate developers. These laws, however, are easy enough to get around, says Tony Burgess. "The only real danger to the saguaro now," he says, "is real estate development. Year by year you see more and more of its habitat taken away, chunk by chunk." So it seems. In the Tucson area development has completely encircled the eastern part of the Saguaro National Monument, and roads now cut up through the Tucson Mountains to the very border of the monument's western portion. Few Tucsonians doubt that development will follow where these roads lead. The monument grounds themselves are not presently endangered, but all the land outside them is. Considering Arizona's profligate use of its most precious natural resource—water—you cannot feel sanguine about its long-term protectiveness of a plant, however majestic.

The Papago and Pima tribes, original human dwellers within the saguaro's domain, traditionally seem to have held the plant in more tender regard, perhaps because their long and intimate experience with it had taught them its hidden vulnerability. The Papago calendar was partly based on the saguaro's yearly cycle, and a Papago myth tells that the plant once was human. In that long ago, they say, the saguaro (*hash'an*) was a little girl whose father was dead and whose mother often left her alone. In her neglect the girl resigned her human condition, sank into the earth, and later reappeared as a strange plant none of the people had ever seen before. Taller and taller it grew, and when it had reached its full height it bore luscious fruit by which the people have been refreshed to this day.

Perhaps the myth's specific content reflects the Papagos' understanding that, just as the young saguaro needs its nurse plant, so all things require nurture. Certainly life in the arid, lonesome stretches of their portion of the Sonoran Desert would have profoundly taught them this truth every day. In their lands, the living is not easy, and all things seem held, poised in precarious, mutually sustained balance. Gary Nabhan, the distinguished desert naturalist who has spent considerable time in Papagueria, once heard a young boy asking an elderly woman if it was ever permitted to throw rocks at a saguaro to knock down its fruit. The boy knew well enough that the traditional way was to dislodge the fruit gently with a long saguaro rib-turned-pole, but he thought maybe there might be a shortcut—and a playful one at that. But the elderly woman exclaimed in horror that the "saguaros—they are Indians too. You don't EVER throw anything at them. If you hit them in the head with rocks, you could kill them. You don't ever stick anything sharp into their skin, either, or they will just dry up and die. You don't do anything to hurt them. They are Indians."

The Pima have made somewhat less of the saguaro, both in tribal lore and in practical ways, than the Papago, but the giant cactus is very much a presence in their world view. Pima legend ascribes the making of the first saguaro wine to the desert birds, several of whom quickly got drunk on their new invention. The mockingbird, the Pimas say, was one of these drunkards, and it began to talk incessantly; it is still doing so. The tribal pharmacopoeia says that to stimulate a mother's milk after childbirth a gruel should be prepared from the saguaro's fruit mixed with water and whole wheat. There were many other uses. The fruit was eaten as a dessert, and saguaro seeds, ground and roasted, were a substitute for lard. The Pima also used the seeds as chicken feed and for tanning leather, while the long ribs were used for shelter construction, splints, and basket frames.

● ● ●

A half-hour's drive west-northwest of Tucson lie the western portion of Saguaro National Monument and, adjoining it, the remarkable Arizona–Sonora Desert Museum. The narrow, twisting road from the city takes you up through the Tucson Mountains, and on their other side another reality greets you and seems to close in behind. The illusion of Tucson, where at least temporarily the desert has been made to blossom, vanishes as if it had never been. Spread out before you in its strange, beguiling suite of grays, mauves, and browns is the unreconstructed, unimproved desert, spiky, jagged, naked.

Perhaps it is the fact that you know Tucson is there backing you with its air-conditioned comforts that allows you to feel suddenly, immensely grateful for this reality on the mountains' other side. Say this is so: still, there is this feeling of gratitude, and as I rode down to the desert floor I thought of Thoreau's bell-like words in *Walden*: "Be it life or death, we crave only reality." Maybe beneath all our fears, our cravings for "creature comforts," we truly do so.

If this be true, it might account for the visitor's mingled feelings of awe, surprise, and delight at the museum, for here is an older—and unsuspected—reality about the desert, a magical glimpse into the way things were here before "here" was the New World. Here the desert really does blossom, not in the gaseous blazes of a city's neon, but as it had for thousands of years before the white man arrived and commenced his ceaseless, ingenious improvements. It is not, to be sure, the sort of blossoming that modern-day developers have in mind, nor is it that envisioned thousands of years ago by the peoples of the ancient Near East when they imagined Paradise as a well-watered and fruitful oasis. No, this is a wholly natural and unimproved blossoming. Here the otter still swims and plays as it did before the few streams were diverted and dammed. Turkeys cackle and flit from one low branch to another. Javelinas grunt and root, and in the shade of caves and bushes jaguars and bobcats loll at noon. Here also the curious can learn something of the rich variety of a place that scant minutes before had seemed monolithic—of the hundreds of microhabitats that make the desert a mosaic, and of the hundreds of relatives the saguaro has living in the same neighborhood.

If the Saguaro National Monument were not a natural extension of the museum, it would be too much to take in after the museum's almost overwhelming surprises. But the monument continues and extends the museum, and it seems right to travel into it. But however much you may be enthralled by this place, it will not do to wander off into it, lost in bucolic rapture. That you might safely do in a Vermont meadow or along the verdurous banks of a Midwestern stream, where the only caution might be for poison ivy. Here in the desert, though, heat stroke and dehydration are present possibilities and the unequipped human does well to remember he has none of a cactus's natural solar defenses. Moreover, surrounding you is an armed host of desert dwellers who may inflict casual penalty on you for your reverie.

I walked a couple of miles into the monument's grounds, keeping an eye out for the natives: pencil and pincushion cacti hidden beneath the creosote bushes; varieties of cholla cacti, including the Teddy Bear cholla that looks so cuddly until you see its furry spines up close; big clumps of prickly pear bearing in this season the brilliant fruit on which the old explorer Cabeza de Vaca subsisted during his eight years' sojourn among the tribes of the Gulf Coast and Southwest; great rotund barrel cacti with gorgeous scarlet blossoms. In the dry washes zebra-tailed lizards shot out of my path, and the rasping calls of unfamiliar birds seemed to warn me off. Under the pendulous arms of saguaros I inspected the holes made in the trunks by Gila woodpeckers and that now were homes to dwarf owls. I poked with a fragment of saguaro rib into the rotting remains of a fallen monarch and found it tenanted by thousands of insects. At every step something new and wonderful appeared, so that the imposed vigilance of this desert hiker was richly repaid: my necessarily sharpened attention to the immediate landscape allowed me really to *see* it. Watching where you put your feet or swung your arm, keeping your bearings carefully lined up on a distant mountain hump—these precautionary measures brought the land into a brilliant and startling detail. Compared to this brief, blazing excursion, all my other hikes now seemed mere slothful saunters.

• • •

Because I wished to taste yet more deeply of the desert and to stretch civilization's tether a bit farther, I left Tucson early one morning, heading for Organ Pipe National Monument, 120 miles west of the city. It was August 6, anniversary of that fateful, mushrooming event in 1945; and that fact rode beside me, a ghostly passenger in my rented Japanese car.

In the early gray the desert seemed still wrapped in the relieving robes of night as I entered the Papago reservation on Route 86. All along this lonesome stretch of asphalt there were small white crosses and some more elaborate shrines marking the sites of fatal auto accidents, consequences of faulty tie rods, worn wheel bearings, peeling recaps, too much speed, too much drink. The memorials were all bedizened with garlands of deathless plastic flowers that remained stiffly unruffled by the wind of my passing. I gave up counting when I got to the twentieth one.

Out away from the roadside the land had flattened into an expanse of red sand dotted with creosote bush, the splayed spires of the ocotillo, mesquite, prickly pear, and occasional stands of saguaro. Raw-headed turkey vultures sat on the cross-ties of telephone poles. A roadrunner, that curious traitor to its kind, who would rather run than fly, raced the car for fifty yards. At Sells, largest settlement on the reservation, a coyote loped across the road and disappeared into the brush. Here I turned off, following the side road into the center of town.

In *The Desert Smells Like Rain*, Gary Nabhan describes his experiences at a Papago wine feast, a rite that Sir James G. Frazer and other nineteenth-century ethnologists would surely have styled "sympathetic magic." The elders at that feast advised their fellow tribal members that the purpose of the feast was not to get sick drunk but to encourage the coming of the rainclouds to the crops. Then the wine was brought from the ceremonial house and blessed by the medicine men. After the passing of the consecrated cup, the serious business of consumption commenced.

I had no desire to ritually "throw up the clouds," as the participants did at that feast, but I did want a taste of the saguaro's fermented fruit if I could get it. The manager of the Texaco station was a big Papago man with black-lensed sunglasses and a T-shirt covered with great honorific blobs of grease. We chatted a bit while he pumped, of the weather, of the new tribal shopping complex going up across the road. Finally I

61

asked whether the people thereabouts still harvested the saguaro for wine and whether this was the right time for it. "Oh, yeah," he said from behind those impenetrable shades.

"Well," I went on slowly, "I was wondering what it tastes like. I'd like to try some if I could."

"You mean you'd like to try some saguaro jelly, you say?"

"No, no. The wine. The wine they make from the saguaro."

"Oh, yeah. Well, there's a lot of people around here who do that, only I don't know where they're living. But I'll tell you what: have you ever tasted Ripple when it's good and cold? It tastes a good bit like that." Clearly that approximation was as close to the wine itself as I was meant to get.

Back on the road to Organ Pipe I saw in the pure distance the stony upthrusts of the Ajo Mountains that surround the monument. I saw, too, more of the white crosses and a fatal species of mistletoe sucking the life out of palo verdes. At one point a javelina burst from the brush, then saw the car and plunged snorting back into cover. A little pall of dust hung for a moment over the place of its retreat.

Why, Arizona, squats at the junction of Routes 86 and 85, hence its name, originally spelled "Y." In its current spelling this huddle of gas stations and curio shops presents the lone desert traveler with an existential question: Why, indeed? I mulled that one over as I turned south on 85 toward the monument, but once inside its boundaries the question seemed reinforced rather than answered by arrival at my destination: a sign at the entrance to the twenty-one-mile Ajo Loop through the grounds warned that once embarked on this course there could be *no turning back*: you must go on. It seemed like a sign on the road to the Beyond, requiring that the pilgrim ask himself whether he had the necessary viaticum.

Once securely on the loop I parked the car near the beginning of the Estes Canyon—Bull Pasture Trail and struck off through a country that was even more stripped and stony than the desert at the Saguaro National Monument. And hotter. The mere movement of my body through the air produced a sensation of profound and encompassing friction. The heat was so intense it seemed to have an audible dimension. But here in the intense noon were the saguaros and the organ pipe cacti I'd come to see, and it was easy enough after a while to forget the heat and simply attend to these stately beings.

Some of the organ pipes I came upon as I scrambled upward toward a craggy canyon had trunks at least thirty feet tall. Branching from a common base, their pipes curved gracefully outward, each plant constituting a sort of thicket. Most of them were now just past the full blush of flowering, their fruits a tarnished, rusty red. Surrounded by them, and with the ocher-colored volcanic crags of the Ajos towering directly over me, I seemed here in yet another new, strange world. The feeling brought back to me the question posed a few hours ago by the hamlet of Why.

What is it that historically has drawn humans to the desert and that has made desert dwellers sages and metaphysicians? Certainly history is replete with those like Anthony, Rufinus, and Jerome who sought out what the latter called "that vast solitude parched with the fires of the sun." Certainly a Christian eremite in this desert would find his fill of solitude and sun, would find also visual confirmation of his quest in the cruciform shapes of the cholla cacti. And what of the late cleric/dropout Bishop James Pike in our own time: was he simply deranged by the desert's heat, or was his search but another for the answer to the question the desert and its life seem to pose?

In the loud glare of this place the question seemed obscurely to involve these grand plants that stood all about me. They were literally *wonderful* and worth any trip to see. And so was everything else of the desert that I had seen—the vultures, the javelina, the covey of Gambel's quail that fled from me, their topknots jerking. *That* was maybe the answer to the question: in its apparent inhospitality to humankind, the desert is nonetheless a unique expression of the Life Force, more evident in such stripped conditions than in smiling lands or in the weltering centers of civilization. Perhaps it was this fact that made the desert-dwelling Arabs such deep thinkers, speculators, tellers of tales; that drew the ancient Desert Fathers out into Egyptian sands. In the desert you see that Force in all its undifferentiated, impersonal power. And it might just be what draws us still to spots such as this.

At any given place, someone once remarked, Nature is doing everything it can. In the desert you see this truth everywhere. Within the lordly branched saguaro as a popular image of the American West may lie our ultimate assent to the principle of Life, triumphant in its circumstances.

Wind on the Buffalo Grass

Our old food we used to eat was good. The meat from buffalo and game was good. These cows are good to eat, soft, tender, but they are not like that meat. Our people used to live a long time. Today we eat white man's food, we cannot live so long ... Sweet Medicine told us that. He said the white man was too strong. He said his food would be sweet, and after we taste that food we want it, and forget our own foods ... We eat it and forget.

—Fred Last Bull, Keeper of the Sacred Arrows of the Northern Cheyennes, as told to Margot Liberty, 1957

A people without history is like wind on the buffalo grass.

—Lakota proverb

I

They put on a buffalo hunt in Dakota Territory in September 1882. Considering the aboriginal scale of such things on the Great Plains it wasn't much of an event—maybe only ten thousand buff taken over a few days' time, whereas well over ten times that had been taken in the year's preceding months. But it did break the odd lull that had settled over the region as summer turned to fall and the buffalo had been so scarce it didn't pay a runner to go out after them. Some whites, hanging about the towns and forts with little more than time on their hands, had even begun muttering that the northern herd had been hunted out just like the southern herd had a couple of years before. But most of the runners scoffed at such an idea. Men, red and white alike, had been killing buffalo in great numbers for half a century out here, and no man knew how long before that the Indians had been hunting them. And still the

65

supply seemed endless. Yet, fall's first weeks *had* been a peculiar time
with the herds strangely absent and only a few old and solitary bulls
sighted in out-of-the-way draws. Now came welcome word that a pretty
good-sized herd had been sighted between Bismarck and the Black Hills,
meaning, surely, that the herds were back. Probably they'd just migrated
over the line into Canada and were coming south for the winter.

The boys got their gear together, including, of course, their Sharp's
rifles. These were beautifully evolved weapons of the trade, many of
them .40-90-420 models (a .40 caliber bullet propelled by ninety grams
of black powder and weighing 420 grains) with German-made tele-
scopic sights. If you hit a buff far enough back in the body with one of
these slugs, it made him instantly sick and basically immobile, and so
you were free to go on with your killing of others in the herd. When the
runners were ready, they rode out to the slaughter and made short work
of the herd, only about a thousand of which escaped and went on
toward the Black Hills. But these remnant creatures were not to escape,
either, because the Lakotas, imprisoned on what remained of their reservations, had heard about the buffalo, too, and had finally gotten permission from their agents to join the hunt. They were slowly starving at
Standing Rock, Cheyenne River, and Pine Ridge, and the case was fairly
easy to make that the men ought to be allowed off the reservations for
this occasion. The problem was that except for the headmen and the
tribal police the Lakotas had been pretty well disarmed, and when they
went out after the buffalo, they went with bows and arrows and some
old and not very reliable rifles. Some of the older men who remembered
traditional ways before the popularity of the gun hunted with their
short bows and were still capable of pumping a stream of arrows into a
buffalo almost as fast as a white man could fire his Sharp's. The younger
men, though, no longer possessed this skill, and some were ashamed of
those who had no guns and had to resort to such primitive weaponry.
Here a few sympathetic whites stepped forward and lent rifles to the
Lakota hunters, and then they went out and took the rest of the herd.

Like the white runners, the Lakotas and most of the other Plains
tribes could hardly believe that humans had hunted out the buffalo, and
when the men returned to their reservations laden with meat for the fam-
ished it appeared the rumored disappearance of the herds was unfounded.
The red harvest was proof to many that the old times were not yet gone

and that even though the people were penned up on reservations, they need not starve there. The Lakotas, Cheyennes, Crows, Blackfeet, Arapahoes, and the others believed the buffalo had been the special gift of the Great Spirit to the people, and so surely that gift could not be finite. As the white men rightly said, the people had been hunting the buffalo almost forever. Their sacred stories did however speak of a time before the hunting of the buffalo, a time when the people had been poor, ragged, and living in a kind of shadow world beneath the earth. Some stories said the people had followed a buffalo cow out of the subterranean darkness, up into the brilliant light of a world of sun, grass, and wind.

Other stories said the buffalo used to hunt the people in that long-ago world. The Cheyennes said the order of things was decided in a great race held in the Black Hills. All the animals sent representatives to run in it, including the head buffalo and a certain young man representing the human beings. In the race the head buffalo planned to butt the young man off the side of the mountain, but thanks to the intervention and advice of the magpie, the young man was able to avoid the buffalo's murderous charge, and then the magpie went on and won the race for the human beings. "Well," said the head buffalo when it was all over, "you have won. From now on the buffalo will serve the human beings, instead of the other way around."

The narrative reflected the fact that before the Cheyennes became a buffalo people out on the Great Plains they lived a far more precarious existence in what is now westernmost Minnesota. There they harvested wild rice, planted some corn, and hunted deer, elk, moose, and the small game of the woodlands. When they were lucky enough to take buffalo, it was almost always one or two at a time and had to be accomplished from ambush. Skunk hunts were an important feature of tribal economic life, and dogs (part wolf) were their beasts of burden. Gradually, though, they moved out of the shadow of the woods onto the Plains, began to follow the huge, shaggy beasts that were to remake the tribal culture, and with the acquisition of the horse became far-ranging nomadic huntsmen. Swiftly the buffalo became a sacred animal for the Cheyennes (and the other Plains tribes as well), probably *the* sacred animal, the four-footed manifestation of the Great Spirit's imminent regard for the welfare of the people, and the hunting of it came to be surrounded by a bristling hedge of ritual observances designed to insure the continuance

of plenitude. Infractions, such as freelance hunting, were severely punished, and the mixed-blood Cheyenne George Bent said a man who
went out buffalo hunting by himself might be so badly beaten by one of
the tribal soldier societies that he could hardly walk. For a subsequent
offense all his possessions might be destroyed.

To the whites who came in contact with the Cheyennes at this period
the ritual calling of the buffalo by the specially charged shamans, the
omnipresence of the sanctified buffalo skulls, and the prohibitions against
freelancing or other forms of carelessness seemed like the grossest illustrations of savagery. There were so many buffalo: maybe forty million at
the turn of the nineteenth century. What was the point of all this mumbo
jumbo? Now history has positioned us to see what those early nineteenth-
century whites could not: that in any given place there exists a natural
order of things that human beings are bound to divine and respect.

For a while the Cheyennes and the other buffalo tribes surely did
respect the natural order of the Plains. They killed only what buffalo
they could use, and they used every part of the beast, from the horns to
the hooves. Even when they succeeded in driving a herd through the
V-shaped wings of a human chute and over the edge of a bluff they
endeavored to make efficient use of this grand harvest, drying the excess
meat and storing it for later use and pounding some of it, together with
the tallow and chokecherries, to make pemmican. Meanwhile, they told
their sacred stories and sang their sacred songs in which the buffalo figured as the primal link between this world and the spirit world beyond.

Around 1820 matters began to change. For one thing, more and
more aboriginal hunters were coming onto the Plains, displaced by the
gun-wielding tribes farther east, by the sprawl of white civilization, and
by the consequent forced land cessions; the Cheyennes themselves had
been such a group back in the middle of the eighteenth century. There
was still plenty of space and tens of millions of buffalo, but there were
more hunters now, some of them armed with guns, and they were
mounted as well. Some of the hunters were white, too, tough, resourceful
harbingers of a populous civilization as yet still west of the Mississippi
but on the move. So the Plains bioregion felt now a first faint pressure.
By the 1830s when the Cheyennes, the Lakotas, Blackfeet, and the others
rode and hunted in all their gaudy glory a very few whites, looking
ahead, foresaw their doom and the doom of every aspect of their world:

tribal cultures, buffalo, elk, pronghorns, even the grasses of the Plains. Between 1832 and 1839 the artist George Catlin moved among the Plains tribes, recording in picture and word their lifeways and the flora and fauna of that place. What he saw happening there provoked in him an appalling apocalyptic vision in which he beheld the buffalo herds wheeling in blind and mortal confusion and the Plains littered with their flayed, reddened carcasses, while "bands of wolves, and dogs, and buzzards were seen devouring them." In the distance, the artist wrote, "were the feeble smokes of the wigwams and villages, where the skins were dragged, and dressed for white man's luxury! where they were all sold for *whiskey*, and the poor Indians laid drunk and were crying." Casting his eyes eastward, Catlin beheld the white man's towns and cities, where before every door there hung a buffalo robe, the life force of the region stripped from it in exchange for the poison of whiskey.

What had happened between 1820 and the time of Catlin's return to white civilization was the creation of a market for buffalo—dead buffalo. Except for a very limited trade in hides with the Pueblo peoples to the south the Plains tribes had no market for buffalo and hardly a conception of what a market was. Quickly, though, they came to learn that what they had in such abundance might be exchanged for blankets, iron kettles, rifles, bullet molds, powder, coffee, sugar, and whiskey, which became the sovereign lubricant of trade on the Plains just as it had earlier in other parts of the country. Catlin thought the only thing that could possibly prevent the awful fate he foresaw for the buffalo and its people was an American government strong enough and wise enough to say to its people, "*Enough*: we have enough territory already. Let us leave the Plains to the buffalo and the tribes." The region, Catlin said, was far too arid and treeless to suit the needs of an agricultural people, and the buffalo and the tribes too marvelous to destroy.

Catlin's voice was unheeded. The national government proved neither wise enough nor strong enough to check the flood tide of westering, and, in fact, in a good many ways it underwrote the most rapacious and cynical tendencies of its land-greedy settlers. In the years between 1840 and the buffalo hunt held in Dakota Territory in the fall of 1882, the government did everything it could to open the West to white settlement and to encourage the belief that all the natural resources of those vast new lands existed solely to be exploited by whites. Nor did the tribal governments prove strong enough or wise enough to help their peoples resist the many seductions of white civilization, among which the greatest (and worst) was the market for buffalo. Thus, the tribes' military defeats were compounded by the interior disintegration of the tribal cultures, and as the 1870s became the 1880s the Indian hunters teamed with the white ones to create a mighty crescendo of killing.

But by late fall 1882, the great herds were all but gone. The frontier rumors were true. Upwards of two hundred thousand hides had been shipped east in the earlier months of that year, but the year following "only" forty thousand went east to be fashioned into robes, coats, machine belts and pulleys, and gentlemen's gloves. The next year only three hundred hides could be had in all the West, and by 1884 virtually none were shipped. Now it remained only for the scavengers to start up a brief business in buffalo bones, gathering them in white piles that in some places extended for half a mile along railroad sidings. Virtually the only buffalo left in the United States was a remnant herd in Yellowstone Park, and even these were the subject of intense pressure from poachers and vandals. By 1894 the herd had been whittled down to less than two hundred. This was the year, however, that public sentiment—much of it generated in the East—was sufficiently strong to motivate lawmakers to frame and pass a bill (HR 6442) protecting what was left of the Yellowstone herd. It had always been against the law to kill buffalo within the boundaries of the nation's first national park, but enforcement had heretofore been ineffectual, and because the government itself had been so significant a contributor to the rapacious approach to America's natural resources, it found itself in an awkward position defending the park's buffalo. Once, the Indian hunters had driven herds over the bluffs to their deaths. Now the entire species of *Bison bison* stood precariously poised on the bluff, beneath which lay extinction. HR 6442 was a decisive step back towards the animal's salvation, and following it there came the dedicated buffalo preservationists C. J. "Buffalo" Jones, Charles Goodnight, and William T. Hornaday who worked to educate the public and politicians about the unique national treasure that had almost been destroyed. The herd in Yellowstone survived and began to prosper and, in the early years of the twentieth century, served as a crucial source for herds in other parks like Custer State Park in South Dakota and the Wichita Mountains National Wildlife Refuge in Oklahoma.

Thus the buffalo lived on, not, of course, as it once had, roaming the Plains in dark millions, but instead as a rare icon like the bald eagle, the giant sequoia, and the solemn, war-bonneted Indian chief who was trotted out for ceremonial poses with visiting dignitaries.

II

From May–November 1995, the Buffalo Bill Historical Center in Cody, Wyoming, put on an exhibit tracing most of the history of the buffalo, from the Ice Age to the present. The setting could hardly have been more apposite. The town sits at the eastern gateway to Yellowstone Park whose relict herd was instrumental in bringing back the *Bison bison*, while the town itself was founded by the celebrated buffalo killer, William F. Cody. The exhibit took you from fossil skulls of the huge *Bison latifrons* and *Bison antiquus*, to the aftermath of the great slaughter, to the successful efforts to save the species from extinction. Along the way you encountered milestones in the buffalo's history, perhaps most impressively the display of 11,000-year-old Clovis points found in what is now southeastern Wyoming. Crystal quartz, chalcedony, obsidian chert, these projectiles shaped by hands long ago turned to dust and whirled away by the Plains' winds still appeared superbly lethal and so spare of form and mass they were transparent. Looking at them, you had to be impressed with a species capable of making them to compensate for the physical deficiencies that placed it at so great a disadvantage in competition with other animals in what the Cheyennes called the Great Race. A bit farther on was a copy of the petroglyph from the Bighorn Mountains labeled, "The Horse Arrives." It showed a snaky, four-legged shape leaping forward, and astride it a shadowy, indistinct figure with a sheaf of scratches for a head. In the timeline you were being directed along, humans were now armed and mounted—huge changes—whereas the buffalo, though uniquely adapted to the grasslands, had made no corresponding adaptations. The buffalo was big and very powerful and possibly it had picked up some speed as it evolved from *Bison antiquus* to *Bison occidentalis* to *Bison bison* and *Bison athabascae* (the mountain or wood buffalo). But, if so, this hardly compensated for its hunters' technological inventions and acquisitions.

And then you came to the gun, a Sharp's mounted on a swivel so that you could effectively hold it, feel its heft, and sight along its octagonal barrel to the buffalo depicted on the wall opposite. From behind the Sharp's the buffalo pinned to the wall looked like a very big and very vulnerable target, and that was the point. "Hell of an effective display item," I wrote in my notebook.

Then came artifacts of the ultimate slaughter of the 1870s and '80s: photographs and engravings of the hide hunters at work and of those carcasses Catlin had seen in his vision a half century earlier; plus mounted heads, almost a dozen of them, trophies of a phenomenon that still has the emotional force of one of those .40-90-420 slugs.

The ultimate display item, so it seemed to me, was a 1908 painting done in Munich by Irving R. Bacon, entitled, "The Conquest of the Prairie." A heroic 47" x 118", it depicts Buffalo Bill on a white charger, his famous buffalo rifle, "Lucretia Borgia," aslant his saddle, leading an apparently endless train of prairie schooners up a draw while in the foreground a group of mounted Indians watches helplessly as white civilization invades their homeland. In the middle distance a smoking locomotive crosses a bridge, while in the far distance rise the faint but unmistakable spires of the modern city. But what made Bacon's painting the ultimate display item of "Seasons of the Buffalo" was that the artist includes a herd of buffalo fleeing the advance of white civilization and passing just beneath the group of Indian horsemen. The beasts, Bacon's composition says, are doomed, pinioned between the old order and the new one, and as the artist worked on this over in Germany in the first years of this century, it must have looked that way.

At the entrance to the exhibit a TV screen set in a wall ran a video of a buffalo herd out on the range. They were seen grazing, fording a stream, and galloping in a dusty mass over the grasslands, and since the camera focus was so tight you were invited to imagine that here was a scene out of the New World's primeval past. The video was short, maybe only ten minutes in all, but it caught and held the attention of the visitors, as it had mine, and I found myself drawn to this ancillary display of white men and women standing in a loose semicircle about the screen and watching the film over and again. What is it about the buffalo that so captivates us? I asked a man who'd seen the film twice through and showed no sign of leaving. "I don't know," he replied, glancing over briefly to see who had spoken to him. "Something majestic about them, I guess. That and how the white man used them up. A shame; but we'll do it." Another man said the buffalo was a symbol of the American West, and to see them "live," so to speak, was thrilling. Most Americans, he said, had never seen a herd on the run. The most comprehensive response came from a man who said it was the animal's history that fascinated him: "The fact that it was brought back from the very edge of extinction to where today it's a commercially viable animal again. If it had become extinct, that would have been a tragedy, but a few people saw the problem, and we've corrected it. I find that interesting." He was from Colorado, he told me, and "many people don't know it, but Colorado has gotten into buffalo raising in a really big way." Here was the newest chapter in the history of the buffalo, beginning where "Seasons of the Buffalo" left off.

• • •

The Great Sand Dunes Country Club and Inn was an improbable place in many ways. In the arid lands that form the border of Colorado and New Mexico you don't expect to find a country club with a championship golf course or one that offered gourmet meals and rooms that went for around $200 a night in high season. Nor was there anything in the immediate vicinity that would suggest the commercial or social viability of such an operation situated here: the increasingly tony town of Santa Fe was more than two hours south while Denver was four more to the north. The only settlements of any consequence in the vicinity were Alamosa and Monte Vista, and neither appeared to have a significant country club set. In short you had to *want* the GSDCC&I to go there.

Once you were there, you could play the course with its stunning views of the Sangre de Cristo Mountains and the adjacent Great Sand Dunes National Monument, and do so at your complete leisure: the inn had but fifteen rooms, and you were thus assured of the sort of meditative round that must be rare enough on any golf course, American or foreign. You could also hike to nearby Zapata Falls on the slopes of the Sangre de Cristos or even wrangle cows with the hands, for the inn sat in the middle of two working ranches and would accommodate you if you wished to attempt a small-scale version of the adventures dramatized in the film *City Slickers*. At night, sated by your gourmet meal, you could, if you wished, relax in the hot tub and wait for a shooting star to remind you of the transitory nature of even such luxury as you presently enjoy.

But these considerable attractions were not what brought me to the GSDCC&I. Rather it was that on these 110,000 acres there are 2,800 buffalo, one of the larger private herds in America. Here, then, was a perfect place to observe something of one of the most extraordinary phenomena in recent American history: the return of the buffalo. The history we have thus far enacted in the New World has moved relentlessly in one direction: toward the obliteration of that New World we found and its replacement with a facsimile of the Old World we left behind. The return of the buffalo in numbers to America may symbolize not so much the old American West as it does a shift in our thinking about our country. For there currently are among us in what once was the New World those trying to restore some of what was so speedily plowed under, cut down, and slaughtered in the names of Progress and Civilization. A significant number of these people are working west of the Mississippi, and some of them have turned their attention to the buffalo.

The man behind the operations at the GSDCC&I was Hisayoshi Ota, a Japanese-born architect who as a teenager came to America for schooling, became fascinated with the country and particularly with the West, and stayed on. And the operations here, I was to learn, encompassed both the new business of buffalo raising as well as what I have come to think of as the "inner work": the nurture of the buffalo as part of the long-term reconstruction of the West. More on the latter shortly.

Ota's bison managers (he insists on the proper term) were Bill Homeyer and his wife, Cam, and it was to them that I went with my first, primitive questions. I found them at ranch headquarters, about a mile away from the modest, rustic complex that was the country club, Cam on the telephone and Bill out by some corrals. He was a bull-shouldered fellow who under his black cowboy hat looked like the younger Tom Mix; later, when he removed the hat inside the office I could see the stockman's identifying markings: below the hatline his handsome, regular features were creased and tanned; above it, his forehead was a curiously vulnerable-looking white. Just now he was looking at some yearling bulls in the corral but in particular at a lone bull that almost sagged against the metal bars. "He's pretty sick,"

Homeyer said at last, his eyes still on the invalid. "This spring he perked up pretty good, and I thought he was gonna make it. Now I guess he won't."

Like the great majority of those in the buffalo business Homeyer's background was in cattle, he told me. He was from Kenedy, Texas, where his father had worked with cattle, and the boy grew up around cattle, horses, corrals, center-pivot irrigation rigs, vets, and feedlots—the whole complex of commercial cattle raising—and that made him suitable in a general way for this job. There were, he said, really no buffalo stockmen, only those like himself and his wife who knew cattle and could adapt to the special requirements of a business still in its Dawn Age. And to give me an idea how truly the buffalo business was in its Dawn Age he told me that whereas there were "something like ten thousand bison slaughtered in a year, there are one hundred thirty thousand cattle slaughtered every day." But, he went on, there was no doubt that the bison herds were growing, both in size and in geographical distribution. From the relict herd in Yellowstone (which numbered about thirty-five hundred), the buffalo population in the lower forty-eight states totalled well over one hundred fifty thousand in 1995, and as Bill Homeyer pointed out, that number was only going to continue climbing since the market for breeders was the fastest growing part of the business. The federal government held title to about five thousand of this number on refuges in Wyoming, Montana, the Dakotas, Nebraska, Oklahoma, and Kentucky. State governments from Minnesota to Arizona had herds totalling another four thousand. The rest were in private hands, and could be found, Bill Homeyer said, in places like Pennsylvania, Virginia, and Florida, "but all the really big herds are out here."

Why, I asked, had so many ranchers decided to get into the buffalo business, and what was its future? Homeyer said it was primarily because they'd discovered that a buffalo cost half as much to raise as a beef cow and currently brought twice as much at the supermarket. They required much less water than cows, could get along well without the expensive petrochemically fertilized grasses that Herefords and Angus required, and could survive quite handily the often severe Plains winters because with their huge shovel heads they burrowed beneath the snow cover to where the cured grasses lay waiting with their stored nutrients. "Bottom line is they were bred to this environment, whereas cows

75

weren't," Homeyer concluded. As for the future, both Homeyers said it remained to be seen and depended a lot on things like national dietary changes, marketing strategies, even the international market for an exotic meat. Some people were already predicting, however, that there would come a day when buffalo would replace beef as Americans' meat of choice. Cam Homeyer thought that might be unrealistic given the numbers now in play and the changes in ranching that would have to occur for buffalo to exceed beef in popularity. But there was no question, she said, that buffalo was a remarkable exception to the current trend of red meat consumption, which was down in America and still going down, while consumption of buffalo—steaks, hamburger, sausage—was steadily going up. And this despite the fact that buffalo routinely cost about twice what beef did, even more than that on the Eastern seaboard. But consumers were buying it because it was a leaner, healthier meat with less fat and cholesterol per serving than beef.

We talked some about what new techniques they'd had to master in working with buffalo, about practicalities like the height of fencing required to control the movements of these amazingly agile animals, about strictly grass-fed buffalo as compared to those who were shipped to feedlots to be fattened up on corn before slaughter, and about the advantages of herding them on trail bikes rather than with quarter horses. Up to this point, I thought, we might have been talking about a special breed of cow, and I confessed I'd been a trifle disappointed that my first glimpse of Ota's herd had been those few yearling bulls in the corral out back. That, I said, somehow didn't answer to my vague but real notion of what buffalo were. Like most Americans, I continued, I hadn't seen that many buffalo, and to me they were still an almost mythic animal. Wasn't there something special about them, something that radically distinguished them from beef cattle other than that they were potentially more profitable to raise? Oh, there definitely was, they rejoined together. "I compare 'em to a thousand-pound goat," Bill Homeyer said with one of his small smiles, "'cause they're so playful and agile. Plus they can eat just about anything and get along." Cam said they were a lot less predictable than cattle and a lot more playful. Yet this still didn't move me closer to what I obscurely felt was lurking there in these shaggy, bearded creatures, and I told the Homeyers that when I'd first come onto the ranch and had seen signs announcing the presence of bison (WARNING! BISON! DO NOT APPROACH) my heart had lifted and begun to beat faster. "I don't know where this comes from," I told them, "but I do know I felt it, and I wanted to see these animals—lots of them together—out on the range."

"Well," said Bill Homeyer, picking his hat from the desk top, "let's go do just that. We have to move 350 yearling bulls out of one pasture and into another, so why don't you ride along with us?"

In a pickup we ran down a network of ranch roads, went through a gate, then jounced across a pasture, and there they were, dark and huddled on the pasture's western margin. Bill drove very slowly toward them, and fifty yards distant swung the truck around and began calling them out the window, beeping his horn as he did so. Bison were easy enough to herd, he told me, provided you exercised caution and patience. Now he said, "They're playing a little hard to get, but they'll come eventually." He raised his voice and turned once more to call out the window, "Come on now, you guys! Don't make a liar out of me!" The herd milled and shuffled but made little movement toward the truck, and while we waited, the sky that had grown dark over the Sangre de Cristos erupted in a single long zag of lightning and there was a rumble of thunder. I wondered aloud if electrical storms ever spooked the bison, and Cam said storms never seemed to bother them in the least. Now Bill got out of the truck, and I followed him, and we stood there in the instantly frigid air and the wind-whipped pellets of rain and whizzing bits of grass, watching as the bulls began to form a phalanx forty yards wide and amble toward us, the dust rising beneath them and whirling away into the luminous, lead-colored air. As they began to close the distance Bill got casually back in the truck, and I was right behind him, having heard more than a few stories about the unpredictability of these creatures. Bill called again, an odd alto hoot such as I'd never heard before and which he said was the same he'd learned to use with cattle, and now the herd was definitely on the move, following as Bill swung the pickup about, going east across the pasture and through two gates, the farther one opening on a spread whose lush grasses announced it hadn't been grazed in some time. The bulls passed through the gates at a rocking gallop, their heads low, beards suddenly etched against the lunar brightness of the sand dunes to the north where the sun still shone. The line of animals stretched half a mile, and once a fair number had come onto the new grass Bill drove carefully into their midst, and suddenly I was given a view of the buffalo—and of America—I never expected to have: completely surrounded by blackish, hairy, heaving bodies, some with the rags of last year's robes still clinging to their humps and hindquarters as if the animal was a giant kind of chrysalis, emerging from one season into another while you watched. I was close enough to see their eyes—large, black, and watchful—and even to see the shreds of grass that clung to their coats. Only the fact that all of them were the same age and gender with horns that had yet to take on the curve of maturity gave an indication that these animals were after all managed—that and the red plastic ear tags they wore.

• • •

Over the next several days I learned a good deal more about the burgeoning buffalo business, of which Colorado was indeed a center, as the man at the Buffalo Bill Historical Center had told me. In the Denver area I talked with ranchers, with a packer and distributor, and with Rusty Seedig, Secretary of the National Bison Association. Like so many things associated with buffalo the Association was growing in numbers, strength, and sophistication of its outreach, he told me, and had recently put on a very successful conference in La Crosse, Wisconsin, where seminars were held on such topics as "Getting Into the Buffalo Business," "Feed Lot Management," and "Does Our Industry Want a Federally Controlled Grading System?" Jane Fonda and Ted Turner had been featured speakers, Seedig said, "and she was just great. Gave a really good talk." Turner had recently become a major player in the business, Seedig told me, through his purchases of four western ranches on which he ran buffalo or had plans to do so. "Well, he isn't *a* major player," Seedig amended, "he's *the* player. He has the ability to blow this thing wide open all by himself. He can make this industry, simple as that. Nobody else has his power, his money, or his access to the media. He could, if he wanted to, thoroughly educate the public to the health benefits of eating buffalo, and if he did that, the industry would just take off. All the animals we presently have would be spoken for, and so would the next generation of them. But as yet, we don't know what his plans are. At La Crosse he didn't say very much. He's been extremely close-mouthed." It was known, though, that Turner's original esthetic and historical interest in the buffalo had now also become economic and commercial, because, Seedig pointed out, he had discovered that by converting his ranches from cows to buffalo he could cut his labor force by two-thirds, save money on feed and water, and get twice as much at the market for his meat. Turner, perhaps surprised by all the economic benefits of buffalo ranching, is said to have remarked, "Hell, this could be a business."

Since the buffalo business is about meat, it was clearly necessary that I eat some, and that I did—ribs, steak, tongue, marrow. At The Fort, a popular restaurant that sits just below Buffalo Bill's mountaintop grave west of Denver, I ate buffalo and talked about it as the guest of the owner, Sam Arnold. Arnold, an ebullient fellow with a sense of humor as well as of history, had modelled the place on the famous trade fort built in 1833 by Charles and William Bent, the latter the father of that George Bent who rode with the Cheyennes in the 1860s and lived on to write about it. In addition to buffalo tongue, marrow, testicles, and various other cuts from the animal, Arnold had on his menu "Trade Whiskey," the authentic rotgut, made with bourbon, red peppers, tobacco, and gun powder. It went for $4.50 a pop. For a dollar more you could have a "St. Vrain's Mule"—ginger brandy and ginger beer and named after the Bents' partner, Ceran St. Vrain. At the Trade Room within the fort you could buy a Green River skinning knife as well as a copy of Sam Arnold's history of eating habits along the Santa Fe Trail.

The eating habits at The Fort suggested that Americans remained attracted to red meat even if they don't these days consume it in the gargantuan quantities the pioneers did when those uncouth men gobbled down half-raw, half-singed buffalo intestines as well as antelope, dog, and moose nostrils. Kip Halligan, the restaurant's manager, told me the restaurant served 5,000 buffalo dinners yearly, almost all of the meat coming from animals raised on Arnold's own ranch. But the buffalo served at The Fort, at the Denver Buffalo Company and other Denver-area restaurants, and that appearing with increasing frequency in American supermarkets is primarily meat from animals that have been fattened in feedlots prior to slaughter. It is not the wild, purely grass-fed meat the pioneers ate or that once formed the basis of the Plains tribe's diet. The buffalo businessmen will tell you there is nothing wrong with this, that it's a simple matter of economics. Still, the practice symbolizes what may be the long-range problem with the buffalo business: that the more it resembles the cattle industry, the more it risks failing to capitalize on its unique advantages and its historic opportunity. At this point at least, it is a business run by those with traditional cattlemen's backgrounds who have many of the thought patterns long associated with that industry. Inevitably, these men and women see themselves competing with cattlemen for a bigger share of the red meat market. Their slogan, "Buffalo tastes like beef wishes it did," tells more about the preoccupations of the new business than it does about the new product. Fifty years from now it may be that they will have succeeded, and buffalo meat will be successfully competing with beef, but if that is because the buffalo has been so micromanaged by genetic engineers, breeders, and ranch managers that it is virtually indistinguishable from cattle, that may not be much of a gain for anybody but the producers. Nor would the spectacle of de-horned creatures standing listlessly in corrals and feedlots be likely to inspire the rapt attention of people who flocked to "Seasons of the Buffalo" at the Buffalo Bill Historical Center.

The buffalo business has not arrived at such a point yet, but there are certainly signs that at least some sectors of the business have that in mind. Currently, it is against the law to feed buffalo any of the chemicals that are daily pumped into beef cattle, but it isn't against the law to treat them as much like cattle as is practicable. It isn't against the law to de-horn them, a common enough practice since it has been discovered that when herded together for business purposes the animals become stressed and may gore each other, a business loss. It isn't against the law to try to breed and cull toward a more docile, tractable animal than nature intended. Nor is it against the law to feed them like Angus, Herefords, or Limousins, topping them off in the feedlots with a diet calculated to add hundreds of pounds of fat to an animal that naturally would not eat that way. Indeed, it has been the dismay of some of the new buffalo men that the animal seems to resist this final temptation, even in the unnatural confinement of the feedlot where by design there is nothing else to do but eat.

There are some in the buffalo business who oppose the emerging tendency to treat buffalo like cattle, and it was interesting to learn that among them the most vocal are the Indian tribes who have gotten into the business or are in the process of doing so. Down on the Osage reservation in northernmost Oklahoma I talked with the Standing Bear brothers, Geoffrey and Sean, at the Osage Tribal Museum in Pawhuska. Geoffrey was the tribe's chief counsel and Sean the museum's director. While I waited to talk with them I went through the exhibits that narrated the tribe's history, including a photograph showing a group of Osage men in camp. "Men of the Last Buffalo Hunt, ca. 1875," the caption read: "This buffalo hunt failed due to the extinction of the buffalo by white hide hunters."

When I met with the brothers I learned that the tribe had recently participated in the release of three hundred buffalo into the Nature Conservancy's Tallgrass Prairie Preserve above Pawhuska, yet that participation had not been completely enthusiastic because many tribal members were uneasy about white attitudes toward the buffalo. It was very difficult, Geoffrey Standing Bear said, after these many years of white betrayals, legal chicanery—even the murders of tribal members— to get the people to believe that the Nature Conservancy folks weren't interested in profiting from the buffalo but rather in the reintroduction of the species to its natural habitat. All some Osages saw, he went on, were the trucks, the corrals, and the computer wands that connected the white men to their captive animals, each of which had a microchip implanted in its ear. Some tribal members wanted the tribe itself to get into the buffalo business but to do so in a respectful and traditional way; he mentioned an organization that was promoting such activity, the InterTribal Bison Cooperative. But as yet the Osages didn't have any buffalo of their own. All they had was the knowledge that the whites had those three hundred head roaming over what had been ancestral lands.

The difference between white methods of buffalo raising and Indian ones, Sean Standing Bear cut in, was simply that "for us it's basically a spiritual matter that's hard to deal with in commercial terms. The buffalo is like a living, walking church. There must be some connection to it in our DNA. Our ancestors ate so much bison through the generations that when we see one it just runs through us—spiritual, physical, everything. When I see one everything within me rumbles."

The president and founding father of the InterTribal Bison Cooperative was Fred DuBray, a Lakota from the Cheyenne River Reservation. The ITBC, he told me, had been born out of his sense that raising buffalo might be a way to restore some balance and harmony to tribal life. During the 1980s DuBray had done an analysis of economic programs, past and present, on the reservation. Most of them, he concluded, had been failures "because we really didn't understand the white economic system and its goals—we still don't. But going into buffalo, that we could understand because it was culturally compatible. People could relate to it, and so the buffalo could become a way of rebuilding tribal culture in a way that brings economics, culture, religion, and politics together. Ideally, raising buffalo will be a way of putting things back into balance that have been knocked out of balance since the buffalo disappeared." Once DuBray and a few others began asking those on other reservations whether they might be interested in a buffalo-raising cooperative they found a deep aquifer of interest, and currently, he said, there were thirty-six tribal groups participating.

But the ITBC was emphatically not interested in going into the buffalo business in the white way. DuBray was quietly forceful in detailing the cooperative's opposition to certain white management practices. "We don't believe in de-horning [buffalo]," he told me. "We don't believe in the feedlot process at all. We want buffalo to be buffalo. We follow a strictly natural program of grazing with adequate acreage so that they won't have to overgraze an area."

"You know," he went on in a quiet, gentle voice that here took on a kind of ruminative tone as if he were reciting an old, old story, "these animals prospered and grew into the millions eating just the native grasses, and that's what we allow them to do. The reservations have probably the largest acreage of native grasses left in America, and this land base can be the basis of a long-range sustainable operation." White ranchers, on the other hand, "don't appear to understand that these are wild creatures—big, dangerous ones that should be kept that way. They want to domesticate them. Again here, it's a matter of *control*: they want to totally control their buffalo herds to maximize the profit. But they're not looking at the long-range aspects. If you domesticate the buffalo, then you haven't got a buffalo anymore. You've got something else. When you intensively manage bison, you change them. You gradually take away their instincts. You tend to eliminate the ones that are the hardest to handle, and that eventually shrinks the gene pool, whereas we should be working to expand it. And," he concluded, "if you stock the range to maximize profits, then you're right back where you started because you've re-created the same problems with buffalo that you had with cattle."

Such views are not widely shared among those in the new buffalo business, perhaps nowhere less so than among those whose work it is to cater to the rising American appetite for buffalo meat. Kip Halligan at The Fort, for instance.

"People want to tell their friends and family they've eaten buffalo," he said, as I dug into a complimentary plate of buffalo tongue with a caper and horseradish sauce, "but they don't *really* want it to taste wild and gamy." Nor, he went on, did they want it to look any different from beef on their plate, and this, he claimed, was as big a reason for topping buffalo off on corn as was simple weight gain. "A purely grass-fed buffalo will have a distinct orange-ish quality to the fat," Halligan asserted, "and, just visually, that's going to give you some customer resistance right there." Rod Schichel, the restaurant's French-trained chef, said that even corn-fed buffalo left hanging too long in the meat locker grew gamier in taste than most customers were used to.

"If you're ready for the taste of buffalo," Schichel explained, "it's okay. Most people aren't. They're ready for the *idea* of buffalo, but actually their palates are set for the taste of beef." An Italian restaurant, he said, drawing an analogy broad enough for me, had to answer to certain taste expectations, and so it was here at The Fort with the meat they served. His job, apparently, was to make buffalo seem like the old, wild creature while it actually tasted close enough to beef to comfort the customers. The hybrid creation called the beefalo (three-eighths buffalo) had been a failed experiment in that direction, but it appeared now that between the genetic engineers, stock managers, and chefs they were going to have another go at it.

While I was eating my way through the tongue, some marrow ("prairie butter," they used to call it), and a buffalo filet, Kip Halligan and I talked Western history, a subject he'd learned quite a bit about, and when at last I'd finished he said there was something he was certain I'd be interested in seeing. We crossed The Fort's courtyard, climbed the stairs, and entered a small room that Sam Arnold and his wife used as a guest bedroom. There against the wall was a big, old-time leather-covered trunk, its top scarred and held together with crude, wide-spaced stitches that were black with age. "Open it up," Halligan suggested, and I did so. On the underside of the lid was written in a firm, fair, and fading hand, "George Bent."

III

What I earlier called the "inner work" of the buffalo phenomenon has proceeded along other lines, though to an important extent it has been dependent on the business of buffalo in that the sheer increase in the herds the producers have sponsored has made it possible for some to think of the animal in esthetic, spiritual, and ecological ways. As Bob Dineen of Rocky Mountain Natural Meats pungently put the current situation, buffalo were now to be found in numbers "simply because they're commercially viable. If they weren't, then you wouldn't see the herds you do now. The only ones you'd see would be on preserves or in zoos." When the herds were small and mostly confined to federal and state lands the buffalo was an exotic in its native territory. But with the population zooming well beyond the 200,000 level there was suddenly a sort of latitude that allowed people like Hisayoshi Ota to see the animal in ways having little to do with whether buffalo tastes the way beef wished it did.

Not that Ota was unworldly or disdainful of commercial realities. I couldn't, of course, have asked for a look at the books of the Great Sand Dunes Country Club and Inn, but visual evidence suggested a thriving operation. Which, as I learned from Ota, had been the original plan: profit. Back in the late 1980s he'd been partners with a Japanese developer who'd had the idea of creating a huge resort here—high-rise hotels, jet port, Japanese tourists—but who subsequently came to feel that these isolated lands weren't suitable for what he had in mind. To his young partner, though, these same lands extended an obscure promise. The West, of course, has always been long on promise to newcomers, but for Ota the promise was a bit different: the freedom to enact here an ideal of land stewardship he'd received in his Tokyo childhood from a family retainer. He told me this as we sat in the sun on the deck behind the club's pro shop. His family had owned extensive property in Tokyo, including a very large garden that once had belonged to a shogun. The caretaker, he said, was a man of intense and meditative frugality, cooking his spare meals with charcoal, heating his bathwater with a wood fire, hunting pheasants through the garden with bow and arrow—all this, Ota emphasized, even though all the conveniences of postwar urban life were readily available to him. His example was deeply impressive to the boy and remained so even after the family lost its Tokyo property and with it the garden. The young man who came to America to study architecture at Columbia carried in mind the example of the caretaker and found that it jarred with his new realities. Living in New York, he told me, was both immensely stimulating and at the same time unsettling because there he saw up close the almost incredible wastefulness of American culture: mountains of waste material trucked daily out of the city, seemingly without a thought of what the future consequences would be of a throwaway, disposable culture. Frugality and recycling seemed fantasies there, and the caretaker would have been as out of place as would a Stone Age huntsman. But when the opportunity on the Colorado ranchlands came his way, Ota saw it for what it was and seized it, buying out his partner and completely reformulating the idea of the resort. This, he decided, would still be a resort, but it would be one with heart and intention. He would use its lands not to generate enormous profits but to restore those lands to something of what they once had been before the primitive profiteers—the sheepmen and cattlemen—had strip-mined them. "I had been wanting to get back to the land ever since my childhood," Ota told me, "and out here I could do it, whereas I couldn't possibly do this in Japan: too little land and far too expensive."

Originally Ota had been drawn to bison on esthetic grounds, like Ted Turner, but then he learned that there was a great deal more to them than how they looked and what their history had been. He learned that the gigantic sweep of grasslands that once stretched from Illinois to the Rockies and from south Saskatchewan to mid-Texas had in effect been maintained by the great herds that grazed them. In recent years the increase in the herds has permitted researchers to study this process, and they have discovered that left to their own devices bison will intensively graze an area and then move along. By not staying on a spot and nibbling the grasses down to the roots—as domestic livestock will—they move over the land and allow the plants to recover and regenerate.

Their grazing pattern, one buffalo researcher told me, "is kind of like a lawn mower that trims the plants and in doing that throws strength back into them." Moreover, bison will not herd up in riparian areas, compacting the soil, stripping the banks of vegetation, and causing massive erosion. Nor do they routinely defecate and urinate in streams as cows do. In sum, bison, the researchers have found, are a great deal easier on rangeland than domestic livestock, while at the same time these natives actually help the rangelands to prosper—just as they had been doing for thousands of years before they were hunted out and replaced by the white man's "blooded" cattle.

In the bison Hisayoshi Ota saw both an animate mechanism for rangeland restoration and at the same time a unique opportunity to practice the kind of careful stewardship he had learned from the caretaker in that Tokyo garden. "The land itself is the most important thing here," he said, half-turning to look toward the stubbled range that stretched west beyond the green of his golf course. "Five years ago I could never have imagined myself doing this. But now, for whatever reason, I've been given this opportunity." The golf course, the inn, and the sale of some of the herd for breeding and feeding, he wished me to understand, were sources of income that enabled him to pursue his goal of rangeland restoration.

What, I asked him, was the optimum figure for the herd on his two ranches? It was hard to say at this point: "Too many bison, and they'll overgraze because they'll have to. People will tell you bison will never overgraze. Ted Turner will tell you that. It's not true. But if they have enough range, then they won't; they'll keep moving. When you see a herd grazing, you notice that they keep moving right along. On the other hand, I think if we have too few bison here, they can't do their work, and the range will continue to deteriorate. Well," he concluded, standing up to indicate he had other matters to attend to, "I have the rest of my life to work on this."

• • •

Hisayoshi Ota may have been a visionary in the way he wanted to run his ranches, but he was certainly not alone in wanting to help restore America's Western rangelands. The condition of those grasslands over which the buffalo once roamed and the related decline of ranching and farming beyond the 98th Parallel have become so obvious over the past two decades that ecologists and land use planners, botanists and hydrologists have begun to say publicly what some of them had been saying privately almost since the time John Wesley Powell made his now-famous report in 1878 on the lands beyond the anhydrous line. Everywhere the grasslands' carrying capacity has been greatly reduced by a century and a half of hard, ignorant usage. Everywhere riparian areas are badly damaged and eroded while their vital supplies of water run off instead of reaching the soil. Water tables throughout the region have been dangerously lowered because of the massive amounts of water needed for breeds of livestock developed in the lavishly watered climate of northern Europe. (In *Diet for a New America* John Robbins estimates that each pound of beef produced requires an expenditure of some two thousand five hundred gallons of water.) Because of years of overgrazing, an armed host of spiky nutritionless plants has invaded the domain of the native grasses, requiring ranchers to plant feed fence post to fence post. The successors of those farmers who ripped into the grasslands with their oxen and heavy plows, breaking the dense root systems with a sound like pistol shots, have suffered the region's endemic cycles of drought. Many of them have failed and moved off the land, leaving it either fallow or else in the hands of gigantic agribusiness concerns. As far as the cattle industry itself is concerned, it has become evident to all who will really look at the phenomenon in the largest context that the substitution of those blooded northern European cattle for bison hasn't worked. The Western cattle industry, it is clear, cannot continue another century and a half without inflicting environmental damage from which the bioregion might never fully recover.

Major Powell foresaw much of this. Crudely simplified, what he said in his report was that west of the anhydrous line the land was too arid to be settled according to plans and habits that had worked well enough east of it. Few listened, especially in Congress, for this was just two years after Little Bighorn, and white Americans, sure they understood what Manifest Destiny meant and even more certain that the tribes were wasting the grasslands' potential, were hell-bent on dispossessing the tribes, killing off the buffalo, and making the whole region into a wider, handsomer version of the Eastern half of the country. The sturdy yeoman would supplant the savage, and the cow would replace the buffalo. When Walt Whitman got his first look at the grasslands in the year following Powell's report he foresaw ten million farms springing up out there and a hundred million inhabitants working them.

It never happened, of course, despite the relentless, often heroic— and even more often tragic—efforts of the generations of settlers who hurled themselves against the vast, dry spaces of the West. In fact, the region has been steadily losing population since the Dust Bowl Thirties, and the geographers and land use planners Frank and Deborah Popper have discovered that large portions of the grasslands have quietly reverted to a frontierlike population density—the two-persons-per-square-mile standard once used by the Census Bureau to define "frontier." The Poppers have found 143 Western counties that currently would qualify as frontier under that definition, counties whose land mass makes up over a quarter of the United States. Nobody has been able to refute the Poppers' statistics, but what has made so many Westerners so angry is the Poppers' suggestion that it might be best to turn a large swath of the grasslands into what they have termed a "Buffalo Commons": a huge ecological reserve through which herds of buffalo would range with a carefully designed freedom. The very idea, to be sure, goes smack up against one of America's essential secular myths, the Winning of the West, but when you travel through some of the country that would be parts of the Poppers' audacious proposal you are moved to wonder how audacious it really is. And the Poppers themselves point out that their proposal is actually quite modest compared to the settlers' attempts to totally transform most of the West into farms and ranches in defiance of the immutable natural specifics of the region. Try, for instance, the country from Denver east to Manhattan, Kansas; or west from Pawhuska, Oklahoma, to Las Vegas, New Mexico. These are long, lonesome stretches by anyone's reckoning, and they never seem more so than when you pass through the warped, boarded-up settlements that are dead or dying. Siebert, Bethune, Arriba (all in Colorado); Colby, Oakley, Ogallah (Kansas); Cherokee, Buffalo, Boise City (Oklahoma); Clayton, Springer, Wagon Mound (New Mexico). If Horace Greeley, Senator Thomas Hart Benton, or Whitman—Western boosters all—could see these places now, they would be aghast.

IV

I use these stretches because that was the way I went out and came back from a tour of tallgrass prairie preserves and their native maintenance crews, the buffalo. At the Konza Prairie Research Natural Area (KPRNA) in the Flint Hills outside Manhattan I walked and rode through the 8,000-acre preserve with site manager Tom Van Slyke who explained to me that the two main areas of prairie research here were the effects of fire and of native grazers. Fire, he explained, was a prime agent in the health of grasslands because it cleared off dead, matted vegetation and exposed the soil to the sun's heat, thereby stimulating new growth. Fire's beneficial effects had long been suspected, he told me, ever since the first-coming whites had observed the Indians setting fire to stretches of the Plains, creating what the tribes termed the "red buffalo." Here researchers were doing controlled burns in selected areas at intervals of one, two, four, ten, and twenty years. "You asked where the buffalo were grazing," he said as we drove around a bend in the a dirt road lined with prairie cone flowers. "Well, they're grazing where we've been burning." We pulled up a sharp incline, parked, and got out into a firebreak between two stands of grass. "Buffalo can smell or sense where a place has been burned," Van Slyke said, "and they'll go for it, because they know that the forage will be better there." We entered the stand that was being burned at two-year intervals. "See this here?" Van Slyke said, inviting me to a closer inspection of the grasses that waved in a blast-furnace August wind. Beneath their tops you could plainly see a layer of gray, matted vegetation. Across the break in the one-year burn pasture the grass plants were a clean, vigorous green right down to the roots, and you could see plenty of dark soil.

Before coming to the KPRNA Van Slyke had worked with cattle, and now as we drove toward where he thought we might find a herd of buffalo grazing he said that, compared with these native grazers, cows were really pretty stupid and not nearly as resourceful as buffalo. "Heat doesn't seem to bother bison at all," he told me (like others he used the terms interchangeably, sometimes switching in the same sentence). "We had four straight days here recently where it was a hundred-and-ten or more every day, and there they were, up on the ridge in the sun. Cattle, on the other hand, will head for the trees and the water and just stand down there all day, mashing it to bits. But when lightning comes the bison will move off high ground, but unlike cattle who'll go to the trees and stand under them, the bison will go to open, lower ground. They just seem to understand this region in a way cattle don't." We now had arrived on a crest of a hill, and there below us were maybe thirty buffalo. Van Slyke was silent a moment, simply looking down at the scene, then he said, "They understand where they are because they're natives. They're natural, they fit in better, they *flow* better with the land. Heck," he smiled broadly, "they just *look* better."

Indeed they did. We alighted from the truck, walked to the point, and watched as a line storm raced towards us, the grasses shivering under the hard wind and the buffalo standing, waiting for the rain, many of them with their heads turned into the wind, massive and dense as haystacks. As the first rain came an eight-year-old bull got up from his wallow and ambled slowly through the flank-high grasses towards the main group. He looked like no cow I'd ever seen, and as Tom Van Slyke had so aptly put it, he seemed to flow with the land as he crossed a swale, went up its far side and came to the edge of the group.

Now the rain came on in earnest, and we retreated to the shelter of the truck's cab where we sat, chewing on Black Sampson plants that Tom Van Slyke said once were used on the Plains as a sort of novocaine. The wind gently rocked the truck, the rain came sheeting across the hills, and in something less than half an hour the storm had blown itself eastward. Then the sun glinted again on the grasses, and the buffalo continued their work of maintenance, just as they had been doing for thousands of years before the arrival of the horse, the gun, whiskey, and the hide hunters.

● ● ●

A few days thereafter, having visited the Tallgrass Prairie Preserve above Pawhuska, Oklahoma, I was on my way back to New Mexico along Oklahoma 64 when I stopped for a cup of coffee in Cherokee. The digital display of the bank's thermometer said ninety-four, though it was just mid-morning, and the sign in the cafe window advised that the place would be closing at 1:00 P.M. due to the failure of its air conditioner. Inside, the waitress told me I might be cooler in back where they had two big fans going, but I noticed that the few customers were all sitting up front, and I said a seat at the counter would be fine. I wasn't surprised to find that all the others there were well along in years, for the grasslands that once beckoned the young and hardy have become the last stand of old folks; the young and hardy have moved off the land and into the larger towns and to the cities. Sipping the scalding and bitter brew, I might have been in any one of the little towns I'd passed through on my grasslands expedition, and I thought again of the Poppers' suggestion of turning all this into a Buffalo Commons; I thought too of kindred schemes for huge-scale restoration projects like the "Big Open" in Montana. Cherokee and all the other blasted towns and the miles and miles of badly hammered rangeland made you wonder—and wonder hard—whether the West ought to have been settled this way, or even settled at all. Maybe Catlin had been right in saying the region ought to have been set aside as a magnificent park, a kind of living monument to that unspoiled New World we broke into with our plans, our ingenuity, our restlessness.

I thought back also to another cup of coffee I'd stopped for, this one in Cottonwood Falls, Kansas, on my way down to Pawhuska, and of the little library they'd made in the cafe on one of the unused shelves. William Least Heat Moon had written of this village in his monumental study of the Flint Hills, but *PrairyErth* wasn't to be found alongside *Pioneer Women of Kansas* and *Ghost Towns of Kansas*. Examining the few holdings up close, my eye locked with that of a lone woman seated nearby. "I was just looking to see what they had here," I said, somewhat lamely.

"Yes," she said, "I looked, too. I thought they'd surely have *PrairyErth*."

From across the small room an elderly man joined in. "I have that book," he announced. "Haven't read it yet, but it's sure interesting to have someone like that come in and look at your place with other eyes, you know? And it's not every county that has two townships in it where no one lives, and we have that here. Now, if you *do* live here, you best live conservatively—that and keep a garden."

Roping a Dream

The middle-aged cowboy sits slumped on the running board of a truck parked in the middle of some Nevada salt flats, holding his head in his hands. Dark rivulets of blood course down one side of his face, and he fights almost pitifully to get his breath. A few yards away on the flats, a wild stallion lies trussed up with a rope, the other end of which is tied to the truck's bumper. At last the man gets enough breath to speak and begins to mumble about the end of the old mustanging days. Everything's changed, he keeps saying with an imponderable weariness, as if now in this fading desert half-light the gathered weight of four centuries of New World history had come to rest on his shoulders: everything's changed. "It's like roping a dream now," he says.

The scene is from the last moments of the John Huston/Arthur Miller film *The Misfits* (1961), in which Clark Gable plays the cowboy who has lived long enough and at the right time to find his West, its life and unexamined customs like mustanging, mysteriously altered. What once seemed an innocent, if mortal, way to make a buck has now been transmogrified into a vicious and inhumane business in which the cowboy is a kind of ignorant serf to the faceless men from the city. Gay, the cowboy on the running board, is no thinker, but he is no dummy either, and he knows when it is time to give something up. It is not, he knows too well, only age that sits on his shoulders now. In the film's final scene, Gay and Roselyn (Marilyn Monroe), the blonde divorcée who has unwittingly brought the news of the end of the old ways, are seen pointing the truck for Reno—where, presumably, the future lies.

Some years back this off-beat, haunting film came suddenly to mind when my wife and I were in the company of two ranchers whose summer sheep and cattle range was in Nevada's Ruby Mountains, across the state from some of the film's locations. The county we were driving through has to be one of the most unpopulated nonwilderness areas

93

left in the lower forty-eight—a hundred square miles and more of big, silent space crossed by one or two sandy roads that can quickly turn into axle-sucking quagmires in the fitful span of an afternoon thundershower. Nothing here but sky, sagebrush, mountains, a few hawks, an occasional band of antelope. Then, off in the distance, we saw some forms, bunched, dark, and indistinct against the light. I wondered aloud what they were.

"Oh," said one of the ranchers, barely giving the forms a glance, "those are our pets." They were, he amplified, a band of wild horses that had come down out of the Humboldt National Forest to graze on the flats. "And you know," said the other rancher with a wry smile, "it's just a lot of fun to come along behind 'em with your sheep or cows. They leave a lot of forage for you." The other man smiled with that same wryness, and so I asked them if they wished the days of the old mustangers were back. "You know," I said, "like in that Gable/ Marilyn Monroe movie where they spooked them with airplanes, then roped them from trucks and used truck tires as drags."

"We don't favor cruelty to animals," the driver said. "But I'll tell you what: with these new regulations, there's just too many of them."

The same view was cautiously expressed by Bruce Portwood of the Bureau of Land Management, which oversees the wild horses and burros that range on the West's public lands. Portwood had been with the BLM more than a quarter of a century, was a native of Nevada, and had seen it all from the days of mustangers like the film's Gay to the current period of federal regulations protecting the wild ones. "Our situation is that we have a real population problem," he told me. We were sitting at the bar of the Stockmen's Hotel in Elko. The only light in there came from the slot machines surrounding us and from the small video screens inset into the bar's surface so customers could play mechanized games of blackjack or poker while they drank. In this gloom Portwood gestured with his huge mitts, detailing the BLM's wild horse program while images of aces and hearts flickered up into his eyes.

"In the past, before there was any federal regulation, there were a lot of abuses, for sure. The mustangers didn't care what happened to the horses, just so they delivered a horse to the canners—wouldn't feed 'em or water 'em, for days maybe, while they trucked 'em in. Then after Wild Horse Annie and the other horse sympathizers got active you

94

couldn't do that kind of thing anymore. But there was about a ten-year period in there before our program got into operation where nobody was doing any roundups. The horses have no natural enemies. They can die in a severe winter. They can die of starvation, which is what happens when you have overpopulation. They can die of natural causes. But we regularly pick up studs that're twenty-five years old. Not so often mares that old, because they get worn down having colts. But you find 'em seventeen years old sometimes. The point is, over that span of years you can build up pretty sizable herds. We have thirty thousand right here [in Nevada]. Wyoming is next. They might have five or six thousand. Then Oregon. That's a lot of competition with cattle and sheep and game animals for the available forage." He wagged his head at the size of the problem, touched the broad brim of his straw hat, and swirled his drink. I asked him to explain how the BLM hoped to relieve pressure on the range by removing horses judged to exceed the carrying capacity of a given portion of public lands.

"The way it works," he said, "is pretty simple, really. We advertise for bids for a gather [roundup]. Generally, we'll take the low bid unless there's a compelling reason not to—if the contractor has a bad reputation, for instance. The contractor is responsible for everything: the trucks, the feed, the helicopter, and so forth. We identify a likely place for the horses to be, then we set up a trap, generally in a draw or on the other side of a hill where there's a trail that goes in that direction. The helicopter drives the band towards the trap, and it's hard and tricky work here because there's a lot of hovering and you're really straining the machine's capabilities. We generally have another copter up to make sure the contractor doesn't drive the horses too fast or separate a band or leave any colts behind. When we get them near the trap there's a rider hidden there with a haltered horse—what's called a 'Judas horse'—and he lets the horse go. It's trained to run to the trap, and it leads the band in. After that we ship 'em to our holding center at Palomino Valley, and there they get their vet work—shots, whatever they need. Then we put 'em up for adoption.

"The way it worked in the past was private individuals could buy the horses, up to four per person, and after a year they could apply for title to them. What happened to the horses after that was their business. Yes, they could be sold to the canners. But there came to be abuses in this operation. A fellow could buy his four horses and get his friends and relatives and so forth to buy their four, and after a year he could get power of attorney and get their horses and sell the whole bunch—generally to the canners. So we stopped that. Now no one can acquire more than four in any way."

It sounded, I said, like a workable, humane program. Why, then, had I heard from ranchers and others that it wasn't working?

"Well," he said, again wagging his head, "the adoption program really isn't that effective in reducing pressures on the range. Oh, there's some adoptions, sure. The colts get adopted. A pretty young stud might get adopted. The ones with good conformations. But the rest, they just stay there in those feed lots, eating hay until they die. I wonder if this is good business. There is a provision in the Wild Horse Act for humane destruction of the old and the sick, but it can't be used: it's politically too dangerous. And now we have the penitentiary programs, and they have been successful in gentling a few horses and making them attractive for adoption. But this isn't going to solve the problem, even if all these operations were greatly expanded. There's too many of 'em, and we don't have a real good way to deal with 'em."

I told him I had a friend who was an ardent conservationist and who had worked all over North America for the preservation of endangered species and habitats and who said he had a way to deal with the horses. "He told me he thought the whole campaign for the horses was the most insane, irrational thing in current conservation policy," I said. "He said his solution was a simple one: 'Shoot the fuckers!'" Portwood laughed shortly, but he wasn't about to touch that one. Neither is anyone else in government, though there are others in Nevada willing enough to apply just this solution—about which more presently.

Whatever your attitude toward the wild horses, it must be admitted that they excite feelings out of proportion to their actual physical presence and maybe even their impact on the public lands. One reason for this emotionalism is easy to determine. As has often been observed, without the horse it would be impossible to imagine the American West, and the wild horse of today is presumed to be the lineal descendant of the mustang that was so significant in the "making" of the West. In Austin, Texas, there is a large outdoor sculpture of a group of plunging, rearing mustangs, tribute to the role of the horse in the history of the West, and at the sculpture's base are these words of J. Frank Dobie:

> These horses bore Spanish explorers across two continents.
> They brought the Plains Indians the age of horse culture. Texas
> cowboys rode them to extend the ranching occupation clear to
> the plains of Alberta. Spanish horse, Texas cow pony, and mus-
> tang were all one in those times when, as sayings went, a man
> was no better than his horse and a man afoot was no man at all.
> Like the Longhorn, the mustang has been virtually bred out of
> existence. But mustang horses will always symbolize western
> frontiers, long trails of Longhorn herds, seas of pristine grass,
> and men riding free in a free land.

You could, of course, write the sculpture off to the well-known (and
misunderstood) excesses of Texas culture, with its grandiosity, sentimentality, and chauvinism—but you would be missing the point. The Texas
tribute is only a recent and regional manifestation of a far larger phenomenon that encompasses Texas and the whole of the American West
as well, and that is humankind's ageless fascination with the horse.
Without even a passing sense of this deep prologue, the current drama
of the West's wild horses would have to seem as irrational and foolish
as it evidently does to my conservationist friend with his draconian
solution. For what rides on the slumped shoulders of the unhorsed
rider of *The Misfits* rides also on those of the BLM officials charged
with protecting the wild ones and even on those of the ranchers,
hunters, and miners who are most stubbornly determined to rid the
ranges of every last free-roaming horse: the horse as dream creature,
as an artifact of the human imagination.

As far down as we can let out our rope into what Thomas Mann
called the "well of the past," there we find the horse, galloping, soaring
on impossibly slender legs, defying gravity and time: in Greek myths of
centaurs and winged horses; on Roman friezes and columns; in Greek
and Roman memories of the Scythians, who were memorable because
they were memorable horsemen; and beyond this, too, to the walls of
Old World caves whereon, thirty thousand years ago, our ancestors
drew the big-bellied horses they knew.

From the first, humans' homage to the horse sprang from the

notion that a man on horseback drew into himself the dream of freedom. No longer earthbound, doomed to know in his bones each weary step of his way, the man on horseback achieved the creative illusion that he could go where he would, that he had risen above the old limits—as, in some measure, he really had. Thus in the ancient records the admiration of the horse as deliverer; thus, too, the mingled admiration and fear sedentary peoples had of the horseback nomads, those drinkers of the wind, the bridles of their horses adorned with human scalps (as Herodotus reports of the Scythians). Journeying ever deeper into the unknown East, Marco Polo comments with undisguised admiration on the horseback life of the Tartars, how, dressed in flame-hardened skins, living on mare's milk, they traveled incredible distances on their shaggy ponies. When in extremity, says Polo, they opened the veins of their mounts and drank the blood. "Most of the bright luster of history," writes Glenn R. Vernam,

> would be missing if the mounted man had not ridden through
> its pages, leaving a passage marked by the glint of bold, free
> eyes and shining armor. In all ages civilization's stirring deeds
> have centered around him. Be he barbarian, warrior, crusader,
> knight, conquistador, cowboy, or cavalryman, it was the man on
> horseback who created the sagas of valor and carried the ban-
> ner of romance throughout the world. His is the figure that has
> excited the admiration of footmen for a hundred centuries; he it
> is to whom the man on foot has always instinctively lifted his
> eyes, both physically and spiritually.

For the native peoples of the Americas, the horseborne dream of freedom began as the nightmare of history with the return of the horse to the New World, its original home—for now the horse bore its implacable white rider. And it was the conquistadors' horses (along with their gunpowder) that gave the numerically inferior invaders an edge in their critical first encounters with the powerful empires of the Aztecs and Incas.

The horses that so terrorized these proud native warriors, that allowed the invaders to attack, retreat, transport supplies over distances, and carry the war to the enemy, were the ancestors of the mustangs that became synonymous with the wild horses of the West. They were descendants of the horses the Moors had ridden to victory when they invaded Spain in 711, called "Barbs," short for Barbary, the northern coastal region of Africa from which the Moors launched their invasion. The Barbs had some Arabian blood in them but were not Arabian, as some have supposed. They had the swiftness and bottom of the Arabian, though, and after seven centuries of breeding following the Moorish invasion, the Spanish Barb, as the type was now known, was famed throughout the Old World for its speed, quickness, courage, and companionability. It was on the small side, deep through the heart, and often had a dark dorsal line running along its back. The predominant colors were shades of brown—dun, beige, buckskin—and many had black points and curious zebralike markings on their legs. Above all, however, the Spanish Barb had endurance and an indomitable heart, and it was these qualities that persisted in the American West, like a vein of iron, through all the centuries of random breeding on the range. Here again, J. Frank Dobie speaks to the point with a traditional saying that cuts across time and cultures:

> A white man will ride the mustang until he is played out; a Mexican will take him and ride him another day until he thinks he is played out; then a Comanche will mount him and ride him to where he is going.

From the beginning, the whites were careful to try to keep their herds to themselves and away from the tribes, for they understood the advantages their horses conferred on them and how unfortunate it would be if the tribes were to learn the uses of the horse. The Aztecs, the Incas, and the tribes of the Southeast who encountered de Soto and Narváez had learned—too late—that the horse was not a mythological beast but mortal. As the Spaniards pushed into present-day California and the Southwest, however, the natives came into more sustained contact with these marvelous creatures: in the missions, for example, they were forced to work with the stock and so learned to ride and care for horses. In the Southwest, when Coronado made his *entrada* in 1540 the tribes contented themselves with stealing a few horses and eating them; by the time of Oñate's expedition into present-day New Mexico at the end of that century, this was still the favored practice of the raiding Apaches.*

Gradually, though, the longer-term uses of the horse became evident to the tribes, and so once again, in a new context, the horse figured in the dream of freedom, and made the Comanches, Kiowas, Apaches, Cheyennes, Crow, and Sioux nomads and buffalo hunters whose most evident stock of wealth was their outsized herds of horses. Yet perhaps in part because of the lateness of this acquisition and the profound cultural changes thereby introduced, there remained among the tribes a sense of the horse as a sacred animal, the special subject of dances, myths, prayers, and songs. In Greek mythology the horse stood in some special, if ill-defined, relationship to the gods, and so it was in the nineteenth-century American West, where among the Indians the horse seemed less a gift of the whites than of the powers.

Inevitably, in the years following Coronado and Oñate horses from these explorers' large herds turned wild—for horses, too, may dream of freedom. Once a horse had escaped, it was unlikely to be recovered; and if it had offspring, they would remain wild as well. By the middle of the nineteenth century immense herds of wild horses were to be encountered west of the Mississippi. Any estimate of their numbers would be at best educated guesswork, but some have said there may have been as many as seven million by the time of the Civil War. A young lieutenant who was later to achieve prominence in that war saw a huge feral herd in 1846 a few days out of Corpus Christi on his way into Mexico in the war against that country. Ulysses S. Grant was himself mounted on a mustang lately caught from that same herd. When the horses were sighted, Grant wrote years afterward,

---

*What a people will eat and what they consider repugnant is in itself an oddly interesting subject, one treated in Peter Farb and George Armelagos, *Consuming Passions* (Boston: Houghton Mifflin, 1980). As for the consumption of flesh, the critical issue seems to be the people's relationship to the creature involved. Several Plains tribes ate dog and served it on special occasions, but the Blackfeet were nauseated by the very suggestion because they remembered the days before the horse when dogs had been their faithful bearers and servants. The Spaniards would not eat horse, but the Southwestern tribes and those of the Plains would—at first. Later, having learned the other virtues of the horse, they did not make a practice of eating it. No Westerner I have talked with will admit to having eaten horse, and a good many are revolted by the idea. Yet in Paris, the most sophisticated city in the Western world, horsemeat is fairly widely sold by the *boucheries chevalines* and is considered a delicacy. Some of the *chevalines'* meat is even imported from the American West.

a number of officers, myself among them, rode out two or three miles to see the extent of the herd. The country was rolling prairie, and, from the higher ground, the vision was obscured only by the earth's curvature. As far as the eye could reach to our right, the herd extended. To the left, it extended equally. There was no estimating the animals in it; I have no idea that they could all have been corralled in the State of Rhode Island, or Delaware, at one time. If they had been, they would have been so thick that the pasturage would have given out the first day. People who saw the Southern herd of buffalo, fifteen or twenty years ago, can appreciate the size of the Texas band of wild horses in 1846.

Little wonder, then, that, like the huge, vanished herds of those days, the horse is remembered in place-names all over the contemporary West, for, in fact the horse was once everywhere: in the wild, as the stock of the whites, as the semisacred status symbol of the Indians, as the mounts of the cavalrymen who fought the native tribes. Dobie gives just a sample few: Mustang Prairie, Pinto Canyon, Wild Horse Draw, Wild Horse Lake, Wild Horse Butte, Wild Horse Mountain, Horse Pen Creek ... Some years ago, tracing the origins of John Steinbeck down through the Salinas Valley, I followed Wild Horse Canyon into the dry and bony hills east of King City. Another time, in the Big Bend of Texas, my brother and I wandered about on a windy fall afternoon in Dead Horse Canyon, a place even drier and more bony than the Salinas Valley one. Big Bend old-timers say it was named that because a dead horse was found there in the long ago.

• • •

Roselyn: Do you kill 'em?
Gay: No, no. We, uh, sell 'em to the dealer.
Roselyn: He kills 'em.
Gay: Well, they're what they call chicken-feed horses—you know, turn 'em into chicken feed: like you buy in the store for the dog and cat?
Roselyn: I thought they were used for riding, or ...

101

Gay: Well, sure. They used to be.

—*The Misfits*

Well, they did used to be used for riding: if a man went after a wild horse and captured it, that was the idea. And many a man left testimony to the qualities of heart, quickness, and bottom of these descendants of the Spanish Barb. Yet though this was so, though there was wide admiration of what was being called by the last years of the nineteenth century the "mustang," death was on the wind for wild horses just as it was for the buffalo.

As far back as the late 1860s some military strategists had seen that the horse and the buffalo meant freedom to the Plains tribes and so encouraged the killing of these creatures. When Custer surprised Black Kettle's peaceable encampment of Cheyennes on the Washita at the end of November 1868, he ordered his men to shoot the 875 ponies the routed Indians had to leave behind. In 1874, Col. Ranald McKenzie ordered the slaughter of 14,000 ponies of the Comanches, Kiowas, and Cheyennes when he jumped them on the Red River. Ten years later, when the Western tribes had been placed in the concentration camps the whites were calling "agencies," the authorities began to take away their horses, since by then it was an article of faith that an Indian afoot was a tractable one.

But the serious business of ridding the West of its wild horse herds was a consequence of the growth and spread of the cattle industry, and to this day it is the cattlemen who remain the horses' chief antagonists. Once it became clear to the new beef barons that feral horses competed with their cattle for forage in the West's semiarid spaces, then and for the first time the wild horse was seen as an anachronism and a nuisance. There is something about all that space, loneliness, and the prevalence of firearms that has always tempted men to randomly kill wild creatures, whether horses, eagles, antelope, or longhorns after these were supplanted by Herefords. But by the opening years of the present century cowhands were being given instructions by their foremen to shoot wild horses whenever encountered. Then came the professional mustanger to join the cowhands in the hunting of the horses, though, to be sure, the mustangers sold many of their captives to the army.

Their prey were resourceful and agile, however, blessed with keen long-range vision that could pick up suspicious movement miles off. They could graze and watch at the same time, and their senses of hearing and smell were acutely developed. Ground vibrations were transmitted to them up their leg bones, and it was almost impossible to surprise them. But the gun-toting cowhands and the mustangers did their work with the same strange, persistent thoroughness that had been evident in the campaigns against the Plains tribes and the buffalo.

Some horse hunters resorted to crude and especially wasteful methods of capture, such as suspending loops from the branches of trees that overhung trails to watering holes. If a band could be spooked along the trail, a few horses might run their heads through the loops and become ensnared. They might just as easily choke themselves to death, but then, there were plenty more of them. A kindred method of capture was what was called "creasing." Here a man would attempt to "crease" a horse's spinal nerve at the top of the neck with a rifle shot, temporarily stunning him. Of course, squeezing off so precise a shot from a running horse (or even from a stationary position) required a considerable feat of marksmanship. More often than not the shot carried too high or too low, in which latter instance it might result in a mortal wound. A far better method of capture—and one metaphorical of the whole process—was simply to walk a band of mustangs into utter exhaustion. Here a team of riders would spell one another as they followed a band, until the horses became so tired, sore, and thirsty that they could no longer run away. Others devised strategically located, cunningly concealed pens in areas with abundant herds, then drove the horses into them. Pens, though, required more time in construction than many of the horse hunters cared to give.

Once caught, the horses might be hobbled or otherwise hindered in movement. Any that proved too fractious were shot. As for the others, some were fettered with drag chains or drag logs. A mustanger might tie a block of wood to a horse's head so that it would knock itself bloody if it tried to run. A more drastic method was to "knee" the captives: a horse would be roped and thrown and then the knee ligament severed and the fluid let out. After a few days the horse would have recovered enough to gimp about, but it would never be able to run again. A single herder could easily move a fair number of "kneed" horses to market.

Ruthless as were the methods of these men, they became even more so as the beef barons continued putting more and more cattle on the range—and thus more and more pressure on it as well. And the greater the pressure, the more evident the need to clear the wild ones from the public lands, which in Western practice were thought to belong solely to those who used them. Mechanized roundups facilitated this task, including, eventually, the coordinated use of planes and trucks. The planes spooked the horses into open terrain, swooping in low after them, their occupants sometimes firing at them with shotguns to make them run faster into exhaustion; then the trucks would take over, coming up alongside the frantic animals where wranglers would lasso them with ropes attached to truck tires, then throw the tires on the ground. It would not take long before even the most frightened of horses could no longer drag the tire along behind it. *The Misfits* depicts this method of operation; Jim Williams, a veteran Nevada horseman, told me the film's chase scenes were based on the methods of one Marsh Banks.

"He was from over in Owhyee County, Idaho, originally, I think," Williams said, "but then he was around Battle Mountain [Nevada]. He was the first fella to figure out how to use airplanes to run horses. Then they'd rope 'em from trucks. If they died, well, all right. And if he couldn't get a horse loaded into the truck, why, he'd cut its throat and leave it there to die." But Williams did not want me to misunderstand Marsh Banks. He was, he said, "a smart fella—don't you think he wasn't. And he was doing what the ranchers wanted done: they wanted those wild horses cleared off, and they weren't particular how it was done, and that's the way Marsh Banks did business."

Williams also wanted to make clear that although he had himself hunted wild horses, he had never been a mustanger like Marsh Banks. He had, he said, hunted the horses and sold them to the canners, but he had never abused them. "We didn't have a wild horse and burro problem," he claimed, "until the do-gooders—Wild Horse Annie and them—got into it. Which is what usually happens when you get pencil pushers butting into the other people's business. Yeah, we sold 'em to the canners, but that's not all: there are dozens of things made out of 'em: they wrapped baseballs in their hides, and so on. I'm not for cruelty, but what they've [the BLM] got now is a hell of a lot worse than what they had before. They ought to have let people hunt these horses who knew what they were doing. Then you wouldn't have a problem. I'll tell you: the BLM won't win no beauty contest out here."

"Wild Horse Annie," of whom Jim Williams and Bruce Portwood both spoke, was Velma B. Johnson, a Nevada woman who earned her nickname through more than twenty years of fighting to "save a memory" (her words). Like some other nicknames ("Uncle Sam" and "Yankee" among them), hers was at first a derisive one, applied by those who found Ms. Johnson's horse advocacy both quixotic and wasteful, but she accepted their "tribute," and by the time her efforts were crowned with success in the passage of the Wild Free-Roaming Horse and Burro Act (1971) it had become a badge of honor.

When Ms. Johnson began her campaign in 1960, the domain of the much-harassed horses had been shrunk to the West's most marginal lands, principally forage-poor lands in Nevada and Wyoming where the supremely adaptable animals were still able to tough out a living. Their numbers had been drastically reduced from the millions of a century previous to about twenty-five thousand, and in 1967, while Ms. Johnson and her colleagues fought on for legislation protecting them, the BLM's population estimate dropped to seventeen thousand. Mechanized roundups had by then been declared illegal, but under the relentless pursuit of the hunters the herds continued to dwindle, and it seemed evident to interested parties that within a couple of decades the wild horse would join the buffalo as an all-but-extinct icon of the Old West. But then the wild horse advocates successfully orchestrated a nationwide children's letter-writing campaign to Congress, and the lawmakers at last responded with the act guaranteeing the horses' protection. Ironically, the BLM, which had consistently recommended against such protective legislation, was now to be the guardian of the herds. The act read in part:

> that Congress finds and declares that wild free-roaming horses and burros are living symbols of the historic and pioneer spirit of the West; that they contribute to the diversity of life forms within the Nation and enrich the lives of the American people; and that these horses and burros are fast disappearing from the American scene. It is the policy of Congress that wild free-roaming horses and burros shall be protected from capture,

105

branding, harassment, or death; and to accomplish this they are to be considered in the area where presently found, as an integral part of the natural system of the public lands.

But if the horses were saved, the travail of the BLM was just beginning. It has not been easy for them, pinioned between the ranchers, hunters, and miners who still want the horses off the public lands—or else their numbers greatly reduced—and those who see the horses as "living symbols of our freedom," as Velma Johnson once put it.

Charles S. Watson, Jr., a self-appointed watchdog/gadfly who monitors the BLM's every move and statement in Nevada, thinks the bureau has been set up to fail in its charge. We were sitting in the living room of his trailer home, right across the street from the BLM's Carson City headquarters. Watson lives alone there and gave the definite impression he preferred it that way: a loner, a maverick, in his untiring defense of his state's public lands acting out one of the inherent possibilities of the American republican experiment. For more than thirty years he has run, out of his home, his Nevada Outdoor Recreation Association (NORA), and the room we sat in was testament to the singleness of his purpose, its bookshelves crammed with volumes like *Our Threatened Heritage*, *Ecodefense*, William O. Douglas's *Farewell to Texas*, and Dobie's *The Mustangers*. On his coffee table reposed an enormous scrapbook he has compiled over the years, *The NORA Index and Survey* of every bit of the state's public lands that contains even the smallest phenomenon of interest. On its right-hand pages were careful maps of the areas, and on the left, color photos of everything from petroglyphs to bristlecone pines. As he talked about the bureau and its wild horse program he was interrupted several times by phone calls from what he called his "whistle-blowers," who helped him keep abreast of the very latest BLM activities.

The first thing I had to understand about the bureau, he told me, was that they were "terribly underfunded and understaffed. They just don't have the money and the manpower to do the job they're supposed to be doing. And this is no accident, let me tell you. It's been the covert policy of the last two [Reagan] administrations to strip the BLM of its credibility and its power of advocacy." He was getting up steam here, leaning toward me from his chair, his hands moving in tense little jerks. "They have been trying to discredit the bureau, make 'em look bad, make 'em look like court jesters, put 'em in compromising situations. This wild horse program is an example. The thing is really a joke. The adopt-a-horse program isn't working to relieve range pressure. It can't work. It isn't *supposed* to work!" And that, he emphasized, was the point. "Washington is trying to subvert the environmental movement by effectively wrecking the one agency that environmentalists should be working most closely with. We call their real policy 'The Great Terrain Robbery.' Across the street [at the BLM offices] they hate us for saying this, but it's true."

Across the street, the mention of Watson's name brought on that expression of mingled reserve and resignation that bureaucrats show when you bring up the name of some "crackpot" who has been tormenting them with questions so troubling they will not quite go away. And it would be easy enough to dismiss Watson's conspiracy theory of the BLM's situation were it not for the fact that BLM personnel themselves so often come close to saying what Watson has been claiming. Without presuming to speak here of the attitudes of officials in the high echelons of the bureau, nor yet of what "back channel" directives may pass from the Secretary of the Interior to the bureau, it can be safely said that what you most often hear from the dedicated, harassed, overworked men and women in the field is that they feel the bureau in fact has been placed in a difficult and ambiguous position, especially on the wild horse question, one where they have scant hope of ever satisfying either ranchers or conservationists. What you hear from them over and again, with variations, is, "We're in a no-win situation here."

One December morning I went out with the BLM on one of their Nevada horse gathers thirty miles above Gerlach, where I had spent the night before. In the steel of the last hours before dawn I wolfed down a huge breakfast of pork chops, eggs, and biscuits at Bruno's Motel in Gerlach, then headed my rental car over the dirt roads to Leadville Canyon, where I was to rendezvous with the BLM crew. True winter had not yet come to the Great Basin, though here and there in the shadowed angles of the hills small patches of last week's snow lay blue amid the sage. As the sun rose I could see against its lifting light the startling white puffs of the many hot springs that dotted the valley floor there and, beyond, the heart-stopping thrust of the Granite Range, snow-clad seemingly all the way down to the foothills.

At the meeting place there were four trucks, a trailer, and two helicopters, and in a matter of a very few minutes I was suited and helmeted and up in one of the latter. The pilot, Ron Crowe, was a lean and taciturn fellow whose last flying had been done for the California drug enforcement people. He had little to say to me until he had spotted one of the two bands the bureau had targeted for removal. "There they are," he said finally over the intercom, pointing down through the ship's Plexiglass bubble. "No, not there. *There*. Just below that ridge." Now he talked quietly into his radio mike to the pilot of the other copter. "I have you. Looks like about eight in that bunch." As he swung toward the band huddled in the shadows of the mountain slope, he switched again to the intercom.

"Usually, the minute they hear us they light out for the next country. These are so docile they probably haven't been bothered much before. Look at 'em: they're just standing there." Indeed they were. A thousand yards beneath the copter as it drifted sideways in the wind I could see the band, silhouetted now as the rising sun drew the mountain slope's shadow into itself. Then, in leisurely fashion, they began to amble down the slope. When the other helicopter came in low behind them, they swung into a trot. Now that the other pilot had them on the move, Ron Crowe moved our ship into a monitoring position above and behind, trying to hold steady against the wind that swept across from the west. The ship swayed and eddied jerkily, and I had reason then to remember my big cowboy breakfast at Bruno's.

When the horses hit the canyon floor their trot became a gallop, the lead copter hovering behind. Less than a mile ahead, the ravine widened, and some stunted cottonwoods and large sagebrush provided cover for a wrangler holding the halter of a bright sorrel gelding. At the moment the band entered the widened ravine and slowed to an uncertain shuffle, the wrangler loosed the gelding's halter, and out he clattered, immediately startling the band into a furious chase behind him. Down the ravine the Judas horse went and into the yawning wings of the trap set there at its end, and then on into a circular corral where he abruptly fetched up next to a feed bag, the band crowding in behind him. Then came the wrangler to close off the way of escape. The barred gates swung shut, and we lifted away from this little scene and headed west again toward the mountains' ridge, Ron Crowe already speaking to the other pilot and exchanging information about the second band in this vicinity.

The second band had been spooked by the herding of the first, and for a few minutes the two copters swooped and sailed, searching the snow-flecked and naked slopes for them. "They can't have gone far," Crowe said over the radio. "When we came down with the others they weren't moving that fast. There they are, to your right, down in that ravine. Can't see 'em too well because of the shadows." There in the blue shadow of a slope the band stood, heads up and looking at the whirling, rackety crafts that now began to circle in behind them. Once they began to move, trotting down the slope toward the ravine and, ahead, the wings of the trap, they proved a less tractable bunch than the first band, principally because of a white horse that resolutely refused to run with the others. He galloped off to one side, then the other, and at last, when the band was well into the ravine above the trap, bolted off to the south. Small clouds of dust puffed up behind him as he struck out for freedom. In the ravine the band bunched and milled uneasily. The herding copter swung up and around behind them once again and came in low for the final push.

They started then, trotting down the treacherous ravine, then slowed, as if they couldn't make up their minds about the meaning of their white fellow's defection. "He's holding the Judas horse too long," Crowe said. And in fact, the band had stopped and was beginning to turn back. Then here came the white one, galloping flat out down the hard-packed run of the ravine, his stretched shadow sharply edged in the brilliant late-fall sun. When the others saw him rejoining them they turned again toward the trap, and now the wrangler sprang the Judas horse, who went like an arrow to his feed bag, and behind them all the gates again swung shut.

That was it for this morning; Ron Crowe set his helicopter down a hundred yards from the portable corrals that were now filled with horses. Off by himself in the shute into which he had lured his fellows stood the sorrel gelding, unconcernedly munching his reward. Up close, the horses that had looked so wonderfully wild from the air, their long tails and manes flowing in the wind, their action thrillingly fluid against the brown and white of earth and snow patches, looked far different. They were mostly undersized (the consequence of their marginal existence in these marginal rangelands) and bony. There was one buckskin of heavy build, but the others were small, some swaybacked with high withers, their lathered hides dirty, their manes and tails tangled. Some had sores and cuts on flanks and legs. The independent-minded white one proved to be a runty albino who rolled his slitted red eyes at the approach of the wranglers with their trucks, prods, and plastic sheets.

The men spread the sheets over the bars of the first corral, blocking the horses' vision, then spooked them toward the waiting gangplank of a van that had been wheeled into position. They shook the stiff, rattling sheets and used their prods, and the trembling, bolting, jerking horses entered the van's barred shadows, their hooves like thunder on the flooring, their eyes wild in the dim light. When the first van was loaded, it rumbled off down the road toward the bureau's holding facility at Palomino Valley (where some of *The Misfits* had been shot). Then the second van was tightly loaded, and it too was gone down the road, leaving behind only a thin gauze of dun-colored dust that hung for a moment before it was whisked by the wind out into the burnished and benignant blue. I walked up the road toward the trailer with the BLM's Dick Wheeler, and we went for coffee while Wheeler spoke of the bureau's horse program and its problems.

Wheeler was the bureau's wild horse and burro specialist for the Winnemucca District. A rumpled, pleasant fellow with an easy manner and shrewd eyes, he explained to me that the horses gathered this morning were what had been determined as "excess animals," which simply meant that he and the bureau's range specialists had determined that this area of the range had too many horses foraging on it. He said the cover in the Leadville Allotment was about standard in abundance and variety for northern Nevada: Kentucky bluegrass, squirreltail grass, Thurber's needlegrass, bluebunch wheatgrass, and, in spring, cheatgrass—which, as Aldo Leopold once eloquently showed, is the telltale sign of persistent overgrazing. There are also, of course, the abundant sagebrush and saltbrush, Wheeler said, and the creatures who graze here would eat these bushes if they had to. Actually, by this time of year the antelope would be living off sagebrush and saltbrush, but the horses much preferred the grasses, and "the structure of the horse's mouth is such that they can do a pretty good job of mowin' 'em down. I've seen it where it's down about like this," holding a thumb and forefinger a quarter-inch apart. "Of course," he said, glancing down at his cup, "sheep do a pretty thorough job themselves."

Within Wheeler's district there were close to six thousand horses, a figure that Wheeler and his staff had determined should be pared to thirty-six hundred. But the job of doing this was hardly so easy a matter as it had seemed on this December morning gather, when all that had been necessary was to locate the horses, drive them into the trap, and load and ship them. To begin with, he wanted me to understand, there were those money and manpower shortages of which Charles Watson had spoken. And then there were the challenges of the various conservation groups who have protested (rightly, it would seem) that overgrazing is overgrazing, and that limits needed to be established for cattle and sheep just as they had been for horses. Wheeler said he had no complaints himself about these challenges: "That's the way democracy is supposed to work." But, he said, while the lengthy process works its way through the courts, the horse population continues to grow. One BLM estimate I saw claimed a given band could be expected to increase yearly by as much as twenty percent—or as little as three percent. But whatever the figure, Wheeler explained, the bureau may actually be losing ground in some areas in its effort to reduce the horse population.

"If you base your whole program on the amount of available forage in a given area and on a horse census that tells you that you have X number of animals on it, and then, while the challenge is being made and heard, the population increases, where are you? What's your base of calculation? It's off, is where it is. So you have to start all over. Administratively, it's just hard to say, 'Okay, this area is managed correctly when there are X number of horses.' There'll be more than X by the time the appeals process is worked through." He smiled a bit ruefully and said again that democracy wasn't perfect, but it was a good system and one he felt comfortable working within, whatever its daily frustrations might be for him.

Others, he knew, were not so sure democracy was workable when it came to the use of the range. These were the folks who paid the government fees to graze their cattle and sheep on the public lands. "They feel they pay for the range and they should have the full use of it," Wheeler said. "So their attitude toward the horses is, 'Get rid of the sons-of-bitches. Shoot 'em, poison 'em. But get 'em off the range.' And it's not just the ranchers. It's game hunters, too, who want the range forage preserved for deer, antelope, and bighorn sheep. But I can see this attitude is dwindling, kind of. I mean, those who have it are fewer and fewer. Part of this is due to simple turnover: the real old-timers are dying out, they're selling out, or else their children are taking over. And the younger people seem to feel, 'Well, a few are all right.' They have a much better idea what 'multiple use' really means. Before that it was, 'This is *my* land!'"*

On the well-known other hand are the conservationists and wild horse advocates. "There's just a lot of sentiment and sentimentality when it comes to wild horses," Wheeler said, with just the slightest shake of his head. "Have you ever eaten horse? Well, among wild horse lovers or even most Westerners the idea is sickening. The wild horse is not meat. He's part of the Old West, the Lone Ranger, whatever. ... He's a symbol of freedom, and you can't sell freedom for your dinner table, let alone to the canners. Under the Reagan administrations, two or three runs were made at Congress to give the BLM sale authority— which, yes, means essentially selling to the canners. Now, if the Reagan administration couldn't get this done, it isn't going to be done. Period. And as far as our own disposal provision is concerned [for the old, the lame, and the sick], even that is political dynamite. We're already in a no-win situation with the conservationists on one side and the hunters and permittees on the other, and so there's no way we're going to make things even worse on ourselves by killing off sick or elderly wild horses. *No way*."

· · ·

Late that afternoon I watched the captives of the morning's Leadville Canyon gather being processed at the bureau's holding facility in Palomino Valley. Supervising the operation was Fred Wyatt, a tall, laconic, leathery cowboy straight out of a Marlboro ad. He stood in a corral with a length of rope in his hands, watching as the horses were fed through a shute into a stall where they were chalked on the rump to identify the place and date of their capture, then shot with a serum

* Recent developments in the West illustrate that this attitude dies hard, especially since it is periodically encouraged by political conservatives within both major national parties.

to protect them against all the diseases to which they would now be exposed in civilization. As a horse was prodded into the stall a metal door slid down behind him and Joe, a big man who looked as if he had Mexican and Indian blood in him, chalked on the identification, then deftly administered the shot. The gate at the stall head clanged up, and the horse came snorting out, rounded a corner of fencing, and trotted into the midst of his familiar bunch. I saw the big buckskin come through, and Fred Wyatt said to Joe, "Pretty nice horse there, Joe. Put a couple of hundred pounds on him, he'll look good." Joe nodded his black hat and went on chalking and shooting. "They'll all put on a couple hundred pounds in here," Wyatt told me in his quiet voice, his eyes steady on the stream of horses going through the shute and stall. "They get nutrients here they just don't get on the range."

In the various corrals surrounding us were segregated bunches of mares, studs, and yearlings. Those horses one, two, or three years old, he explained, went to the BLM's facility at Bloomfield, Nebraska, and from there to satellite adoption centers. Those four, five, and six went to the few prisons where the inmates worked at gentling the horses. Those seven and up went to two wild horse sanctuaries in South Dakota. The bureau assists the sanctuaries with some of the costs for the first two years of a horse's stay, but after that the sanctuaries must bear the costs themselves. Those horses, Wyatt said, would never be adopted and presumably would die there.

I asked Wyatt his feelings about the program as a whole and about the BLM's situation in trying to run it. To him the wild horse program, he said slowly, was a natural consequence of the national feeling about the wild horse of the West. "The horse had so much to do with the settlement of this country that people naturally feel a real attachment to them. And you know, even these runty little horses we get in here can be good, useful horses if people will take the trouble to work 'em the right way. I've been riding a horse we caught over here last year, and he's really a good animal. But, you get people who don't have patience with these creatures, and you get others who say they're useless and we ought to get rid of 'em. And then there are those who're just antimanagement, period. Those are the ones who don't believe the range—any public land—ought to be managed at all. 'Let it alone.' What they mean is, 'Let us alone to use it in the right way.' Of course, they're against the program. The Sagebrush Rebellion was, I'd guess, partly a statement of that attitude."

The sun had set by the time the last horse had been inoculated and sent to its appropriate corral, and winter was on the night wind, sweeping dust, feed, and the scent of manure across the beaten expanse of the holding facility. Fred Wyatt led me through a system of locked gates to a small corral in which stood a lone horse, a black three-year-old stud the BLM had captured earlier in the year. "He's going to be a good-sized horse," Wyatt said as we approached him. "When he gets his growth, you might have to use a stepladder to get up on him. I've been working with him some, and he has a good disposition." The black followed Wyatt around the enclosure like a dog, and then, as we stood chatting at the bars, he nipped my sleeve smartly. Wyatt slapped his jaw lightly, and the horse moved off a few steps into the closing dusk. "People have been giving him things to eat out of their hands," he explained. "Teaches him bad habits."

• • •

I told 'em when they got these new laws and so forth that the next step would be the rifle. These ranchers weren't gonna stand for these horses eatin' everything in sight. And that's just what's happening now.

—Jim Williams, Austin, Nevada

That night at a Reno 7-11 I saw my first reward poster for the killers of the wild horses. The offer was twenty thousand dollars. At that time (the end of 1988), the count stood at 506. Since then there have been twenty-eight authenticated shootings in the Ely area and a report the BLM cannot confirm of an additional four hundred killed and bulldozed under in White Pine County. The bureau will say the total is now over six hundred, and there have been no convictions yet. In three separate cases where arrests had been made the defendants were acquitted or the case was dismissed for lack of sufficient evidence; one case was dismissed on a legal technicality. In one case a woman was accused of taking a wild burro off public land and appropriating it for her own uses: this, too, was dismissed. The bulk of the killings discovered thus far, said Bob Stewart, the BLM's chief of public affairs in the state, had been discovered in the area north of Austin and south of Battle Mountain, with most of the horses gut-shot near watering places. "There have been some," he said cautiously, "that might have been thought to have died of starvation or thirst. But usually when a horse dies of either of these causes, he'll lie down and paw the ground for a while, perhaps as long as a day or two. These carcasses were so decomposed it would have been hard to tell, except that we found no evidence of slow death. No feces, either, which is another sign of starvation or death from thirst. So, we're satisfied that all these deaths [in the Austin-Battle Mountain area] have been from the same cause: gun shot. Our evidence tells us these animals were shot with civilian-issue, single-shot, small-bore weapons."

He veered sharply away from any talk of conspiracy, directing my attention instead to isolated cases in the past where individuals had killed wild horses and been caught and punished. Some kids, for instance, had shot and killed a couple of horses—and a cow as well. A sheepherder had killed one and then used its carcass to bait wolves that had been plaguing his flock.

Charles Watson and other conservationists and wild horse advocates believed there is more to the story than the BLM is willing to admit. Watson believed the killings represent a "full-fledged conspiracy," though perhaps not of the organized sort. "You must know," he said, "how poorly paid these wranglers and ranch hands are in this state. And that twenty thousand dollars hasn't flushed *anyone* who has seen *anything*! I mean, we're no longer talking about a few killings here, a few there. This is pretty serious stuff we're talking about now. The kind of conspiracy I'm talking about is a de facto kind. I mean, the Claude Dallas mentality that is still so prevalent out here.*

"Why wasn't Claude Dallas apprehended out here? He wasn't apprehended until he stepped out of the protective environment of the Great Basin where activities like his are not only tolerated but praised. People who tell you this is now the Mild, Mild West don't know what

---

* Dallas achieved an odd, and perhaps telling, notoriety in the West of the early 1980s, when he shot and killed two Idaho game wardens, then broke jail. He was recaptured in California.

they're talking about, let me tell you. This is still the Wild, Wild West. I mean, there is still a spirit here that refuses to admit there even are such things as 'public lands.'"

Dawn Lappin of the Reno-based Wild Horse Assistance Organization (WHOA), who fought with Velma Johnson for the horses' protection, also believed there was a conspiracy of silence. She was critical of the BLM and the U.S. Attorney's office for their handling of those few cases that had been brought before the courts. In those, she said, either the "BLM moved too quickly, or else they didn't do their work properly. It could be, of course, that the heat was on, and they felt they had to get some indictments when they didn't really have strong cases. I went to the first two trials, but they were such a mess I didn't even bother to attend the third one." Now, she said, the whole matter had been smeared over with such a thick coating of perceived incompetence that it was possible no convictions would ever be handed down. "It's very hard in the state of Nevada to get a conviction for this, even if you have witnesses," she said—and who now would risk volunteering information given the way the previous cases had been botched? "Despite the fact these cases didn't hold up," she said, "I still believe the ranching interests are behind this, and no one will ever make me believe otherwise." I had to understand the climate in the state, she concluded, with more than a trace of deep weariness. "When you have a U.S. Attorney like [William] Maddox who comes right out in the front page of the *Reno Gazette Journal* and says he can understand people's frustration with too many horses and that maybe Congress should do something about it—this is just the same as telling people that their crimes will be condoned. And so far, they have been."

• • •

At the Central New Mexico Correctional Institution in Los Lunas, the inmates were more concerned with working their horses than with speculating about the Nevada killings. An inmate named Robert Leach simply shrugged when I asked him about the killings and said he didn't concern himself with problems he had no chance of solving. Right now, he told me, his problem was Butter, a skittish three-year-old buckskin the BLM had captured a few months ago and with whom he had been

116

working the past two weeks. "Out here," he said, his eyes on Butter at the far end of a pie-shaped corral, "it could be anybody, because everybody's got a gun." Then he entered the corral and with a careful casualness approached the horse, who stood stiffly watching him. A small audience gathered at the corral gate, their arms resting on the iron fence bars. A chill winter wind blew out of a leaden sky, whipping dust and hay around the watchers. "Robert's been working with him real well," said Larry Pointer of the BLM's Santa Fe headquarters, one of the watchers at the gate. "You wouldn't believe how *he's* come along since he first started working with the horses. It's really amazing. When we first got him in here he was sized up as a troublemaker, and to tell you the truth, we had some problems with him at first. But now he's one of our best workers." Inside the corral the captive man and the captive horse were enacting a tight little drama of trust, the man time and again hoisting himself up to rest his elbows on the horse's back, letting Butter feel that full weight, talking to him in a low voice. Finally, while another inmate held Butter's halter, Leach hoisted himself up again and this time threw his leg over the buckskin's back. Almost at the same instant he was sailing through the air, landing with a dusty *thwump* in the dirt. He picked himself up and smiled thinly at the audience on the other side of the bars.

"The younger they are," said a soft voice at my elbow, "the less they understand. The real young ones don't understand at all that you're not going to kill them. They don't understand that you've got a halter on them, and that that halter's attached to a rope. They just get real excited, and their eyes cloud over, and when they get that way you can't work with them. They're liable to hurt themselves real bad. This one here almost broke both his front feet he got so excited: got 'em caught in the bars." The speaker was a young man with an angelic fuzz of beard circling his jaws, scholarly wire-rim glasses, and a straw hat that made him look as if he'd once toiled in the sunny wheat fields of Arles. But no, he was from Montana and had worked with horses all his life. Now he was working with them again, here in the joint, where he was doing a stretch for second-degree murder. "The thing you learn," he said, "is that they're much more afraid of you than you are of them. You can walk into that corral [he pointed behind us to a corral filled with yearlings] and walk toward them, and they'll just part for you like the Red

Sea." He smiled and held his arms outstretched to show the horses part-ing before him. "And pretty soon, after you're around them a few days, they get used to you and find you're not going to kill them. They get used to good treatment pretty quick. I guess it's just like people: we can get used to that, too."

Triumph of the "Bascos"

In written reminiscences of his visit to the French Basque village of his forebears, writer Robert Laxalt includes a vignette of the funeral of an old man lately returned there from a lifetime following the sheep across the daunting stretches of the American West. The villagers told Laxalt of the man's impoverished youth, how at age ten he'd been loaned by his family to watch others' flocks in the mountains above the village, sleeping in a stone hut, subsisting on the hard fare of corn cakes and skim milk, in winter his wooden shoes stuffed with ferns that served for socks. For such a boy there were no prospects here in the village, and so at eighteen he'd seized the chance to herd sheep in America, exchanging, Laxalt writes, "one form of servitude for another."

Unknown as American realities were to the youth, its prospects were, in the general way, understood: others from the village had gone, had become what the villagers called the *Amerikanuak*, the Americans. Some had prospered over there, had come back wearing hats (instead of berets), the symbol of an achieved affluence. Such, anyway, was the dream, and the boy, having little choice, had gone off with it, had hugged it to him through the bleak vicissitudes of a shepherd's life in the West, always looking toward that future when he might return to the village and spend his declining years at ease. Too late the return, though, and now no ease but that last one in the old earth. The villagers shook their heads and went on with life: the story was familiar enough.

For more than 150 years Basques—at first, mostly the men—had been leaving their villages along the French-Spanish border, where the opportunities seemed as circumscribed as the homeland itself. The Basque country was after all barely a hundred miles across in any direction, and every acre of it had been in intensive use for centuries. Here there was no waiting, wide-open frontier into which a young man might take himself for a new start. Everything was deeply, immemorially settled: the very houses bore the names of those who had originally owned them. The properties were small, self-sustaining farms with a few cattle, horses, and sheep. In May the sheep were taken up into the mountains, the shepherds following them out of the village and up to the *olhak*, pastoral cooperatives where the sheep browsed under watchful eyes and the men made cheese and slept four to a bed in smoky stone huts. Below in the village, the women and children went on with their portion of the old round, planting, harvesting, slaughtering.

If a household had too few to do its work, it might be lent a child from a neighbor whose household had too many. And when it was time for the household head to step aside, or when death paid its call, then the total inheritance, the *etxalte*—house, fields, livestock—would be passed undivided to one of the children. The rest were given some sort of going-away gift and forced to think of a life elsewhere. The daughters might marry and so stay on in the village, but of those surviving sons whom fate had disinherited it came to be said, "One to the Church, one as the village artisan, and the rest to America."

Most went away with heavy hearts, carrying with them that dream of eventual return. But one path leads on to another, and in the New World many a Basque forgot how to retrace his steps. Some died there. Others procrastinated so long that at last they knew themselves to be strangers to their old home and so became by default *Amerikanuak*. Others suffered the mischances of life on the foreign fringes of America and lost the painfully gathered savings of years: a trusted employer had gone bankrupt; a bank had failed; a supposed friend had made off with a bankroll hoarded for years in the safety of a suitcase.

Often, when they did return, it was to find that their American experiences had so altered them that they no longer fit into that snug landscape. John Ospital, who had followed his father and uncles to America and who now ran the Villa Basque restaurant in Stockton, said of his recent visit to the Basque country that he'd been amazed at how small it was. He and his bartender, Jeano Hirigoyen, had taken their American wives to the Basque provinces for what was to be a grand tour. "But it was all over in a week," he said, shaking his head at the mystery of the thing. "It was so *small*. We did everything in a week, and then there was nothing more to do." Mary Jean Paris, a French Basque living in Nevada, came to America in 1949. Only four years later she went back for a visit, but everything in the old place made her feel suddenly like a foreigner. "It seemed so small—tiny, really," she said.

"When I opened the windows [of her old home] it seemed like I could touch the mountains, where before they had seemed at a distance. My husband says that's when I became an American. Before that, I guess I was still thinking maybe I'd go back."

Nor was it only a matter of scale. "I wasn't understood," Mary Jean Paris said wonderingly. "I couldn't seem to communicate, somehow. One of my sisters said, 'Write, if you think of us.' It wasn't as if I was out here leading an exciting life." She made a brief, eloquent gesture that included her kitchen and the ranch that surrounded it. "Here all you have to think about is your family and your work. It isn't as if I was living in a big city. But to them, I was a rich tourist: six weeks without working. Boy!" she laughed with a tinge of rue. "That six weeks I took to go home, it took me two *years* to make that up!"

• • •

It shouldn't be supposed, however, that the Basques are naturally unadventurous folk and that under other circumstances they would all have stayed happily at home ever after. Probably Europe's most ancient ethnic group, the Basques have also been its most venturesome. They were Europe's first whalers and cod fishermen as far back as the sixth century A.D. Fearless mariners in frail barks, they are said to have sailed the dark green Atlantic all the way to the New World long before Columbus, and it is certain that in Columbus's wake Basques were in the forefront of exploration and settlement. John Ospital claimed that Columbus was himself a Basque; certainly his flagship, the *Santa Maria*, was a Basque ship, and its master was a Basque, Juan de la Cosa, the famed cartographer/navigator. There were Basques with Cortés, and Magellan's first mate, Juan Sebastian del Cano, who completed the circumnavigation of the globe after the captain had fallen to native spears, was a Basque. Basques played significant roles in the settlement of Mexico, Argentina, Uruguay, Chile, Colombia, and Peru. Stockmen, fence stringers, bricklayers, longshoremen—everywhere the Basques went they earned a reputation for industry, frugality, and probity: the word of a Basque, they said in South America, was better than a written contract.

Basques were in North America as early as 1598, when Juan de Oñate followed the Rio Grande north out of Mexico into what is now

New Mexico. Oñate became governor of the new province and introduced the first sheep herds into what would one day be the United States. But it wasn't until the Gold Rush of 1849 that Basques made a real entry here. Earlier, in the Rio de la Plata region between Uruguay and Argentina, they had established themselves as expert sheepmen in the great, solemn stretches of the pampas. Now some of them saw a new opportunity: the economic collapse of the Spanish dons and the availability of free grazing lands presented another sort of golden chance, the opportunity to become sheepmen in California and supply the mining camps and instant towns with much-needed meat. In California as in South America the field was open to them, because the Californios, like the gauchos, despised sheepherding as a low occupation. John Ospital claimed that many Basques had been cowboys in Paraguay, Uruguay, and Argentina. "They only went into sheepherding here," Ospital said, "because the cowboy trade was all full." The Basques, while fiercely proud, were not particular about the kind of livestock they worked with. "Basques," Ospital said, "can do anything connected with either farming or ranching."

Sheepherding had certain "advantages" for the newcomers. In addition to the availability of grazing land and the ever-expanding market for mutton, the incoming Basques knew that sheepherding required no knowledge of English and relatively little initial capital. It didn't take a man much to get started, and if he did not mind his wandering, isolated existence on the fringes of America, he might eventually prosper in the new land. So the Basques began to move north, and by the turn of the century they had become California's preeminent sheepmen.

But by that time, too, conditions in California had changed. Land values had become grossly inflated, the result of a rapidly expanding population and the irrigation and cultivation of the valley lands. Forest reserves and parklands had been created in the Sierra, further limiting grazing and transhumant patterns. The days of limitless space—and commensurate opportunities—were over. Some Basques saw this, got out of the sheep business, and sank roots in California's soil to become the basis of the state's Basque population, still the largest in America. But the others were still dreaming of the Pyrenees and of their eventual return to them. Besides, they said, they were Basques: rural people, mountain people. "They could have settled down then," said the

Stockton bartender, Jeano Hirigoyen, "but they preferred the mountains. We still do." Better to be in the mountains or on the range, said the Basques, than to be *errikuak*, those of the town, a term connoting misery, dishonesty, nervousness.

So they went east, over the Sierra, back against the tide of migration, down into what was the last American frontier, that bleakly beautiful territory of northern Nevada, eastern Oregon, and southern Idaho. This was the Great Basin, most of which is also the Great Basin Desert, the largest desert in North America. It is a place of seasonally extreme cold and blasting heat; of stunted vegetation where trees are events; of little water, alkaline soils, and sparse population. For the Basques it was to prove a place of trial—and eventually of triumph. Here, in the American equivalent of the Sahara's Empty Quarter, they were yet again to emerge as peerless herders of sheep, until in our time the Basque had become a figure of the national folklore: the heroic, bronzed loner with shepherd's crook and dusty, moving flock, merged against the background of a stony and unforgiving landscape.

• • •

Between the easily stated fact of that Great Basin migration and the enshrinement of the Basque sheepman in American folklore, however, lay a hard, often terrible way that thousands of nameless men and women had to travel, its traces graven in the faces of the survivors, heard like the whispers of past winds in the words of those few old-timers whose histories were later recorded: men like Beltran Paris and Emmett Elizondo and Dominique Laxalt, Robert Laxalt's father. If to survive absolute solitude, harsh weather, a harsher terrain, poverty, cultural dislocation, predators, and prejudice is to be heroic, then the "Bascos," as they were derisively called, deserve the title—and deserve, too, their honored place in our folklore.

Those who came into the new country from California had the advantage of that primary experience with American realities. But for those many more who followed from the Basque provinces, the contrast between the known and the Great Basin was shocking. These newcomers had heard the village talk of opportunity in the new lands, how a man might take his wages in ewes and so in time build his own flock, hive off, and earn enough money to come back home. If you had a relative over there, the rite of passage seemed not so fearsome a thing, and success, though hard, almost assured. But nothing they'd ever known or imagined could have prepared them for what awaited them on arrival in New York, friendless, often equipped with only their native tongue, a mysterious language utterly impenetrable to others, the ancient roots of which still elude the researches of philologists. And then westward, each mile seeming to impose an ever more impassable gulf between them and home, the scale of things exploding into ever more vast proportions. Mary Jean Paris recalled making the last leg of her journey to Nevada by plane. "Going over the Rockies," she said, "I looked out of the window and said to myself, 'Oh! Now I'll never be able to get back.'"

Finally the new country—barren and stony like the desert it really was and without a single familiar feature for orientation. "Oh, how cruel that country was," Robert Laxalt quotes his father as saying:

It wasn't like the Pyrenees, where the feed was rich. ... There, for as far as you could see, there was sagebrush and rocks, and the only trees were runted little junipers. Herding in that country was something I never dreamed could be. There was so little feed the sheep would wake up before daylight and never stop until it was dark, and it was all even a young man could do to keep up with them. If I didn't have a dog, I couldn't have done it.

The young man cried himself to sleep at night, cursing with a sick heart his decision to come to America. "I would get up in the morning," he told his son, "when it was still dark, as soon as I heard the sheep moving, and make my coffee, and I would hate for the day to come so that I would have to look at that terrible land."

Beltran Paris, a French Basque who came over in 1912, told his biographer, William Douglas, that he'd gone immediately to herding with only a dog and a bedroll—no tent, no horse. "I wasn't used to sleeping outside," Paris said, "and the stars and moonlight kept me awake." He recalled those slow night hours when he'd lie awake in his bedroll, surrounded by the sheep, watching the constellations arc toward dawn and another dusty, windy, lonely day on the move. "Some guys

124

cried when they were like that," Beltran Paris said, "but I don't remember crying."

As a young man, Emmett Elizondo came over in 1915 from Sumbilla in Navarra. Nearing ninety, he still bore the marks of that hard American initiation. "Was I lonely?" he answered a visitor to his mountain ranch above Montrose, Colorado. "Well, no, I don't think I was." But his sister, Maria, quickly corrected him.

"You were, too, Emmett. You know you were. You told me you were so lonely at first that if you'd had the money, you'd have gone back." Elizondo said nothing, merely looked at her over the rims of his thick glasses and scratched meditatively at a dry spot on his brick-red face. In his silence you could see the lone eighteen-year-old boy in the middle of that strange new country.

There were other severe hardships to be faced there—weather, accidents that so far from help often proved fatal, predators. But of all these the hardest was the simple, hope-defeating fact of isolation, month after month. Some went crazy from it, and over the years the Basques developed terms for the condition: *basatia*, "sheeped," they called it; or *ardigaldu*, "sagebrushed." Sometimes a herder would feel this condition coming upon him and still have the presence of mind to shoot himself before he went over the edge. Among the cluster of slurring stereotypes was that of the "crazy Basco" seen wandering aimless and empty-eyed through the streets of some Western town.

Then there were the cowboys. Although Western folklore and Hollywood have made too much of the range wars between cattlemen and sheepmen, the antagonism was real, sometimes violent. In the Great Basin good grazing lands and water were scarce, and competition for them was fierce. The cattlemen regarded the itinerant Basques as interlopers and tramps, sheepherding as an inferior trade. Whenever they could, they harassed and threatened the "Bascos," whose flocks, so they claimed, spoiled the range and watering holes for their cattle. "When I was first here," said Emmett Elizondo, "they [the cattlemen] kept calling me 'son of a bitch.' That was okay with me: I didn't know what it meant. Later, they called me 'Basco son of a bitch.' By then I knew what that meant, all right."

Elizondo was reluctant to discuss some of his more violent confrontations with cattlemen, except to allude vaguely to one shootout that left a cowboy dead and a Basque herder crippled for life. But he did recall a cowboy who had threatened to kill him. "I knew then I was safe," he said, the eyes hard and steady behind the lenses. "If I was gonna do something to you, I wouldn't tell you about it: the dog you got to watch is the one that doesn't bark. Anyway," he went on, "one day I see this fellow riding towards the same gate I'm coming to. So I waited for him to get there first so he'd have to get off his horse and open the gate. Then I rode through. 'Nice day,' he says. 'Beautiful,' I says. Then I turned my horse around and watched him all the way till he'd ridden into the trees."

On another occasion, a group of cattlemen came to pay him an unsocial call at a house below the one in which he now lived. "They kept calling me," Elizondo remembered. "'Come out here, Emmett. We just want to talk to you.' I was standing just inside the door with a .30-.30 and I called back to them, 'I ain't deef. I can hear you good right where I am.' They kept calling, so finally I said, 'You sons-a-bitches, you may get me, but one of you will sure get it too!' They rode off after that."

● ● ●

Through these years some few comforts began to come to the sheep-men—but not many. One was the development of the Basque hotel, the *ostatua*, as a significant cultural institution in the Great Basin. As it had in California, here the Basque hotel provided the itinerant sheepman with an array of crucial services unavailable elsewhere. It was at once an employment agency, providing job information to both employers and herders; a post office; a bank and savings deposit; a locker where town clothing and other effects might be stored while the owner was out on the range; and, above all, a major source of ethnic identification and solidarity, where a man might hear once again the warm flow of the mother tongue, taste Basque cooking, play *pelota* (Basque handball), and exchange memories of the old country. Usually the proprietor was a Basque deeply familiar with the sheep business and about as much at home in America as his boarders were foreign to it. Thus he could serve them as an advisor, paralegal aide, and confidant. It was a terrifically demanding role, and in order to fill it a man needed a good wife. While he tended bar and advised the men, his wife cooked, cleaned, supervised the personnel, nursed those ill or injured, and sometimes even laid them out for burial. Benerita Urutty and her husband, Jean, ran the La Salle Hotel in Grand Junction, Colorado, for twenty-one tough years. "We had twenty-five rooms for anyone—herders, camp tenders, cowpunchers—who couldn't get back to wherever it was they'd come from," she recalled. And had she done more there than simply cook, clean, and supervise? "Oh, God, yes," she sighed. "I took care of many of 'em just as if I'd been their mother or sister."

The hotel served another function as well, for very often the personnel were Basque girls over from the homeland. Many of them became the wives of the sheepmen, following a path as hard as that of their men and fully as heroic. To them fell the full burden of raising their children, and they could count on seeing their husbands but rarely. Robert Laxalt's mother told him once that his father, Dominique, should never have gotten married, because a man like that "didn't go with a house." Theresa Laxalt raised her six children in sheep camps, at the Carson City hotel she ran, and later in a house in that same town. Dominique Laxalt was usually off in the hills with the sheep, the only daily reminders of him being a wedding picture and his good suit hanging stiff and unused in the dimness of the closet.

Pete Paris, son of Beltran Paris, paid a moving tribute to the Basque wives and mothers of the West. They were the real heroes, he said. His mother, Marie, ran an Ely, Nevada, boardinghouse all through the Depression and after, renting out rooms for twenty-five cents a night, doing the cleaning, raising her children. "Dad would come through pretty regular," Pete Paris said, "at least as regular as he could. My poor mother, she'd say to him, 'You better spank these boys. They've been mean all week.' But we'd climb up into his lap, crazy to see him. How was he going to spank us for something we'd done a week ago?" He shook his head, recalling all his mother had gone through to keep the family going. "She worked herself to death right there in Ely," he said at last. Behind him, Mary Jean, his wife, nodded knowingly from the big Wolf stove where she was frying mutton for supper. She'd been through all of it. For sixteen years she'd lived in Ely with her four children so they could get some schooling, and then on weekends had driven the sixty miles of broken roads to the ranch. At the end of a weekend of cooking for Pete and his brother Bert and cleaning up their bachelors' quarters, she'd bundled the cranky kids back into the car and retraced her way through the night.

● ● ●

In addition to these considerable hazards, the Basques had to contend with the sort of prejudice that seems always the lot of an ethnic group that monopolizes a particular trade and sticks largely to itself. Like the Chinese in California (and to whom they were sometimes compared), in the Great Basin the "Black Bascos" were resented for their in-group attachments, their competitiveness, their frugality and industriousness, even for their language, that secret code. "We got called 'Black Bascos' a lot," Pete Paris said with more wonderment than bitterness in his voice. "Hell, we weren't *black*! And we got called 'Sheep.' Once when I was a freshman in high school, I was in the drugstore in Ely, and this big-talking senior walked in with his pals. He says to me, 'Hello, Sheep, what do you say?' I answered him back, 'Hello, horse doctor.' His father was a doctor, and I guess I stung him a little. That was the last time *he* called me 'Sheep.'" But the prejudice was deep; it was in the schools, too, Paris said, where "we were told, 'If you don't do your work, you're going to end up herding sheep.'"

Pete Cenarrusa, a second-generation Spanish Basque and for many years the Idaho Secretary of State, offered an explanation of anti-Basque prejudice. "You see," he said, hunching his heavy shoulders as he leaned across his desk at the state house, "the Basques were looking for new opportunities here, and when they found them, why, they took advantage. They were aggressive. They didn't sit around waiting for things to come to them."

Cenarrusa said that most of the Basque immigrants in this century actually had little experience herding sheep, but they learned quickly, were rugged enough to stand that life, "and they were very competitive. This made the natives envious. When it came time to ship the lambs, the Basque boys were always down at the scales: 'How much my lambs weigh?' Always trying to be the best, improve production. That's the root of it." Most of them never got rich, but enough, like Pete Cenarrusa himself, became sufficiently successful to provoke hostility. He arose from his desk and went to a bookshelf from which he pulled William

Douglas's and Jon Bilboa's definitive study of American Basques, *Amerikanuak*. "Listen to this," Cenarrusa said, "this tells it all"; and he read an item from the Humboldt *Star* of 1912, a poem concerning some "Basquos" just over from Spain. On their way to herd sheep, the newcomers pass a gang of loafers who jeer at them, make jokes about sheepherding, and complain about the condition of the country. But the "Basquos" keep steadfastly on their way. The concluding lines read:

> Five years the Basque will follow sheep,
> And every cent he gets he'll keep
> Except what little goes for clothes.
> And then the first thing someone knows
> He's jumped his job and bought a band
> And taken up some vacant land;
> And then the fellows who still prate,
> About hard luck and unkind fate,
> And wail because they have no pull,
> May help the "Basquo" clip his wool.

Pete Cenarrusa snapped the book shut, and in his hearty laugh there rang a note of triumph.

• • •

Emile Etchart, his wife, Anna, and their neighbors Jean-Baptiste and Helen Massonde sat around a kitchen table on which stood a jug of red wine and a plate of thickly sliced sausage. It was sunset in the fields outside Grand Junction, and a strong west-blowing wind brought the heady scent of new-mown alfalfa through the open windows. They were patiently explaining to a visitor some of the major changes that have impelled Basques into work other than the sheep business. They mentioned foreign competition from New Zealand and Australia, and, especially, the proliferation of governmental regulations. The Taylor Grazing Act of 1934 effectively put an end to free grazing on the public domain, and in doing so put the itinerant Basque sheepman out of business. The spread of the forest reserve idea was another significant factor. "The rangers," claimed Emile Etchart, "are after you all the time: 'Don't graze here. Too much grazing there.'" His tone conveyed a weariness with all that red tape. Leaning across the table toward the visitor, he gestured with his great, work-blunted hands. "I tell you," he said earnestly, "those old guys like Beltran Paris and Elizondo that made it good, if they had to start out today, they wouldn't make it."

Emile Etchart has made it—but by getting out of the sheep business. He'd come to America in 1956 to herd for his brother, Martin, determined like so many before him to branch off one day with his own band. "I went to work for him right away," said Etchart with slow emphasis. "That was in May 1956. When do you think I first came to town? November 1961." His handsome, ruddy face creased into a small smile then, and he added laconically, "I stayed a few weeks." But his hard work and dedication paid off eventually, and Etchart had his own band of seven thousand head. In 1976, though, he quit the business and now raises corn, alfalfa, and barley.

In 1975, Etchart said, he lost five hundred lambs to that most persistent of the sheep predators, the coyote. That's when he told his brothers, "'You want to go on raising coyotes, fine. Me, I'm through.'" He cited the current restrictions on the use of poisons, especially the controversial 1080. "That," he said, "was one of the best poisons we ever had. But we have so many funny people from the city: 'Oh, we just *love* the coyote.' I don't mind the lions that eat what they kill, but the coyote, he doesn't even eat what every day he kills."

Jean-Baptiste Massonde joined in heatedly. "Every night, every night! They pull the baby lambs right out of the ewe. They kill *you* like that!"

Etchart mentioned other factors in the decline of the sheep industry and the steadily dwindling importance of the Basques in it. Immigration quotas, for one thing. "Now we have Peruvians and Mexicans instead of Basques," he said. "We have no luck with the Peruvians when they get into the second year [of a three-year contract]. They act like they're the Incas. The Mexicans are much better. But when they make enough money, they go home." He shrugged tolerantly, understanding the Mexicans' desire to return home in comparative wealth from an exile in foreign servitude. He knew too well what that was like. "But lambing comes, where are they? Maybe they will come, maybe not."

There was, too, the problem of rising expectations, the real inflation. "We're ruining this country," Etchart claimed. "Don't get me wrong:

130

this is a great country. This is the greatest country," raising a great hand ceilingward in sworn testimony. "But now everything is credit, credit, credit. Credit is killing us. We buy on credit, and then we can't pay. We've gotten spoiled. I'm spoiled now, too. We do too much for our kids: Atari games, bicycles. But you *got* to do too much, you know? In the old country at Christmas we'd line up our shoes. If we were good, maybe an orange or two. If not, a potato."

• • •

You could hear many of the same things at other Basque homes and gathering places in the Great Basin. At the Silver Dollar Bar in the Basque quarter of Elko, Nevada, Pilar Gastenega Fagoagoa, a handsome woman in her early forties, spoke of the changes in her lifetime. Her father, a Spanish Basque, began as a herder, took his wages in ewes, and eventually built his own band. Her husband, a French Basque, had herded for eleven years but was now in construction, an occupation, she said, attracting many younger Basques. Her eldest son was a helicopter mechanic and her youngest a mine supervisor. "We never discouraged them from going into the sheep business," Pilar Fagoagoa said. "But it's for sure they're making a lot more money at what they're doing than they could herding sheep." That, she said with a smile, is "a *hard* way to make a dollar."

The town and its bastions of Basque ethnicity had changed also. The Star Hotel down the street, she said, used to take in herders. It was an old-time *ostatua*. "But now there aren't any Basque herders any more, so it's strictly a restaurant, and they're trying to sell, I hear. These places were filled once. This place [the Silver Dollar] used to go twenty-four hours straight with four bartenders. One time Old Pete [a locally renowned sheepman] came in here when it was just booming along—big greasy overalls, hadn't shaved in days—and he was refused a drink by the owner. 'You're too dirty,' he told Old Pete." She laughed easily. "Well, Old Pete went across the street to the bank, bought the bar, and came back in. He knew the place was for sale, and like a lot of the old sheepmen, he'd saved every penny he ever earned. So he'd just gone over there to his friend at the bank and signed the papers. Then he came back in here and told the guy who'd refused him, 'You're through.' The guy says, 'What do you mean, I'm through?' Old Pete says to him, 'I own this place now. Get.'" She laughed again. "He didn't even have the keys to the front door.

"You say you want to buy one of these big *botas*? Well, let me blow some air in it for you. That way you'll have some Basque breath in it as long as you own it. They last practically forever."

• • •

"What really gets me," I said, "is when I compare in my mind this country we're looking at with what I've seen of the Basque homeland. For me, even as a tourist there, the contrast is simply stunning. Think what it must have been for them!"

I was talking with Don Oliver of NBC News as we stood in a crowd on Elko's main drag, watching a parade during the Twenty-fifth National Basque Festival. In front of us a camera crew from the network's "Today" show was videotaping the procession as it danced, strutted, and rumbled its way to the fairgrounds a few blocks north. We stood in a flood of high desert sun. Beyond the roofs of the town's westward buildings hide-brown mountains rose naked into the cloudless blue. There wasn't a tree in sight, although we had earlier seen a grove at the park adjacent to the fairgrounds. Oliver said he'd never been to the Basque country—though his work has taken him just about everywhere else in the world—and he asked me if I could describe some of what I had seen. I told him I had by no means seen all of it, but what impressed me most in what I had seen was the *density* of that landscape. It was a sensation, I thought, produced in part by the sheer up-and-down-ness of that mountainous terrain. When you were in it, it surrounded you, enfolded you. True, there were places where you could look out over the tumbled mass of mountains and see where the slopes went, how they opened one into the next like a fan. But mostly your attention was compelled by the facts of where you now were, and you felt very much as if you were in the midst of a deeply historical landscape where the human hand had long been felt everywhere on it. The few mountain roads ran just beneath the summits, brackened and craggy, through pastures filled with cattle and sheep, their bells tinkling as they moved steadily through the verdure. Here and there was a stone hut, as if sunk into a humus of history as well as soil. Many looked deserted, but at one, some dusty, red-faced men hung about the dark entrance, a scarf of purple smoke standing out from the chimneyless roof. Below in the narrow valleys you could see fields of wheat and hay, and beneath them the neat gardens of the individual homes. Everything seemed in intense use, and the narrow, irregular sizes of the fields bore testament to the subdividings of the generations. When you passed down into the villages, you saw on the lintels of the houses the incised names and dates of the first owners. (Later, at St.-Jean-Pied-de-Port I noticed that in the phone book the town's residents appeared to be listed by the old names of their dwellings rather than by street address.) It seemed to me in talking with Basques who had emigrated to America, I told Oliver, that they had all been permanently bent by the shocking exchange of these landscapes. You could see that old shock in their eyes, I said, a sort of burnt stare that was not a daze but yet partook somewhat of that, a sort of perpetually musing look.

Out at the fairgrounds and the park, the musing took the form of a communal celebration of the past. The festival's theme was the "New Generation." The theme, explained the master of ceremonies, was "a tribute to our forefathers who preserved our precious cultural heritage so that we could pass it on to this new generation." There were dances; a contest between women who gave the traditional Basque yell, a high, oddly moving tremolo; weight-carrying and wood-chopping contests; singing debates. Pete Paris, Jr., son of Pete and Mary Jean, easily won the sheep-crooking contest. "No wonder," said the announcer over the public address system. "He's the only active sheepherder left around here." Under the welcome, rustling shade of the trees in the park the prize loaf of sheepherder's bread was auctioned off for $110 to a Bakersfield man. Nearby a group watched the final stages of a codfish casserole contest: the contestants rapidly and dexterously swirled pans of codfish chunks submerged in garlic and olive oil, the trick, apparently, being eventually to turn the whole dish to the consistency of mayonnaise.

The Basques have always identified themselves by their language: *Euskaldunak*, speakers of *Euskera*, the Basque tongue. So it was a fair guess that beneath all the festivities lay the special, singular pleasure these people took in hearing the music of the ancient tongue. Many have supposed, and with reason, that the Basques were the creators of the astonishing Paleolithic art found in the caves of the Basque homeland

133

and areas just adjacent. Hearing that tongue all around you, in casual conversation, in song, over the PA system, it was easy to imagine you were overhearing the talk of those who tens of thousands of years before had made the aurochs, bison, and shaggy ponies race across the undulant walls of the caves. In the French Basque country this language is dying. Over the border on the Spanish side the fierce Basque nationalism is doing its best to keep it current. Here in America fewer and fewer of the new generation to whom this year's festival was dedicated speak Basque. Even the parents who are native speakers are falling out of the habit. Emile Etchart's American-born nephews speak it, he told me, but his own sons do not, and maybe that meant they were a little less Basque. "For them to be Basque," he said with emphasis, "they have to have both father *and* mother talking Basque. Anna, she's American Basque, and she doesn't speak it. Me? I never lose my Basque. It is me. I think in it."

● ● ●

At Harrison Pass in the Ruby Mountains above Elko, Pete Paris, Jr., and his brother David were paying a visit to one of their herders. The Paris brothers are continuing into the third generation their family's involvement with sheep, though these days they run about as many cattle as sheep. But many Basques their age had gone into construction or gardening. Their younger brother was a CPA in Elko. And as for the younger Basques coming over from the old country to herd, Pete, Jr., said their hearts weren't really in it. "They really don't do that good a job," he claimed. "The Peruvians and the Mexicans actually have better records now than the Bascos do." Life in the old country, he said, had perhaps become too good for those younger Basques to volunteer for the privations of the American sheepherding experience, even with such newer comforts as transistors and pickups.

As the brothers talked, great cloud shadows flitted across the green slopes, and a thousand head of Paris-family sheep stood bunched under the constantly shifting light. Jose Etchart, sixty, watched them over the end of a cigarette, his face dark and roughened by years of exposure, lips blistered, eyes as blue and candid as a mountain pool. "He's bought this life," Pete said simply. "He's in love with it. You see that still in the older Basques." The brothers reminisced then about some of those older Basques who had worked for the family. One had saved every penny and died rich and intestate. "Dad knew the state and the lawyers were gonna get everything," David said, "so he went to Elko and bought old Tony the biggest Basque funeral he could—fancy inlaid casket, big party afterwards, the works." Another Paris-family herder would regularly put in his eleven months and two weeks with the sheep, then blow it all on what Pete called "wine, women, song, the whole nine yards." He died with nothing, Pete said. "He died counting sheep, and he died happy, doing what he wanted."

The little group broke up at last, Jose Etchart, his horse, and border collie moving off with the sheep through the sage, steadily diminishing in the silent vastness. When he was gone Pete said Etchart was another of the old-time savers. "He's got more money in the bank than I do," he laughed. "He invests in the money market, and when I come up to see him, he asks me what the prime is at now." To an outsider, he said, such an existence might seem a strange and lonely one, but there was no reason to feel sorry for Jose Etchart.

Nor did the young Paris brothers feel sorry for themselves, and still less did they appear to regard themselves as an endangered species. There was a cheerful, clear-eyed confidence about them that said they expected to make it as stockmen. As for other Basques like their younger brother Mark, the Elko CPA, they thought it was fine that they were going into other lines of work.

Pete Cenarrusa agreed. "My son tried the sheep business for a while," he said, "but he found that the only way he could make a profit on lamb was to serve it on a plate. Now he owns a restaurant in Bend [Oregon]." This, he said in summation of the Basques' American experience, "is an American success story. We're assimilated now, and they're even going to raise a monument in Nevada to the Basque sheepman. And all within my lifetime."

In the parking lot outside Cenarrusa's office the young attendant offered an almost instant confirmation of what Cenarrusa had just said, as well as a kind of folk history of the *Amerikanuak* experience. Asked if he knew much about Basques, the young man appeared puzzled for a moment. Then he brightened and said, "Oh, yeah: those guys that used to run sheep and now own everything."

Beseda at Deming

By the time the community of Deming, New Mexico, holds its annual
Bohemian sausage festival on the third Sunday in October, chances are
good that the northerly portion of the state will already have tasted the
crust of winter: there will likely have been a frost in the country above
Santa Fe, maybe even snow on the mountains, and the aspens will have
burned their fiery gold into gray ash. Even in Deming, less than forty
miles from the Mexican border, the nights will be cold. That is why the
community holds to the traditional date, for the *klobase* (Bohemian
sausage) is prepared during two days in the open air, and in hot weather
might easily spoil. By the third weekend in October the Deming folks
feel assured they'll be favored by seasonably cool days and crisp nights.

Because I wanted to get the full flavor of the event, I left for
Deming the Friday before the festive Sunday. There was indeed snow
on the Sangre de Cristos, the aspen fire was dead, and though most of
the leaves in the valley were still green, they had the beaten, brittle look
they wear after an early snow. The morning air had a bite to it that felt
good on the face and hands, and when you were encompassed by the
best blue of a New Mexico sky, there was no room left to lament the
death of summer.

South of Albuquerque the magic began. Santa Fe has its undeniable
charm, and there is a rough vigor to Albuquerque that results whenever
a railroad town sprawls into a city. Still, these *are* cities, and in that sense
there is always something ephemeral-seeming about them. Physically
substantial, their lives are yet forfeit to the changes of history. They are
not what they once were nor what they will be. But south of them the
land takes over in an immemorial sweeping gesture, and the towns and
villages scattered over it seem to exist in a kind of minimal, enduring
sufferance: crossing the Rio Grande for the first time on I-25, you feel
you are going over a boundary after which everything opens magically.

On this morning the cottonwoods along the river banks were tipped
yellow, and cranes stood motionless in water that looked smoky in the

137

young light. To the southwest you could see the Gallinas Mountains, while to the east were the Monzanos; the sharp fall sun had cleared them and now shone down directly on peaks and slopes, the ravines still in dusty dark. Between these ranges in a sky suddenly immense, small flocks of birds seemed flung into space like shot. A serenity of the season sat on the landscape as if the earth were taking a deep breath.

Below Lemitar greasewood bushes took over the valley floor, drawing their thin green veil across the gray soil, and there were the San Mateos on your right hand and the big beauty of the San Andres on your left, both of them brown in their foregrounds, a cloudy blue behind, and with a line of green at the base of the San Andres where cottonwoods snaked along the Rio Grande. At Derry there were white and blue shirt backs in the chili fields along the Rio Grande. The big river that is an artery pulsing through the states into Mexico is also a highway for impoverished migrant workers coming north, and when a couple of days later I told a Deming rancher what I'd seen at Derry, she shook her head and said, "They're illegal." Then a pause before adding, "Everyone uses them. Why, you couldn't work most of these places without 'em. You can't get the Americans to do the work anymore."

South of Hatch the curves and dips of Route 26 insisted that you slow down, and the land jumped up at you in suddenly sharp detail: Johnson grass, yucca, Spanish bayonet, cactus. Cooke's Peak, named for a distinguished but now-forgotten American army colonel, jutted out of the small range that also bore his name. Here was the essential landscape that extends all the way down into north-central Mexico; except where water is available for irrigation, the general aspect is hard, flinty, and dry for hundreds of miles southward. In some stretches, but especially down through Sonora, even the nature freak might begin to long for some sign of the human touch on this landscape, but there is little of that unless you count the occasional Mexican bus, swaying terrifically in terminal speed, black smut belching out beneath and behind, and bearing on its visor some grim legend like "Villahermosa."

The Deming town site was traversed for the first time by white Americans in 1780. Two of those rambling, ignorant expeditions dignified in American history by the title "explorations" crisscrossed the Deming area in search of a likely trade route that would link Santa Fe with Nueva España. They failed to find much (or even to find each

138

other) except bands of mobile natives, christened "Apaches" by Juan de
Oñate almost two hundred years before: the area was then home territory to the Mescaleros, the Mimbreños, and, to a lesser degree, the
Chiricahuas—tough customers, as the Spaniards learned to their sorrow,
who did not take easily to interlopers arrogant enough to assume territorial rights by virtue of an alleged cultural superiority.

Until the coming of the Anglo Americans, then (who in their
turn assumed territorial rights because of their alleged superiority to
Mexicans), little of historical note happened here. The Apaches came
and went, raided and retreated, about as usual, and this pattern persisted well into the period of American domination. In the early 1860s a
fort was established just north of the present town site, but the soldiers
weren't safe a hundred yards beyond its adobe walls. Some farming and
ranching had begun, but the civilians were pretty much on their own,
the soldiers being there to protect only California-bound wagon trains.
There was a little settlement called Mowry in honor of a picaresque
army officer who ended up in a French donjon keep: one of his many
swindles involved selling innocent Gauls tracts of paradise in the New
Mexican wilderness. But civilization, American-style, had to await the
coming of the railroad.

The real story of Deming dates from late 1881, when the Southern
Pacific reached here on its way to the coast. The town was named after
the wife of Charles Crocker, one of the "Big Four" of railroad history,
and appropriately its first store utilized two boxcars as storerooms. For
years the grandest building in town was the local Harvey House, which
catered to the rolling trade. With the establishment of the railroad
Deming became, with its near neighbor Columbus, the principal cattle-
shipping point in the southern portion of the state. Cattle is still the
basic industry, though since the discovery of the possibilities of irrigation
in the area there is considerable agriculture too. You see cotton fields
about the town, as well as acres in rye, milo, potatoes, onions, tomatoes,
and that staple of the New Mexican diet, pinto beans.

In the wake of the railroad, those who came here and made it into
a real community instead of just a point on the way to somewhere else
were mostly from Texas, with a scattering of other places of provenance
like Alabama, Mississippi, and Kentucky. But mostly they were Texans
with names like Gibson and Chadborn and Carson. There are also a few

German names in the records of the early settlers, and of course Spanish ones, many of these people native to the area and others refugees from the endemic political unrest south of the border.

What drew Texans to New Mexico then is what draws them yet: a higher, drier climate with fewer insects, good water, and plenty of sunshine (Deming boasts that it averages 331 days of sun a year). And some Texans, then as now, were attracted by the prospect of making a lot of money quickly: there were lead and silver mines in the area, and in the Tres Hermanas district there was some gold. After the Mimbres drainage system was tapped for irrigation early in this century the richness of the valley soil was a magnet as well.

These things attracted another class of Texas migrants in the 1920s: Czechs, or, as the older folks knew themselves, Bohemians. Their Abraham was Frank Florian Kretek, farmer, rancher, butcher, and real estate agent, who moved to Deming with his wife and her sisters in 1923 and for the next ten years zealously promoted Czech immigration there. In such Czech-language newspapers as *Nove Domov*, *Veztnik*, *Vlasatel*, and *Svoboda*, Kretek announced the unique virtues of his new home: the availability of rich, irrigable lands; the sunshine; and the water, tested at 99.99 percent pure—or so he claimed on his letterhead.

In a few years Kretek could offer another inducement, for with more and more Czechs now in Deming, those coming after could be certain of fellowship, of the sound of the mother tongue, of the old customs. Houston had a sizable Czech enclave, and Texas towns like Wallis, Frydek, Navasota, Taylor, and Temple all had their Czech families. Frank Kretek's news sounded good to the Brdeckos, the Culaks, Ligockys, Marcaks, Orsaks, and Kostelniks. They came to Deming to look it over, found it good, and stayed on. Usually Frank and his wife, Bozena ("Bessie" to everybody), would put up the new arrivals and help them get established.

But the early years weren't easy. There was, to begin with, the language barrier. In Texas the older generations had spoken Czech among themselves, but now children were coming along, and here in New Mexico they had to learn English from scratch. One of the children, a man now in his seventies, remembered those days: "When we came here, we couldn't say 'shit' in English," he said with asperity. "But we *learned* English! We didn't have no bilingual schools like these dummies

140

now ... " His voice trailed off as if in recollection of those days when even the Spanish kids, who surely had language and ethnic problems of their own, would laugh at the "Bohunks'" efforts to master a new and difficult tongue.

Nor was the learning continuous, for in those years the children were often needed more in the fields than in the classroom. Sometimes, to make ends meet, parents hired their kids out to other farmers who needed seasonal help. "We only went to school when there was no work at home," Frank Culak recalled. The Culak kids, he said, regularly worked in the fields from eight in the morning until dark. When they were hired out, they made ten cents an hour. On the home farm, of course, there was no pay—and no hired help, either. But the Czechs were tough and built for the long haul, as Willa Cather observed of the pioneering Czech families on the Nebraska frontier. There they hung on through weather, blights, and rapacious land speculators. And so it was in Deming.

How real the need, therefore, in those early years, for gatherings that gave the Czechs a sense of common purpose, of common problems successfully faced, and of other dimensions to life besides work and worry. The *beseda* was a cultural institution of the old country that could answer this need in America. Essentially it meant an extended-family gathering featuring card playing, feasting, music, and dancing. In the Texas towns, and then in Deming, the *beseda* expanded from family gatherings into small celebrations of ethnic solidarity, reaching out from the family base to include friends and neighbors. In Deming, the *beseda* became the most significant centripetal force in the Czech enclave, along with the Holy Family Catholic Church, and in 1928 these forces joined in the first annual *klobase* barbecue.

Again, the main man was Frank Kretek. Holy Family Church was in serious need of funds to pay the priest's salary, property maintenance, fuel bills, and so on, and Frank Kretek had an idea: why not organize a kind of large-scale *beseda* featuring the sale of the popular Bohemian smoked sausage he made at his meat market? He would contribute the *klobase* and the barbecued beef; others would chip in as they could with cole slaw, onions, potato salad, beans, cakes, and pies. All the proceeds would go to Holy Family. It was done, and it was a success. In the festival's first years the nets were modest enough (fragmentary church records show a net of $192 for 1935, $115.72 for the year following); but supplies were cheap then, too. Now the meat alone cost almost four thousand dollars.

From this narrow base the *klobase* barbecue gradually widened into a genuine community event. Deming merchants donated prizes; individuals, whether they happened to be Holy Family parishioners or not, contributed foods; and people came early for the bingo and stayed late for the auction of watermelons, pinto beans, and, in recent years, cotton. All the proceeds still went to Holy Family, but after a while this became relatively unimportant. The important thing was that the third Sunday in October meant a grand community get-together, and even though the *klobase* festival is now an event on the state's calendar of tourist attractions, those who come to it from elsewhere are treated to the increasingly rare and wonderful spectacle of a community in relaxed and genuine play, celebrating itself.

By mid-Friday of this fifty-fourth festival, the men were gathered at Frank Hervol, Jr.'s, farm to cut the meat for the *klobase*. Beside a duck pond and under the clattering shade of big old cottonwoods, several tables were lined up with deep vats parked next to them. Beyond the pond and through the trees you could see broad cotton fields and, away to the west, Cooke's Peak. Ducks glided on abrupt errands across the rippling water, and a pride of farm dogs waited patiently for windfalls as the big knives cleaved through eight hundred pounds of sow and six hundred of bull. "We used to make it almost all of pork," Ed Kretek was saying as he supervised the beginnings of the long process, "but folks have got to where they don't like it that rich. So we've changed the recipe this way." Ed is Frank and Bessie's son, now in his thirtieth year as chairman of the barbecue. A short, squat man whose sloping shoulders and thick forearms suggest power, he moved among the tables, pausing occasionally to cut meat, dividing the piled beef from the pork on the tables, reminding the men not to cut too big and to "throw in all that fat, boys, so she won't be dry." From beneath the slanted bill of a worn engineer's cap his eyes missed nothing.

At the sun-dappled tables the bloodied hands went steadily on with the work, and there was talk now, twenty voices calling jokes and jibes across the tables, reminiscing about past barbecues, telling stories. There was beer and whiskey, but not too much, for the work had its element of hazard and required attention. "I've known some of 'em to leave part of a finger here," said Kretek, and there was a knowing chuckle from one of the cutters. Still, there were occasional trips to the beer cooler, and cups of whiskey and 7-Up ("Seven High") passed out. "*Jesus!*" said a man, tasting from a cup as it came down his way. "Here, Jim, *you* drink this, before it melts the cup!"

"Boys," said a voice, "So-and-So's sick in the hospital, and he's kinda hurt he hasn't had more visitors." Murmurs at the tables. "But if you do go to see him," the speaker continued, "whatever you do, for God's sake don't mention the Republicans. That gets him so mad he just can't breathe, and it's not good for him."

"I know lots of folks not even in the hospital that do that," said another, and there was laughter.

With one or two exceptions the men were along in years. Most were natives of Deming or had been here long enough to be considered so, but a few had come more recently from out of state. One, a man near eighty, was from St. Louis. On his way to Tucson for his lungs, he'd met someone on a bus who told him, "'Tucson ain't worth a shit for asthma. Try Deming.' So I did and been here ever since. The climate suits me."

Another man, a Slav whose parents had come over from Europe to settle outside Chicago, said he'd retired down here simply because he'd heard it was a nice, quiet place and had plenty of good weather. He'd tired of those brutal Midwestern winters, where the snows of November still lay beneath those of March. He had now finished his cutting and was wiping his broad hands on the butcher's apron he wore. Was this sort of community festival new to him? I asked. "Oh, hell no. You know, up near Chicago in the old days, we *really* had these things." On saints' days, he explained, or holidays, or on days that meant something in the old country, the women of the local Catholic church would put on dinners or picnics. "At those shindigs," he said, "they'd rig up a bar just like you'd make it from a big erector set, and you'd have all the beer and whiskey you could hold. And you'd sit at the tables, and the ladies would serve you your chicken right there, whatever you wanted—legs, breasts, wings, assholes." Those were events to behold, he said, "but they don't have 'em anymore, at least not like they used to."

I complimented him on his looks and vigor, this man nearing seventy and still strong and unlined after a career as an iron worker. "Hell, yes,

I'm in good shape," he said with a thin smile. "The doc here told me so himself just last week. He says to me, 'You're in great shape for a guy your age.' Then he says, 'How's your sex life?' Can you beat that? He asks me about my *sex life*! So I says to the guy, 'Sure, I got a sex life. And you know what? I can still go twice.'

"The doc looks at me, and he says, 'Why, that's remarkable. Which do you enjoy more, the first one or the second?' So I says to him, 'Oh, I guess I like the one in the fall better'n I do the one in the spring.' My sex life … ." He moved off toward the beer cooler, shaking his head in wonderment.

By now, the cutting over, they had the meat grinder hooked up to a long, broad belt attached to a tractor parked under the trees, and after a few minutes of tinkering and adjustments the tractor coughed deeply and sputtered into life. The belt rolled toward the grinder, and then the first load of meat went into the cup-shaped maw. But what emerged at the other end was only a gooey, creamy mass that shortly fouled the bit. Wrong bit. Another bit, the right one, was substituted, and in a few minutes the tractor again coughed oil-rich smoke that stood for a moment above the faded red of the engine cab, the belt drove toward the grinder, and this time the meat came spilling out in long, satisfying strings. There were assenting murmurs as the men moved to the tables on which wooden kneading troughs had been placed.

At the grinder, the meat snapped and popped as it was forced out, then fell in ropy coils into the tub beneath. When a tub was filled, it was trundled heavily over the dust and cottonwood roots to the tables and kneading troughs. There Ed Kretek poured on the traditional mix of salt, pepper, sage, caraway seed, and a puree of water and garlic powder. The men bent over the troughs, their hands and forearms plunged into the stiff, heavy mass, kneading in the ingredients. This work was harder than the cutting, and there was less talk. The sun sank toward evening, and the air cooled, making the meat even more resistant.

Finally Ed Kretek was satisfied that enough had been done for the day. "Six o'clock, boys!" he called out. "Six o'clock tomorrow morning! We've got a lot to do, so don't be late."

"Bring the beer, Jim," said one, "and don't be late." The kneaded, mixed meat lay piled in the steel vats, covered with wet towels. It would stand there in the night air, guarded by one of the men, and now there was a general movement toward home, the dust from the farm lane pluming out behind cars and pickups and hanging golden in the lowered sun.

Saturday's dawn was gray and cold. A brisk wind blew over the cotton fields, riffling the waters of the duck pond, clashing the big leaves of the cottonwoods. The smoke of the fires was gray, too, and near one of them men huddled and rubbed their hard hands. "Meat's gonna be *cold* when we put our hands in it this morning," one said. There was worried talk of the weather—references to last year's dust storm that spoiled the festivities and of the rain they had had the year before that, under which the folks had lined up, gotten their plates, and then retreated to their cars and trucks. That defeated the whole idea of the thing.

Over one fire big pots of coffee boiled, and a pickup parked next to the tractor, its tailgate dropped, had boxes of rolls and doughnuts spread out for the taking. The farm dogs were back at their posts, and a dozen chickens pecked about under the tables. This morning, too, there were children, bundled in denim jackets and mesh caps; some stood around Ray Harman, who had a fire of mesquite blazing next to the tin smokehouse.

"We've always used mesquite for the smoking," Harman explained. "Maybe at first it was because there was so much of it around here. But anyway, they found out it's good for smoking 'cause it burns slow and"— he poked at his fire with a long-handled shovel, laughing as he did so— "it burns pretty hot." Indeed. Even in the morning's chill you wanted to stand well back.

After more than a half-century of barbecues less mesquite is immediately available, and the men have to travel a bit farther each year to get it. "But every time someone hereabouts clears a field," Harman said, "he'll give us the wood, and that way we usually can get a pretty good supply. Now these," pointing to a bundle of wooden poles stacked next to the smokehouse, "there are plenty of. And they don't wear out anyway." They were yucca rods, used for hanging the sausages, and preferred for this since they are so durable and don't leave an odor on the links. Some had been in use for twenty-five years.

The job of the morning was to regrind the meat, then case it and hang it in the smokehouse over a bed of slow-burning mesquite until early Sunday. The regrinding was cold, greasy work, the meat a stiffened mass, but by the time it had all been put through a second time and the hand-cranked casing machine set in operation, wives, aunts, and sisters had arrived from town and had a breakfast of sausage patties and toast going. With the smell of the frying sausage and the sound of its spattering juices there was new cheer in the grove. One by one the workers went over to get a helping and another cup of coffee, which steamed out of Styrofoam cups. Handing a man a plate of crisped patties blackened at the edges, one of the women, her plump face reddened by fire, said, "They say you eat to live, but I believe I've got it the other way around."

Geraldine Kretek and her twin sister, Gertrude, were there; they watched admiringly as their brother supervised the work, shuttling back and forth between the casing table and the smokehouse. Gradually the smokehouse began to fill with the racks of pink-tinted links, snugged into their casings and draped over the yucca rods, and Ed Kretek's delight became obvious: Aren't they just beautiful? his eyes said. And you had to agree they were. The first level of coals hadn't been laid yet on the dirt floor of the smokehouse, and inside a large tomcat balanced on hind legs like a boxer, sparring at the lowest links. Then Ray Harman, keeper of the flame, put on the first shovelful, and the cat vanished in the rush of spicy smoke.

With beer in hand, Geraldine Kretek talked a bit wistfully of the festival and its history, of traditions that had fallen into desuetude over the years as the inevitable process called "Americanization" or "acculturation" worked its way. The family *beseda* was pretty much a thing of the past, she said, and the "environmentalists" (apparently the state health authorities) now raised objections to the outdoor preparation of the sausage, its overnight storage, et cetera, et cetera. "They'll shut this down one year, you wait and see," she warned. Still, for all the things lost along the way, the festival had widened to include the whole community, and that, she guessed, was all to the good. "It's just something that brings this whole town together, at least for once," she said. And so maybe it was a kind of trade-off—the Czechs losing some of their traditions, but Deming gaining a genuine festival.

This was the subject late that afternoon as I sat with Ed Kretek in the now-deserted grove at the Hervol place. The sausage was all cased, hung, and smoking in the smokehouse next to us. The tubs, vats, and troughs were gone, the tables scrubbed, the casual litter of the operation

146

piled near the lane. The day had cleared in the afternoon, and the sun was setting now in a strong easterly breeze so that we had the fragrance of the smokehouse drifting past our noses.

Kretek was tired, and he still had a long night of watching ahead ("I sit out here and watch 'em just like a hen"). His fatigue seemed to mingle with the hour of the day and with memories of other barbecues, inducing a reflective mood just tinged with a philosophic melancholy. He talked of the local bakery, where he'd worked for many years and of which he'd eventually been part-owner. Gone now. "See, we had to modernize, and we just didn't have the capital to do that, so ... " Now he works for Rainbo Baking Company out of El Paso. "Rainbo is *Good* Bread," the sides of their delivery trucks proclaim, and I wanted to ask him if it were really so, whether Bessie Kretek would have been proud to turn out that soft, spongy product in her own kitchen where, for so many years, she had made *kolache* (a Czech pastry with cottage cheese filling) and other homemade delights on her wood-burning Quick Meal stove.

"It's just that way nowadays with a lot of things," he said. "A big bakery can make bread cheaper, and they can transport it faster and farther. When they have to modernize, why, they've got the money to do it." The same thing went, he said, for brewers (we were drinking beer made in Portland, Oregon), meat packers, grocers, hardware stores. He used to deliver bread to twenty-five local grocers in this small town; now there were only two. Thus, one by one, the small, locally owned businesses disappeared in favor of the larger outfits, until in places like Deming there was little of the local, the truly indigenous, left. Now it was the community as a whole, not just an ethnic minority, that had need of a big *beseda* to vivify its sense of itself as a community, its sense that it was something other than just a bunch of people living in a place where work was done and money changed hands.

Look ahead, I said to him: will the festival be going on fifty years from now? He gritted his teeth, looking into the breeze, and wagged his big head. "Hard to say. Hard to say ... We're getting on, you know. Did you notice how many young folks we had out here helping out? Not many, were there? So, I don't know.

"And you know something else? Some of these people here—why, there was a guy here this morning, cranking: I hadn't seen him more than three, four times this whole year. And in a little town like this!"

147

He shook his head again at the mystery of the thing. "Can you imagine? But that's the way it is now. We're all sped up. I am, I know."

Perhaps, I suggested, it's what's called the "pace of life" that caused the old ways to die: customs, homemade things, even friendships. Your sisters, I added, say that you don't have the *beseda* like you used to. Again he shook his head in vigorous lament. "No, no, we don't. See, before there were so many cars, why, when you went somewhere, you stayed awhile. Now, why, things're so sped up, nobody has time for anything."

TV was another thing that atomized a community. "Oh, hell yes. I'm not married, and I work pretty hard. When I come home, I turn it on. First thing you know, I'm asleep. Try to get a dance together now like we used to: you're liable to end up with a half-empty hall. Everybody's home watching TV, and I'll admit I'm like that, too. So, you ask about this"—gesturing toward the empty tables and full smoke-house. "I just don't know whether the younger generation has the spirit or whatever it takes to carry it on.

"Here," he said, shifting the plane from the theoretical to the con-crete and rising with a swift ease that belied his bulk and fatigue. "Here, you ought to try one of these now." He led me around to the back door of the smokehouse, nailed tightly shut and from which a whisper of smoke escaped. Opening it, Kretek cut off a fat link from the lowest layer and handed it to me, smoking hot. We opened two more beers, and I ate this delicious thing as its juices spattered my boots and dotted the dust beside them in a local shower of fat.

By the time we'd finished our beers the sun was lower than the tree-tops and came slanting at a hard angle. So it was difficult at first to pick out the figure that now emerged from the cottonwoods and the fields behind. It was Frank Hervol, Jr., a man in his early thirties. He would take over Ed Kretek's duties for a while so that Ed could get into town for early mass.

On his way into Deming on the old highway, now bypassed by I-10, Kretek went by Mountain View Cemetery where his parents lay side by side beneath cedars, oaks, cottonwoods, and the journeying clouds.

• • •

148

The fears of Saturday proved empty in the brightness of festival morning: Sunday would be one of those 331 sunny days Frank Kretek advertised when he was luring Czechs here half a century ago. The Florida Mountains (that's "Floreeda") stood up sharply out of the plain, one solid mass of blue against the morning sky. Fields of rusty brown rye and cotton lay as if new-made in the sun. A succession of pickups, their cabs filled with dressy men, women, and kids, sped past the Hervol place on their way to town and church. In between their swishes there seemed a Sabbath silence on the land; even the birds in the cottonwoods were quiet.

In town things were otherwise, and by half past ten the streets around the Luna County Courthouse were lined with cars and pickups. Above the tops of the shade trees of the courthouse square big clouds of smoke hung in the windless air: a crew of men here had been barbecuing two thousand pounds of bottom round all through the night, and by now it had reached a succulent pitch. Deming Packing Company had donated the slaughtering and deboning, Ed Kretek had said, "and they ain't even Catholic: that's what this thing does for us all."

The courthouse was an undistinguished hulk, a combination of unarticulated architectural styles, but the square was pleasant with its broad lawns, bandstand, and clustering shade trees. They hanged six of Pancho Villa's raiders here in the aftermath of the old *caudillo*'s raid on neighboring Columbus, an event still vivid in the minds of old-timers of the region. But today nobody was thinking of that ugly bit of gringo justice. Today was festival day, and people were out from Columbus, Lordsburg, Hatch, Silver City, Las Cruces, even El Paso. In the smoke-filtered shade they stood in lines before the ranked tables on which were piled salads, beans, slaw, onions, and tomatoes. Individuals from the community sign up to contribute ten pounds (that's ten *pounds*) of something, plus a cake or pie, and so there is always a superabundance of food, even these days when the festival draws three thousand or more. At the ends of the tables were the featured items: the barbecued beef and the *klobase*.

From the area of the barbecue pit men ferried heavy trays of beef and sausage to the tables, while others insured a steady supply of the links, dipping ladles of *klobase* into pots of boiling water and holding them under until steaming and ready. At one end of the long pit a team of men sliced the barbecued beef into individual servings, their faces shining in the sun and the fierce glow of the mesquite coals. Three huge cast-iron pots of coffee bubbled over a fire; a man tended them, stirring with a long stick the cloth bags of grounds in the inky depths. The bingo was going, and a man on the bandstand called numbers through a bullhorn.

Beneath the stand families sat on benches, checking their bingo cards while they feasted and visited. Here was a feast for the eye as well as the palate, a more robust and vibrant "Sunday Afternoon" than Seurat allowed himself in his grand painting. Everywhere you looked it was plain these people had not come for a "bargain" meal, nor did they intend to eat and run, however accelerated the pace of daily life now was even in such small communities as this. For this suspended, sunny moment anyway, life regained its old leisure, the inexorably forward-working gears of the historical clock stopped, the hands turned back a half-century and more. All over the square the eye picked out groups on the dappled lawn in attitudes of delightful ease, surrendered to the pleasures of this day. In the foreground my glance rested on a great, heavy farmer in clean and faded bib overalls. He had cleaned his plate by 11:30, and now he mopped his blazing brow and lounged at his ease in the sun and smoke and the sounds of bingo.

Geraldine Kretek, conspicuous like her twin in floppy leather hat ("It's a Juarez special"), introduced me to various Czech families, all of them certainly friendly but naturally more interested in each other and the food and festivities than in any visiting writer. Besides, a Danish television crew was on the grounds with wires, mikes, and cameras—next to which a man with a pocket notebook is not especially impressive. Mary Nemec, one of the pioneer Czech settlers here who raised cotton, beans, and Irish potatoes on a farm twelve miles south, looked up politely from her plate at this inquisitive stranger. Yes, she used to come right by the square in a muledrawn wagon when she and her husband brought their cotton in for sale. She still subscribed to two Czech-language newspapers out of Texas. And was there anything else in particular I wanted to know? Looking into her strong, square face, I thought again of Cather, of the lives of the Nebraska Bohemians she rescued for us by writing of them, their sacrifices, blunted hands, hunched backs, sunbleached eyes—all that toil that went into their hold on the land. Mrs. Nemec's daughter, Sophie Nemec Greenwell, laughed when she asked me whether I'd met enough of the "Bohunks" in town.

During a brief lull in the festivities Ed and Geraldine Kretek took
me to his home to load me up with homemade preserves, pickles, onions,
tomatoes, a pumpkin, and, when we'd come back to the square, pounds
of beef and sausage. Helping me store these treasures in my car, Ed
Kretek was in a hurry and couldn't stay longer to reflect on the glory
of the day, the flavor of the sausage, the weather, the handsome turnout.
He had to get ready for the cotton auction. "All this," he smiled, gesturing to the piled gifts in the back seat, "is just for you to remember us by.
Now you be sure to come back and see us next year."

And I said I would.

A Lot Like it Hot

"What," the poet asked, "is so rare as a day in June?" Since he was from Boston, he had in mind, of course, a New England June day, and indeed nothing is rarer than that, whether in its soft, singular perfection or in its astonishing contrast to the long train of very imperfect days that have led up to it. On such a day all the torments of the previous months are forgiven, and you're ready to swear with the Lowells and the Cabots that this unpromising little bit of geography is specially blessed by God.

It's *getting* to that June day that's so hard, as the English were the first to discover. Governor Bradford's famous description of the weathered wall of woods that confronted the Pilgrims at Cape Cod in November 1620, is deeply familiar to all who have endured New England's harsher hours. "They," wrote Bradford, "that know the winters of that country know them to be sharp and violent, and subject to cruel and fierce storms." The newcomers spent a ghastly New England winter there, awaiting that June day with scarcely a lukewarm bowl of porridge to cheer them. Fifty of the company of 102 died.

Some years ago I wearied of waiting through New England's winters and dreary springs for that rare June day. I had known cold before, had endured winters in Chicago when the wind they call the Hawk had come swooping in off the lake to curl your eyelashes with frost. But somehow the longevity of the New England winters and the miserly character of its springs got me down. Several times my heart was broken when the Red Sox's April opener was snowed out, and it must have been after one such disappointment that I moped into a Concord, Massachusetts, bookshop and emerged with the biggest, sunniest book I could find: a huge coffee table volume on the Southwest. Like Keats wearing out his brief hours in the chilly confines of England, I too longed for a "beaker full of the warm South," and in those pages, anyway, I had it: sun and startling shadow, blue mountains, red mesas, festive tables laden with Spanish-style dishes that made me sweat just looking at them. Subsequently I went out there on a visit and found it all true; then, having no religious stake in staying in New England, I moved to New Mexico, and the picture book's promise was fulfilled.

A few years ago, however, personal errands brought me back to New England, where, Pilgrim-like, I endured a winter on Cape Cod. Nothing I could do there seemed proof against an inclemency that went to my marrow, and I spent most of my days upstairs in a leaky old farmhouse where my view commanded a particularly sullen stretch of beach, sucking my paws in ursine solitude.

One day, having nothing better to do, I bought a can of chili con carne in a Hyannis supermarket, thinking I might thus recapture something of my Southwestern happiness within its tinny confines. Alas, it was a terrible disappointment, this insipid, oleaginous bean soup that in much of the country east of the Mississippi has long passed for chili. It bore not the least resemblance to that pungent, deep-flavored item I'd learned to love in the Southwest. Then and for the first time I understood the poignancy of an anecdote told me by a Santa Fe woman whose son had gone off to college. "We heard nothing from him for months," she said, "until we got a card. It said, 'Send chili.'"

Chili isn't by any means the only product of chile peppers (note the orthographic distinction: "i" for the dish, "e" for the plant). It's simply the most famous ambassador to the rest of America from the chile-saturated culture of the Southwest. There, the pervasive use of chile peppers long preceded the invention of chili con carne, and indeed it's hard to imagine what the Southwest would be like without its peppers. In this region the chile is sign and symbol of a way of life, and you could, if you wished, bathe yourself in chile culture all day long from the beginning of the year to its end: *huevos rancheros* for breakfast, perhaps with a side of tortillas with chile honey; *burritos* at lunch; a chile-pepper martini to start off the evening; and then *chiles rellenos*, with a glass or so of *jalapeño* wine. You could spice up your wardrobe with chile-pepper caps (red or green, depending on your taste), rings and charms, tie clips, necklaces, key rings, and earrings, all of them depicting the chile's distinctive, tapering pod. You could write notes on pads decorated with a frieze of pepper pots, serve your guests on similarly adorned place mats, send a friend a magnet or a flag showing a chile. You could attend any of the numerous chili cook-offs that are held in all seasons, or in the fall take in El Paso's "Fiery Foods Show." There is even a magazine devoted to chiles, *The Whole Chile Pepper*, published in Albuquerque.

Chiles are not, of course, confined to the Southwest. They travel to all parts of America, though often in much-disguised or denatured forms, including that of canned chili con carne. They are widely used in all manner of cocktail and hot sauces, in salad dressings, in processed meats, and as coloring and flavoring agents in a vast variety of foods. A pharmaceutical company uses chiles in its heavy-duty back plaster. Chiles are the active ingredient in a commercial powder alleged to keep feet warm in winter, and they are even widely used as a canine vermifuge.

Yet to many Americans, chili con carne and chile peppers are synonymous, and while this could not be said of the chile-heads of the Southwest, still, a case could be made that to Southwesterners in exile chili represents the whole of a lost homeland. Years ago, in a letter to the late Dallas journalist and chili controversialist, Frank X. Tolbert, a Texan in New York claimed that chili wasn't so much a food as a state of mind. "Addictions to it," this woman wrote, "are formed early in life and the victims never recover. On blue days in October I get this passionate yearning for a bowl of chili, and I nearly lose my mind, for there is nowhere I can go in New York City to buy the real thing." (Things have improved, at least in this respect, in Gotham. There as elsewhere in the country, Mexican cuisine and its stepchild, Tex-Mex, are enjoying an astonishing popularity, both in restaurants and on dinner tables: Mexican foods increased more than 230 percent in grocery store sales in the decade of the eighties, and the trend seems likely to prove a long-term one.) Lady Bird Johnson used to moan the chili-bowl blues when November brought its ashen skies and chilling winds to Washington. Itinerant entertainers who knew authentic chili used to make assiduous searches of the towns they played, trying to score for the real thing: Will Rogers (from Oklahoma) and trumpet star Harry James (who went to school in Texas) were said to spend as long as it took to find what Rogers called the "bowl of blessedness." If they came up empty, their performances lacked warmth. I think there can be little doubt that a bowl of red would have been better for the Puritans suffering their first New England winter than their miserable British gruel. Chili might have kept more of them alive—with what benefit to the country's moral tone, who can say?

• • •

Actually, chile peppers aren't really peppers, though you couldn't tell your tongue that. Technically, they are fruits, members of the *Capsicum* genus. Their distinguishing characteristic is the presence of capsaicin, a clear, highly pungent substance. The more of this stuff there is in a variety, the hotter the pepper. Like British Thermal Units used to measure externally produced heat, in chile culture there are Scoville units that measure the degree of capsaicin-produced pungency in a given variety.* The popular jalapeño, for instance, hot enough for most palates, measures about 10,000 Scoville units, but this is mild compared to the habañero pepper's towering inferno of 100,000 units. The genus name is believed by some to be derived from the Greek *kapto* (to bite), although, like so much else about chiles, this claim is disputed. Whatever the etymology of the chile's name may be, I can ruefully testify that there are hot Greek roots here. Twenty years ago, a kid to slaughter, I was invited into an Athenian garden and offered an innocuous-appearing *Capsicum* that moments later had me doing a spirited fire dance before an amused local audience. There are about three hundred varieties of *Capsicum*, and, as I learned in Athens, they are found all over the globe. I once sat amazed in Alcalde, New Mexico, as a horticulturist easily rattled off the names of more than thirty varieties, described their salient qualities, then ran through the eighteen types commonly used in commercial products.

Like corn, tobacco, and tomatoes, chiles were a New World gift, growing as wild perennials in the West Indies, South and Central America, and Mexico and cultivated by South American natives perhaps as long ago as 7000 B.C. According to a myth of the Cora Indians of Mexico's west coast, chiles were introduced into the world when First Man shook them from his testicles onto the plates of food at a primordial feast. When the other animals had recovered somewhat from the crudeness of this action, they tasted the chile-seasoned food and blessed First Man. The myth, had he known it, would have offended the God-haunted Columbus, but the admiral knew a good thing when he tasted it, and he brought a store of chiles back with him from his first voyage.

---

* The units were developed by Wilbur L. Scoville, a Parke-Davis pharmacologist, in 1912. They are somewhat subjective in nature.

By 1500 chiles were in wide cultivation in Spain and Portugal, and Portuguese traders were taking them to India. From there Indian and Arab traders carried them to Indonesia and Malaysia, while Dutch traders took them into Thailand. The cuisines of all these places would surely be unimaginable without the ubiquitous presence of these little fruits—though the daredevil Westerner who dives into a Thai dish might through his tears have cause to question the wisdom of those pepper-exporting merchants of long ago.

Like so much else from the New World, the fruits were promptly misnamed in the Old. As with their noxious relative tobacco, moreover, a tremendous number of medicinal virtues were early ascribed to them. They were said to relieve gas, aid digestion, ease childbirth, remove warts and pimples, heal stings, prevent cavities, and so on. Most of these alleged virtues are no longer credited, but chiles are a good source of the vitamins A and C, and in recent years it has been soberly suggested that regular chile consumption might be helpful in regulating blood cholesterol levels. Whatever the case, many a chile addict will tell you he needs no scientific validation of the benefits of chiles: however prepared, these burners induce a sense of spiritual and physical well-being that transcends analysis.

In America the locus of chile culture remains those lands that were once the northern portion of Mexico: west Texas, the lands bordering the Rio Grande in New Mexico, and southeastern Arizona. In the 1890s, New Mexican chiles were introduced into California, which now is second only to New Mexico in commercial chile production. Chiles are also grown in Louisiana, Mississippi, South Carolina, Florida, even in Michigan and northern Colorado. But by common consent chiles don't taste—well, like chiles *ought* to—anywhere but in the Southwest. Nobody knows why this is so, but Southwesterners will swear to it. The late Dr. Roy Nakayama, New Mexico State University horticulturist and for many years the world's leading authority on chiles, suggested that the Southwest's high temperatures and aridity might be what gives the region's varieties their unique flavor.

Dr. Nakayama was the creator of two new varieties of chile, the Big Jim and the NuMex R Naky, both remarkable for their size and meatiness and both relatively mild. These have proven extremely popular with commercial producers, but you can't tell northern New Mexicans that. They remain devoted to their native varieties, which centuries ago were brought into the Española Valley around the village of Chimayo by either northward-trading Indians or the Spanish.

One year I followed the cycle of the chile season on three Chimayo farms, from planting in late April to the stringing of the red *ristras* (strings) in September. As on so many of the area's farms worked by descendants of the original Spanish settlers, plots are small and narrow, the result of endless family subdividings down the generations. Thus mechanized cultivation is impossible, and with chiles this means hard hand labor, especially during planting. Here the thin, golden seeds, hot to the touch, must be placed with the thumb and first two fingers in shallow holes, row on row, an acre a day, your back bent toward the sun. Then the opening of the *acequias* (irrigation ditches) to the slow brown crawl of the Santa Cruz River water into the fields.

In three weeks, if not surprised by a late frost or snow, the green shoots are up and the farmers' summer engagement with weeds, pests, and drought begins. By early August the plants bear incongruous-seeming white blossoms and the pods are out on the branches, small green cases conserving their fires within. Nothing now but unseasonably heavy rains can spoil the harvest; heavy rains, though, will rot the roots and stems. At the end of the month the harvesting of the green chile begins; those pods not picked then mature to a scarlet blaze as fall deepens on these high plains.

Standing at the lower edge of his chile field and leaning on a hoe, Abedon Lopez, eighty, looked back over another planting and a life spent, as he put it, "fighting weeds." Nobody, he claimed, "wants to be a farmer anymore: work's too hard. But I have liked it. One of these days I'm gonna die, but I'm ready because I have done the way I want. I grow my chiles and melons. Five o'clock [in the afternoon] I go down to feed my cows. Six in the morning, I get up. That's good." He shook his head in affirmation, and we went up the road to the adobe coolness of his kitchen and the noon dinner.

The day after I'd watched Lopez plant his field he sent me to see his neighbor, Willie Trujillo, and I watched him put in his chiles, dropping the pinches of seed into each hole, then moving on. Like Abedon Lopez, Trujillo still favored the native Chimayo pepper, even though he had been told often by the horticulturist at Alcalde that Dr. Nakayama's new varieties would give him bigger yields. "Those Hatch

chiles," he'd said, referring to the town in the southern part of the state
where Nakayama's chiles are popular, "they're all right for there. But
here, I like the Chimayo." He shook his head at the new rows, and told
me to come back to see his fields in August.

I did that, arriving at his neat house in the waning hours of an
afternoon. "When you come last?" he asked, and when I told him it had
been early May he chuckled. "You gonna have a big surprise when you
see them," he said, and he led the way down to the chile field, passing
through pens with pigs, pecking chickens, and hissing geese, their necks
stretched in menace. We went through a field of alfalfa and another of
carrots, cabbage, and cauliflower. On the other side of the *acequia* were
the chile rows, the plants almost knee high and bearing the telltale white
blooms that announce the nearness of harvest. Trujillo preceded me
down the rows, a spring now to his elderly step. We knelt then amid the
green. His face under the broad hat was as sharp and brown as if
hacked from hardwood, but there was nothing sharp in the tender way
he handled a plant, fingered its leaves, and turned up the pods to my
inspection. "The chile is a temperamental plant," he said. "You got to
treat him right. If you do, he treats you right."

• • •

September, harvest, and the annual chile celebration at Hatch, where on
festival Saturday the thermometer on Main Street read a spanking 109.
At the grounds there was a contest for size and shape of the pods, with
Dr. Nakayama's breeds earning their usual high marks; a fiddler's contest; and a four-wheel drive mud-bog contest that spattered the audience
with liquid desert clay. But I was there for the chili cook-off, a
Southwestern sport that, like chiles themselves, has spread to all parts of
the country.

At eight of a Sunday morning the contestants were gathered under
a canvas tent, the roof of which was already aglow with what promised
to be serious sun. Most were teams of two, one to "prep" the ingredients,
the other to cook them. Ray Walker of Amarillo said he'd placed fourth
a few years back at the International Chili Society Cook-off at Tropico,
California. Basic chili, he told me, hefting a sweating can of Pearl beer,
is meat and an equal amount of chile peppers, onions, garlic, and oregano.

Like other professional chili cooks, Walker was somewhat secretive about his own recipe, but he admitted to blending two varieties of chiles and to using fresh coriander. As for meat, "beef is best. Sometimes I use road meat. 'Course you have to pick it up within twenty-four hours or it's too stringy." He watched me casually out of the corner of his eye. "Couldn't find any on my way over here this morning, so I'm using beef." On the sideboard of his cooking outfit, over which a comely female assistant perspired quietly, stood a bottle of tequila and a six-pack of Pearl.

I supposed those were ingredients too, for chili recipes often call for spirits. "Cactus chili," for instance, calls for tequila, which gives the recipe its needles; beer is ubiquitous. But savage battles have been waged over just what constitutes *authentic* chili, and only the presence of the chiles themselves is undisputed. A championship recipe from Mexico calls for chocolate; Floyd Cunningham's "German Red" uses vitamin E ("it gives the chili a message," he says); Boston chili is basically a bean dish. Meat is found in almost all recipes, but there is no agreement on the kind or on how it should be prepared. Most canned chili (like the brand I bought in Hyannis) uses ground beef, but many will tell you the beef should be cubed. I've also seen recipes calling for pork, chicken, rattlesnake, bear, turtle, even armadillo.

Nor is there consensus on the vegetables to be used. The most commonly included are tomatoes, onions, and beans, but you could start a fight with some purists who'd claim the addition of these ruins chili by turning it into a messy stew. Then there are those who will fight over whether the beans should be navy, or kidney, or pinto. And another of the endless splinter sects holds that the beans must be pinto—but served on the side.

Actually, recipes for chili, like those for gumbo or cassoulet, are like the melody of a jazz performance: structures from which the cook is encouraged to improvise. The following is an improvisation on one I found in a chili cookbook. I call it "Basic Texas Red" because, despite all the controversy surrounding chili, it is generally agreed the dish originated in Texas cowboy culture during the last century. "Basic Texas Red" preserves a good bit of the original style and flavor of the earliest recipes and includes ingredients most commonly found in chili formulas.

A Lot Like It Hot

"Basic Texas Red"

SERVES 6

3 strips bacon, diced
3 lbs. stew beef, cubed small
1 tablespoon oregano
1 3-oz. bottle chili powder (preferably without dried garlic and salt)
1 tablespoon cayenne pepper
3 tablespoons crushed cumin
4 cloves garlic, minced
6 medium-sized fresh tomatoes, diced
2 cans beer
coffee, water, salt to taste

Fry the bacon in a heavy pot or Dutch oven. Add meat and brown quickly over fairly high heat. Add oregano, chili powder, cayenne, cumin, and garlic, mixing thoroughly at lowered heat. Add tomatoes. Add beer and enough coffee (black) and water (if necessary) to cover ingredients. Simmer 3 $1/2$ to 4 hours uncovered, adding water (or coffee) as necessary.

NOTES: *1. A tastier base than the bacon called for could be supplied by the substitution of Italian sausage. I did not list it in the recipe in the interests of authenticity. 2. Nowadays with the enormous popularity of Mexican cuisine it should be possible to come by a good brand of chili powder on grocery store shelves. If you are fortunate enough to live where whole chile peppers, red or green, are sold, these could be substituted for the powder. Just be sure you know what kind of chiles you're buying. In preparing these, remove seeds and stems and puree in a food processor. 3. Whether handling fresh or dried chiles, exercise caution: all this talk about heat and flame is no joke, and an inadvertent touch of a chile-saturated hand to the eyes, mouth, or nose will prove extremely unpleasant for a while afterward. 4. If fresh tomatoes are unavailable, canned ones are far preferable to the tasteless baseballs of the hothouses. 5. Chili's flavor markedly improves if the stew is left to sit overnight, so it is best to prepare it the day before, then let it steep.*

161

There's nothing fancy or esoteric here, but you'll find this chili has wonderful flavor and packs a punch. If you're not accustomed to Southwestern cookery, you might want to consider toning it down a bit by serving side dishes of pinto beans and sour cream. A generous dollop of the latter atop a bowl is of assistance to the thin of spirit and palate. The thing to remember in cooking chili is that any fool can make foods hotter than a baker's belt buckle simply by adding more spices. In order to work its soul-satisfying magic, chili must be hot enough to make you tingle from head to toe, but it shouldn't be so hot (to borrow from Twain) that it would stir the vitals of a cast-iron dog. That is neither fun nor good eating.

"Basic Texas Red" isn't the One True Chili, of course. Despite what Frank X. Tolbert and the other chili controversialists have said, no such Supreme Dish exists. But it is a variety of the authentic article, about which only the deeply disputatious would argue. As such, it is a species of blessing that will light up your life wherever you serve it, whether you live in chili's native habitat of the Southwest, in Manhattan's gleaming canyons, or in the old haunts of the Puritans, patiently abiding there that rare day in June.

Time and the River

"You boys are just gonna have to sit here awhile," Lavar Wells told us.
Todd Langley and I were already sitting in the office of Red Tail
Aviation at the Grand Junction airport, and Wells's news was just fine
with us. Langley was a photographer I'd joined in Denver for a hairy
flight over to Grand Junction along the tops of the clouds with a comely
systems analyst seated between us, spoiling her makeup with great rivers
of frightened tears. While we were being flung about the cabin by the
commuter plane's pitches and swoops Langley and I fruitlessly tried to
convince Susan that the pilot was a pro with no more interest in crashing than she had. We were still recovering from this experience and so
were relieved to hear from our new pilot that we wouldn't have to go
up again for a spell. We had seen Wells's plane, and it was a good deal
smaller and more mature than the one that had bounced us over here
from Denver. A Denver magazine had commissioned us to fly into Rock
Creek on the Green River this afternoon to rendezvous with a river
float featuring nightly concerts by a classical quintet, and Wells was now
explaining to us that he wanted to wait until the afternoon thermals had
calmed. "Right now," he told us with a sly smile on his leathery face,
"that canyon's likely to be a bit active. I don't like to go in until there's
some shadow that quiets things down a little." I looked across the room
at Langley, and we rolled our eyes at each other: if Wells wanted to wait
until dawn, that seemed no more than basic prudence.

We had no trouble filling the interim. Lavar Wells proved to be one
of those marvelously capable and various characters that used to be
found all over the West but now appear endangered, replaced by newcomers like myself, fellows who can't pour piss out of a boot with
instructions written on the heel—to use one of LBJ's tamer apothegms.
Wells was from Hanksville, Utah, a town, so he told us, that used to be
ranching, "but now is mainly filled with bureaucrats from the BLM
that has squeezed the life out of it." He still had a small cattle operation
there, "mainly so I can bitch at the BLM: you have to have somebody to

163

be mad at, right?" Wells was also a musician who played guitar, fiddle, and banjo and sang cowboy songs for tourists in the Grand Junction area. But his main gig was playing in a polka band for fans who would drive fifty and sixty miles to a dance. "Frankie Yankovic is still a bigger name with these folks than Frankie Sinatra ever was," he claimed.

In the late afternoon the three of us took up all the seats in the battered Cessna, but this time we flew beneath the clouds, west into a sinking sun. When we got to Rock Creek on the Green River, Wells did a deft, wing-dipping fly-by to make sure no cattle were occupying the little riverside hay field that served as a landing strip, then expertly set us down in a high cloud of dust and flying bits of grass.

The grass had settled, but the dust was still aloft when Bill Dvořák and his young son Matt came walking up through the cottonwoods. With his wife, Jaci, Dvořák was outfitter and guide of this float and in his bathing trunks looked like a combination of Anthony Quinn and a hit man from a mid-budget action flick. He told us we were just in time for tonight's concert, and as he rowed us over the river to the camp we heard the stately strains of one of Scott Joplin's rags across July's slow-flowing water.

I was too busy that evening clumsily setting up my tent to really listen to the concert, but I was ready for the drinks and dinner that followed. Then, sitting in a circle with my plate of turkey fajitas and plastic cup of wine, I became aware that a night bird of anxiety had come to sit on my shoulder as the sun slid behind the cliffs opposite us. Five days stretched before me, five days in the intimate company of these strangers, five days of apparently unvarying routine, five days without the company of my wife, the comforts of my study, my jazz recordings, workouts, impulsive trips into town—all the daily *choices* I had. Here choices were starkly delimited: there was the river, the canyon it cut through, and you and your newfound companions. As the first stars came out, I turned toward my tent, feeling I had something in common with the quarry-slave of William Cullen Bryant's "Thanatopsis," "scourged to his dungeon." My last glimpse of the outer world was of the other member of the press corps, Todd Langley, standing in front of his man-sized duffle and staring off downriver.

● ● ●

Guided white-water rafting might be as misunderstood by the uninitiated as sport hunting. In both instances you think there *must* be something more than meets the ignorant eye. Surely there was an inner game
in hunting that compensated for the pedestrian thrill of stalking some
creature whose habitat had contracted enough to bring it within range
of your technologically infallible rifle. With guided rafting such
as the Dvořáks so expertly provided, there had to be more to it than
being ferried with other passengers down slackwater to a rapid, running
the rapid, squealing like slaughterhouse pigs, and then the boredom of
slackwater and sun again until the next thrill. But what was it?

I was searching ever harder for an answer on my third day out (day
six for the tour) when I found myself in a raft oared by Wally, an astonishingly high-spirited New Zealander guide who spends his entire year
running rivers in North America and his native country. Langley was in
the raft's front, at work with his cameras, and there was also Anita, a
public relations official from the University of Southern California
before her recent retirement. This trip, she said, as Wally stroked us
steadily over the flat, silty water, was a present she'd made to herself.
And it was turning out well, very well. Only ... "Well, there have been
some things I didn't expect—because I really didn't know much about
rafting." Like being in the constant company of about thirty-five other
people in the midst of a desert wilderness. "I guess," she continued,
"other than worrying about the bathroom arrangements (must be a uni-
versal concern), when I thought about this, I imagined a solitude kind
of thing: you know, out here on a deserted river, no cars, no one around.
But actually, you're around people all the time." She laughed good-
naturedly, looking at the other people around her now, but we laughed
with her and there was no offense to be taken. "I'll be glad," she concluded, "to get to my motel room at the end of the trip and have some
of that solitude."

"I think you've got the wrong idea about rafting," Wally hollered
from the high howdah of his oar bench. "I don't think a rafting trip can
be a solitude-type experience. When you think about it, you see it can't
be. It's a social event. It's about a bunch of people learning to get along
together, people who don't know each other. It's a *team* thing."

Later, at lunch in the clamorous shade of an ancient cottonwood's
dry leaves, the subject arose again in conversation with Jaci Dvořák. She

and Bill had known each other since high school and had made rivers their lives. They guided all over the Rocky Mountain west, she told me, and in Texas, Australia, and New Zealand, spending almost the entire year on the water, with only a month or so off in late fall.

"One thing you see on a trip like this," she said, looking at me so steadily I thought I must be wearing my quizzical misgivings pretty obviously, "is people taking hold of it. A lot of them at first don't really know what they've signed on for, and to begin with they're shy and don't know the routine or one another. And you might get somebody who says, 'I want out of this thing.' But we tell them, 'Look, we can't call a plane in. There's no way out, and you'll just have to stick it out.' By the end of the trip they don't want to come off the river: it's gripped them. Sixty percent of our customers are repeats."

The Dvořáks had been running these music tours for eleven years, and all of the musicians on this one were "repeats." This was not a picnic of a gig for them, either, but rather one they felt compelled to come back to, despite its professional hazards. On my second night out the quintet set up in a field called Lion Hollow and there played Bach, Beethoven, Kurt Weill, and a lovely tango in the blazing heat while the Dvořáks' golden retriever, Cassie, raced to and fro through the foxtails. Nancy Laupheimer, a flutist, was executing some very demanding passages in a Bach piece with beads of sweat visible beneath her bangs when a shout rang down from the canyon wall at the field's edge: it was Jake, Nancy's little boy, who had improved the moment by climbing to a very high and precarious perch, and now he wanted mom to notice. Later on, concert concluded, son rescued, I asked Nancy about the playing conditions. "I've played in worse," she told me, "when it's not only been hot but buggy with lots of little bugs clustered around your face when you're trying to concentrate. But I wouldn't miss this trip for anything. I *love* it, so the conditions don't bother me."

Roy Tanabe, a violinist with the Los Angeles Philharmonic, agreed it had been hot back in Lion Hollow but said that hadn't bothered him as much as the site's acoustics. "We couldn't hear each other very well," he said. "I know I was making noise under my chin, but it was difficult to hear what anybody else was doing." This trip was, he told me, the warmest he'd been on yet—but by no means the most demanding. One year on the Green the company was just putting in at Sand Wash when

166

they saw the mosquitoes, "just a cloud of them, and they plagued us all along the river. One night we set up two tents. The musicians got in one, and everybody else squeezed into the other. We could hardly play we were laughing so hard."

The morning following I was sitting on the dew-dampened sand, sipping coffee in the gray light with Tanabe, cellist Armen Ksajikian, and violinist Barry Socher. The sun hadn't yet swung over the east wall of the canyon, there was a chill on the air, and the coffee tasted a good deal better than it probably would have anywhere else. Ksajikian had been making these tours since the early '80s and now laughingly recalled that once on the Rogue in Oregon the group played "the complete Haydn string quartets—all eighty-three of them. It took thirty-four and a half hours, but we did it." Neither he nor Socher looked like athletic outdoorsy types; together they might have gone five hundred pounds. Yet here they were, and here they had been, summer on summer. What, I asked Socher, was it that kept bringing him back?

"Music and the river," he replied. "The river and music." He smiled at me warmly, gently, as if he were adding, "Doesn't this give you all the explanation you could possibly require?"

• • •

On our last full day before take-out below Swasey Rapids we stopped for lunch near Florence Creek and needing to feel useful I followed Bill Dvořák's huge tanned back up through the meadow to fill some water jugs from the creek. (Despite all the BLM regulations the Green is polluted enough to discourage casual human consumption.) Dvořák filled his two containers and toted them back downhill as if they were a couple of cartons of skim milk while I slogged slowly after him with one on my shoulder, trying the while to imagine how truly essential it was to the group's welfare. Lunch was in progress on the bank, and Julie, a big, well-proportioned guide, was talking at large to the assembled. "Do you all notice," she asked rhetorically, "how much Anita sounds like everyone's mother? 'How are you going to meet anyone on the river?' she asks me. That sounds too much like my own mother: 'How're they going to find you if you keep moving?'" She paused effectively, looked at Anita, then added, "I've got to ask mom how much she's paying this woman."

167

Then we were off again, running at last out of Desolation Canyon, as John Wesley Powell dubbed it and into Gray Canyon. Less than an hour into it there came a giant muttering behind the canyon walls, the sky darkened, and some long fingers of lightning were visible in the far distance. The wind shifted to downriver and became a real force, and the flotilla ran swiftly before it, the rain firing drops at our backs and necks like pellets from a rifle barrel. "I *love* big weather!" Wally bellowed above the blast, and then, just as suddenly, the wind dropped, changed direction, and blew in our faces. High on the gray, scrabbled slope a herd of Rocky Mountain bighorn sheep ignored us, feeding on the tough grasses with their white rumps to the weather. Now it became tough going for the rafts, Wally, Julie, Bill Dvořák, and the others pulling hard at the long sweeps and the opaque waters riffling back against them. Just as suddenly the squall passed over, the mountain god changed mood, and in mild air and calm water we nosed into tonight's bivouac just as the sun cleared the clouds and began to sink toward the canyon's western wall.

By this point I had the camp routine down pretty well, though I was still among the slower campers in setting up my tent, and on this last night I was just finishing up when I heard the first strains of Mozart from down the narrow beach. I stopped what I was about and sat down on the sand to listen, realizing with what felt like a much-belated clarity that what the rafters were being given was extraordinary: this beautiful, this magisterial music, performed by a group that truly cared about giving its very best under any circumstances; and this against the backdrop of the tough riverside fringe of tamarisks, cottonwoods, and black sagebrush, behind which the stark, friable slopes rose toward a deep evening sky with clouds burnished by the last rays of the sun. But when at last the concert ended it was possible for me to remember the obvious—that not too many raft trips have such accompaniment—and this left me pondering still the essential and unadorned lure of the guided river run.

I was still at this when Todd Langley and I had a farewell beer the next afternoon in the dingy bar of the Grand Junction airport, but I came up empty. All I honestly felt then and on the trip home that night was gritty all over, sore from my five nights on the ground, and a weariness with the company of others. The river and its music were already well in the background. Like Anita from USC, I was looking forward to the solitude of civilization. It wasn't until several days later, back home with my river sandals tucked safely away in a remote recess of the closet, that I found myself thinking back to an afternoon on the river that at the time had seemed a nadir.

We'd put in for a day well before high noon. It was very hot, and we'd all gobbled our lunch in the scant shade, then headed back to the river. But even the water wasn't much comfort—silty, slow, and the towering canyon cliffs radiating their heat down upon it. The inside of my tent was like a convection device, and so I sat in the spidery shadow of a tamarisk, wondering what on earth to do. Cloud masses appeared over the canyon walls, followed by thunder, a scatter of raindrops, and a stinging scour of wind-whipped sand. Then the sun again and shadows on the cliffs. I regarded my toenails and found to my surprise they looked like those of Howard Hughes in his terminal dishevelment and so clipped them. Below, on the river bank the dog endlessly retrieved sticks thrown for her. The shadows on the cliffs sharpened and slowly lengthened. A rufous-sided towhee hopped through the inner branches of a tamarisk, and a heavy drowse sat on the encampment. Like Melville's sunken-eyed Platonist, all sorts of vagrant thoughts swam through my head, but time and again the situation brought me back to myself, for there was no escape. For me it wasn't music and the river, as it was for Barry Socher—couldn't be. It was Time and the river and the finite and mortal me, forced by circumstance to be present in that steady and ceaseless flow. That, I realized now in the quiet comfort of my study, had been the singular virtue of the trip, one I hadn't sought and indeed one I would probably have avoided had other diversions been available. But they hadn't been, and so for once I had been fully present, fully conscious of being present. Just *there*.

A Custom of the Country

"No, sir, you fellas aren't fooling me one bit." Calvin Reese was staring at his two visitors out of dark, hooded eyes.* He spat snuff juice into the nearly full plastic bottle he held in one hand. "You're not outsmarting me," he continued with that stare, his face impassive. Then a smile, a very small one. "Say, which of you have a Humane Society card in your pockets—or do you both?" I tried again to assure him that neither my friend nor I was with the Humane Society, that we weren't sailing here under a false flag. Reese had been in the navy in World War II (as had my friend), and I thought maybe the naval metaphor might mollify him. Something was needed here, for sure.

We were sitting in the dim living room of Reese's house on the outskirts of Phoenix. I had been trying for the better part of the past year to get him to talk with me about cockfighting, but until recent days he had been bluntly reluctant. Then in a phone conversation a week before he had said suddenly, "You're a writer, are you? All we ever get from writers is misrepresentation, misquotes, misunderstanding, a whole lot of trouble, that's what." He had paused. "I may have someone kill you after I read your lines." Another pause. "Are you properly scared?" I said I was. "You ought to be," he said. "You know what kind of people we are, don't you? You must be able to read if you can write. Well, all right then. You see what they say about us: we're a bunch of murderers and rapists, and our wives are all prostitutes. But I'm not going to tell you anything more on the telephone. You come out here [to Phoenix] and let me look you in the eye, and then maybe we'll talk."

So here I was. My old navy friend and I had been over in Mesa earlier in the day, watching the leisurely play of a spring-training ball game. Here, however, was a wholly different sort of sport, and the way the talk had been going it didn't look as if we were going to find out very much about it. Clearly Reese had been stung—and badly—in

* Throughout this essay I have changed the names of the cockers.

the past, and he was taking no chances yet with these benign-seeming strangers. A red plastic hummingbird feeder hung under the eaves outside the room's window, and I watched it sway slightly in the desert afternoon's late breeze. Reese spat again into the bottle and leaned forward in his chair, nudging with his slipper the ancient dachshund snoozing in the gloom at his feet.

"There's no whores, there's no dope, and there's no Mafia." Here was another change of pace—but was it an opening? "As far as I know there isn't a game fowl breeder whose wife has her ass on the line. That's contrary to what you may have heard. Most of us are pretty steady middle-class people that have worked for what we've got. You won't find many welfare types among us. Oh, there are some bad eggs mixed in, but you'll find that in any sport, I don't care what it is. You'll find that over there at your baseball game."

In fact, it did prove an opening, and in the next half-hour Reese rapidly described this clandestine custom that has engendered the passionate opposition of just about every conservation consortium and humane organization in America, and the equally passionate determination of the cockers to continue breeding, raising, and pitting their birds. As Calvin Reese had said, we had not outsmarted him. We had not, I am sure, even outwaited him. It was merely that he had decided, for whatever purely private reasons, to tell us a few things, let the consequences be what they would.

A cockfight, he said, beginning at the beginning, "is a contest between two evenly matched, evenly armed gamecocks in which there's a winner and a loser. Without a winner and a loser there is no contest. And a lot of misunderstanding comes right here. People say, 'Well, why do you arm them [the cocks]?' You have to understand that the gaff is an equalizer. It's what makes the contest fair. The gaff or the knife actually inflicts less tissue damage than a natural spur, and there's less risk of infection. Here"—he rose from his seat and disappeared into another room, returning presently with a cigar box filled with the clipped natural spurs of various breeds of gamecocks.

"You think nature's fair?" he snorted, holding up two grossly dissimilar spurs, one of them curved as wickedly as a scimitar and about as long as my thumb, while the other was but an inoffensive stub. He asked us rhetorically how we thought a contest between cocks with such

172

spurs would come out. "Some Spanish people'll fight natural spurs," he said. "Cubans will. Mexicans, Puerto Ricans. In the Philippines they fight knives. But you'll find most white people will use gaffs." He showed us some of these severely beautiful weapons and explained briefly the method of affixing them to the cock's heels with leather and twine.

"Now, here's another thing: people will tell you we *make* these roosters fight. Why, there isn't a thing in this world you can do to make a rooster fight if he doesn't want to. Nothing. But you take a rooster and set him where he can see another one, and nine times out of ten you'll have a fight. That's just the way they are. They're very territorial. All we're really doing is making a regular contest out of what happens anyway. You think humans *invented* this? Hell, they came upon it in the wilds and watched it happening. Who the hell're you"—he was glaring at us now—"or anybody else to come in here and tell me I can't watch two roosters fight? Why does it [the pitting of the cocks] make me less good than you? You're just assuming your greater virtue, aren't you?" Compared with the carefully arranged equality of the contest as he had just described it, this social and moral inequity was to him patently ridiculous, and he digressed from a description of cockfighting to the attacks made on it by those he styled "do-gooders," those in the grip of the "Bambi Syndrome," and especially the Humane Society.

In some places, he told us, "You wouldn't believe what powers they've given them [the Humane Society]. They have jurisdiction over the police! They're like the Nazis or something: go in there, break up the fight, trespass, no warrant, break up your house, search for implements, and so on! They'll see a cock in your backyard and then go phone the TV: 'Look! He's doin' something cruel!'

"There is a definite need for a Humane Society. There's people who'd kick that dog to death," pointing with his toe at the sleeping dachshund, "just for the pure hell of it. But they have gotten to where they're trying to dictate the way of life of everybody in this part of the world. They're actually trying to change us into a vegetarian society from meat eaters. I'll bet you didn't know there are lobbies in Washington right now against *circuses* and *zoos*! A fact!"

Far from being callous about their birds, cockers actually like and admire them, he told us. "But a rooster isn't a human, and we don't confuse the two. That's what you get from TV and the movies where they make the animals talk like humans and have the same feelings: what I call the Bambi Syndrome. Do you hunt? I didn't think you did. Well, if you did, if you *had* to hunt, you wouldn't confuse animals with humans, that's for damn sure." As he spoke I fondled the dachshund's ears, and Reese anticipated the unvoiced drift of my thoughts when he asked, "You wonder why we don't fight dogs? People do fight 'em, but I've never been to a dogfight in my life and wouldn't be interested in attending. I don't mind saying why. It's because a dog is different than a rooster. A dog still isn't human. I care a lot about this dog here, but I don't bring him to the table to eat with me. But a dog is a pet. He's part of the household, sleeps inside, and so forth. That's the difference. Yes, I've had individual roosters I liked. One of them, Old Gray, won eleven times. I had another named Old Bob. He was a good one. My father and grandfather had favorite birds. But none of them were pets, and that's the point."

I wanted to see Reese's birds, never having seen a fighting cock except in the movies, and said so. This set him off again, this time on the sensationalized cinematic depictions of cockfighting: all those scenes of handlers spraying cocks' heads with alcohol, putting their birds' heads in their mouths to revive them, et cetera, et cetera. "You could go to a hundred fights," Reese said, "and never see any of that stuff." But, no, I couldn't have a look at his birds because they were kept out on a farm where they could get good exercise, and in any case the peak of the fighting season was over now in Arizona, and he had no birds that were currently in top fighting condition. If I was seriously interested in the birds and in watching them work, he said, he would give me a few things I could read. "Then you call me along about the end of next January, and we'll talk again. There are some good derbies here in February and March." He turned abruptly from me to engage my friend in naval reminiscences of the Pacific theater, in which they had both served, and he was still talking navy and Japan when we took our leave of him in his small front yard.

"We had a boy here, a Jap boy, lived out here quite a few years. Well, after a while he got homesick for Japan, and he went back. I told him when he showed up here again, 'You dumb bastard. If you'd stayed here, the Americans would've made a rich man out of you just like they have every other Jap.'"

• • •

When I did call Calvin Reese that following January, the first thing he wanted to know was whether I'd read any of the items he'd suggested. I said I had. His list was very short, but I found it took me into hitherto unsuspected territories of culture and history.

I learned, among other matters, that cockfighting is quite probably mankind's oldest spectator sport. As authors Page Smith and Charles Daniel note in their definitive work *The Chicken Book*, it has been argued that "cockfighting was, in fact, the occasion for the domestication of the chicken"—which, if true, would account for the corollary fact that the origins of cockfighting are so ancient as to be unrecoverable. The general region of origin of the gamecock, though, has been pretty securely identified: India or Java or Malaya. In the fourth century B.C., when Persia conquered India, it took over among other things the Indian custom of pitting gamecocks. From Persia cockfighting spread to Greece and thence to Rome. It was said that the famed Greek general Themistocles elevated the custom to the status of a national sport simply because he chanced to see a cockfight as he was about to march against the Persians. "Behold," he said to his troops, "these do not fight for their household gods, for the monuments of their ancestors, for glory, for liberty, or the safety of their children, but only because the one will not give way to the other."

By this time artificial spurs were a common feature of the fights; the Greeks called them "plucks" and fashioned them from steel or bronze. Already, too, there were elaborate procedures for training gamecocks, including special diets, rubdowns, and sparring exercises. The Romans continued and refined these and other associated practices, even though they at first had found the Greek obsession with the sport baffling. When their legions went northward into pagan Europe, the fighting cocks went with them to enliven their campfire hours.

By the Middle Ages in Europe cockfighting was the diversion of kings and commoners and was sufficiently prevalent and expensive of time and money (which were increasingly being equated) that the Church attempted to suppress the sport. The attempts were ineffectual, but they did signal a trend that continues into our own time: that, for various reasons, Christianity and cockfighting were seen to be incompatible.

This view gathered strength through the centuries until in England in 1834 the forces of Christian humanitarianism were successful in forcing passage of a law forbidding the ancient sport. By that time, however, cockfighting had bequeathed the language a clutch of words and phrases that remain testament to the hold the sport has exercised on its devotees: cocky, cock-of-the-walk, cockpit, cockeyed, cocksure, cockade, crestfallen, cockalorum. Opponents are pitted against one another, and one may show the white feather. At times we may get our hackles up or our feathers ruffled. Arguably, the cant phrase "to be hung up" derives from the entanglement of fighting cocks. If one is lacking in capacity, we might say he isn't up to scratch. We might even toast a winner with a cocktail.

By the time of its English prohibition cockfighting had long since taken ship to the Americas. In the Caribbean and throughout Mexico and Latin America it continues to enjoy enormous popularity, apparently impervious to the continuing influence of Victorian morality or contemporary animal rights activists. In the eighteenth and nineteenth centuries in what is now the United States, cockfighting was exceeded in popularity only by the sports of hunting and horse racing; indeed, in the Middle Atlantic states and the South it might have been more popular than either of these still-honored pastimes. Modern American cockers are proud to point out that Washington was a fancier and breeder; that Jefferson often attended cocking mains (meets); that Jackson had a cockpit on the White House grounds; and that in his Illinois lawyer years Lincoln often served as a referee. That is three-quarters of the Mount Rushmore pantheon—and many an aging New Deal Democrat would be happy to tell you that sculptor Gutzon Borglum erred enormously in omitting Old Hickory from that mountain face. Of the four holies, only T. R. was not a cockfighting enthusiast, preferring to be in charge of killing creatures himself on his many hunting expeditions.

Despite its ancient and famous pedigree, cockfighting is under serious attack in America, and the domain of the cocker has become greatly circumscribed in the twentieth century. Currently only three states (Arizona, New Mexico, and Louisiana) permit the custom, and even in these places cockers are under such relentless assault that they routinely manifest the quasi-paranoid behavior of Calvin Reese. In New Mexico, for instance, the state's permissive legal stance on cockfighting comes under yearly challenge when lawmakers convene in Santa Fe for the winter session. In 1987, the Humane Society of the United States made its annual effort to persuade the New Mexico lawmakers to outlaw the custom, alleging that cockfighting fosters callousness in its spectators, "particularly in the children." In addition, the society alleged that "many other illegal activities are associated with these fights. It is rare that illegal gambling is not taking place ... , for one of the primary purpose [*sic*] of these fights is betting. ... Often," the society's letter continued, "we have found during our investigations of these events illegal weapons and drugs which are an obvious danger to the community."

All of the lands where cockfighting is currently legal lie west of the Mississippi, except that portion fo Louisiana above Lake Pontchartrain. Louisiana is, of course, heavily populated along the river, but there is good cover for cockers in the inaccessible coastal parishes and in the Cajun parishes to the west. It may be that this remove is a factor in the siting of one of the biggest events of the American cockfighting year, the tournament at Sunset, Louisiana.

Rivaling the Sunset meet in importance and size, however, is the Copper State Kemper Marley Tribute, a derby held at Avondale, just outside of Phoenix, and it was this event I was hoping to attend when I returned to Phoenix the first week in February. But I knew I would have to pass the scrutiny of Calvin Reese and his associates, a somewhat daunting prospect in view of my previous contacts with Reese and what I had been learning of anticocking pressures.

When I called at his house on this breezy February afternoon, he said the best thing I could do would be to meet some of the cockers who would be fighting birds in the derby, and so we drove ten miles into the country beyond the city's sprawl to a rambling ranch-style house with several vehicles parked in front of it, a high fence behind, and, within the fencing, several outbuildings whose roofs barely protruded above the fence top. I could hear the shrill challenges of unseen cocks rising from the enclosure as we walked to the back of the house. "Put the dope away!" Reese hollered in through a window. "We got a writer here."

Inside, three men sat at an oval table drinking coffee and smoking cigarettes. They regarded me unsmilingly as Reese made the introductions. "There's four of us here now," Reese joked, "so here's our chance to nut 'im." They didn't smile at this, either, but after a long pause they resumed their talk.

Holly, a muscular, stocky man of sixty or so, had worked for the county for thirty years, and it was his cocks I'd heard in back. Over a cigarette his yellow eyes assessed me narrowly while he kept the conversation going with Jackie, a burly cocker from Oklahoma City (where the sport was then legal), and Nick Zacharios, a monument maker from Philadelphia who had come out for the derby with twenty cocks. Zacharios had gold rings on the pudgy, powerful fingers of both hands, and a rooster's spur hung from his bolo tie. When the conversation waned Holly asked if I'd like some coffee; after he'd returned with it the men turned their attention to me and asked about my interest in their sport. I said I'd read a bit about it and was curious enough to want to attend some fights. They listened carefully, glancing occasionally at Calvin Reese for corroboration. When I'd finished, they all began at once: cockfighting, they said, with three voices but one tone, was terribly misunderstood, and one of the reasons for this was writers like me, Holly jabbing a finger in the air toward my chest. Cockers, I needed to understand, were mostly cleanly, upright men, good family men, kind to animals and children. "And you know what?" Holly asked rhetorically, *"you'll* never know the kind of comradeship there is among us. No, sir. You'll never see the like of it. Do you know, I could travel from one end of this country to the other and never have to pay for a meal or a bed. That's a fact." The others grunted. "Just staying with cockers." He nodded curtly in assertion.

"You know one thing I've never understood," Jackie said in an oblique continuation of this subject, "is just this: you'll search for years and years for just the right breed of rooster, and when you think you've got it—then you'll turn right around and give it [the secret of the breeding] to all your friends!" They laughed in assent. Calvin Reese suggested that rather than all this talk it would be better to take the stranger out into the yard and show him some birds and their characteristics.

Outside forty cocks jerkily paced and pecked at the ends of tethers that led to small wooden tepees where they could take shelter. From the looks of the grounds, though, they must have spent the majority of their time doing just what I now saw, for there were grooves in the dirt and grass where the birds had walked around and around, searching perhaps for food, restless in the clamorous company of their fellows. Here and there scurried Holly's dog, a Queensland heeler named Blue. "Blue thinks it's his job to keep the yard in good shape," Holly said. "He'll run a cat outta here, and if he catches it"—*pop*! he snapped his leathery fingers—"he'll kill it. The main thing is, he won't let the roosters fight. Here," he said, untying a rooster and cradling it in his arm, "watch this." He walked the rooster over to another one still tethered. As soon as they saw each other they crowed savagely and strained for contact, at which Blue raced in and chivvied the tethered one back to its tepee.

"Think we make these roosters fight?" Holly asked in a challenge of his own. "You listen to the Humane Society, they'll tell you that. Well, you can't make a bird fight if he don't want to, and that's a fact you can write down. Watch this." And again he introduced the cradled rooster to the tethered one. Again they yearned toward each other, and Blue sailed in as peacemaker. The four men smiled.

Nick Zacharios walked me around the yard, explaining as he went. "The combs and wattles are dubbed off when they get to be stags," he told me. "What's a stag? A stag is a rooster a year old. He moults from July to December, and after that he's a cock. Here," picking up a stag, "see these scales on the legs? They won't be there when he's a cock. Then under here," pulling up a glossy wing, "he'll grow a second row of feathers here. And his legs'll be a good deal harder." He talked about conditioning, standing there in the sunny yard, the spur on his chest glinting dully as he stroked the stag that lay quietly in his big arm. There were many theories, he said, "but basically what you're doing is building stamina and strength, not bulk. It's not like your pro football lineman where you have to have a certain amount of bulk to be able to hold off your man. You want to train a rooster so he'll be tight and lean and with a minimum of fat on him.

"One of the basics is to walk him a lot every day. The best rooster is the farm-walked one, but nowadays there aren't that many opportunities for farm-walking. But you still want to put his feed where he has to work to get it. Some will walk 'em up a ladder. Some guys'll rig up a mattress to run 'em on. Another thing is you work your birds with sparring muffs on." (Later he showed me these, small leather items that fit over the sawed-off spurs and resembled tiny boxing gloves.) "You're trying to develop ring generalship in them along with the stamina and strength."

In my reading some other training practices had struck me as unusual, but here in the face of so much well-intentioned tutelage I forgot to bring them up. I had read, for instance, that a cocker might poke a bird with an ice pick, both to test its reaction to pain and to condition him to it. I had read, too, of the practice of cutting off a bird's legs, the idea here being to see if it would then "face" an unmutilated bird. The mutilated bird would, of course, have to be destroyed, but if it did face, that would augur well for the gameness of his siblings. A cocker I met at the Kemper Marley Tribute the next day said he'd never heard of the ice pick method of conditioning, but he had known of cockers who had applied the drastic technique of amputation. As for himself, he said he would never use it, "because even if a mutilated bird shows game, it isn't certain his siblings will.

"You'll find guys," he continued, "who'll take a bird who's had a real hard fight on Saturday, and then on Sunday, after he's had time to sit and get real sore, they'll take him out and let another bird have a go at him. Just to see how he reacts. Some guys'll do this two, three days in a row. I don't do it because I'm not sure what it proves. All I ask is that on Saturday night the bird gives me all he's got. If he does that, I don't care what else he does. And another thing here: gameness isn't *every-thing*. Of course, you've got to have it, but you've got to have other things, too. A bird can be game all the way through, and I can have a bird who'll run when he's hit, and yet he'll beat that dead-game bird because he's a better fighter."

We stood now beside a long, windowless structure from inside which came the loud sounds of a radio. It was, Zacharios explained, a cockhouse. Part of the training of a gamecock involves conditioning him to the ferocious din of the pit, and the radio was reminding them of this tumult. At the same time it was oddly restful for them, Zacharios said.

We moved on past the cockhouse to the feed barrels, where we were joined by Calvin Reese. "If a man's got a solid reputation as a cocker," Nick Zacharios said, "you'll hear him often referred to as a 'good feeder.' That's because feeding is the single most important thing." Reese opened one of the waist-high barrels and dipped his hand in, bringing out some cracked corn and offering it to me for inspection.

"See," he said, "no dope. The Humane Society, the RSPCA, and I don't know who all will tell you we dope our birds to make 'em more vicious and so they won't feel pain. That's a lot of crap! Look here: this is all good, clean food. Cracked corn. And here's maple peas. And this one's got ... "—pausing as he looked into another barrel, then scooping out a handful of pellets—"this is an alfalfa-based pellet. Over here's Canadian peas. You're feeding for muscle, and your diet should be anywhere between eighteen and twenty-three percent protein."

Since the object of all this training and feeding is to win, it seemed appropriate here to ask about the money that might be won and how the betting was arranged. At derbies, I was told, the amount to be won depended on the number of entries; at the Kemper Marley tomorrow, the purse might be over $100,000, though it might also be split several ways if there should be a tie. As for the wagering itself, I was told the house keeps no book, operates no windows. "It's just me and you," Calvin Reese said, sifting some cracked corn from one hand to the other.

"It's wagering," Nick Zacharios said. "The betting in the big derbies is usually on the man. The spectators there will know the cockers, and they'll bet on the man they think is better, has a better reputation. Now, if the two men are about equal, then they'll bet the roosters according to their breeding, which they can tell by looking. Oh, there's some that have pet schemes, and so forth; some won't bet black roosters, and what have you. And if there should be a difference in weights, they'll bet that. Most times there won't be that much of a [weight] difference, but sometimes there is. The roosters're matched as evenly as possible. At the lower weights, you might sometimes have to give an ounce or two, but you sure as hell hate to. At six pounds, though, it doesn't make any difference if you give an ounce or so."

Jackie was telling stories in the background, his voice swelling louder as he warmed to the narrative flow. Zacharios stopped trying to educate me, and we all turned to listen to Jackie as he told how recently he'd crept up behind a neighborhood kid who was peeping on Jackie's teen-aged daughter. "I put my pistol up behind his ear," Jackie laughed, "and I kind of whispered to him, 'you're a dead mother-fucker.' He 'bout shit his pants! 'Oh, please, Mr. Kendall, don't shoot! I won't ever do it again!' 'You shoulda thought about that when you were peeping on my daughter,' I tell him. Actually, he's a pretty good kid, and I can assure you I haven't had any trouble with him since.

"There are others, though, in that neighborhood that're just trouble. Once I hired one of 'em to mow my lawn, and before he was half done he comes to me and wants his pay. I said, 'Why don't you finish the job, and then I'll pay you.' He got nasty. He said, 'If you don't pay me right away, I'll come back some night and throw a brick right through your picture window!' Can you beat it? So I just look at him real quiet-like"—giving us a flat, level stare—"and I say to him, 'You just do that. You throw a brick through that window, and I'll slit your bag and run your leg through it.' He looks at me and says, 'What's that supposed to mean?' I say, 'Well, you got a bag down there, don't ya, holds your nuts? Well, see this knife? You break my window, I'll slit your bag with this knife and run your leg through it.' He ran home and told his mother, and she called me. She said she'd never heard such language in all her life. I just laughed." He did so again, and we all joined in.

• • •

The afternoon had been a stunning barrage of instruction, exhortation, and anecdote, and through it all Calvin Reese had let the others do most of the talking. Now we sat in his pickup in front of his house, the blue haze of a Phoenix winter evening gathering around us like a great serape. He was wondering what questions I had. "We've spent all of our afternoon," he said, giving me what I was coming to recognize as his stare of challenge (rather like a gamecock's), "telling you this and that about gamecocks, and so forth. Why don't *you* ask some questions now, instead of sitting over there with your finger up your ass." It was not, I felt, meant personally, and I tried to indicate I hadn't taken it so by answering that I was still far too ignorant to have any intelligent questions to ask, but that after the first round tomorrow I was certain I'd have some.

"Well, shit!" he said, leaning back in his seat. "You can't expect us to teach you all you need to know about all this," his hand gesturing vaguely out toward the world beyond the truck's cab, "in a few hours, or even a few days—or *years*, for that matter. It takes a lifetime living around others who do this to understand what we're doing. There's two thousand years going into all of this. No man alive knows it all, though each of us likes to think we do. You ask any man there tomorrow, and *he* thinks he knows all about it. If he did, I guess there wouldn't be any point in having any more fights, at least with his birds."

I said it was clear to me now that cockfighting was a great deal more complex than I had supposed. And I meant this, for I had come to understand, even in my ignorance, that Reese and the others saw themselves as sportsmen in an ancient tradition. In their own view they were entitled to no less honor than that routinely accorded trainers of boxers or racehorses. And if they struck me as outwardly prosaic men, there was something of the poetic—and perhaps even the mystical—in their attachment to those fiercely beautiful creatures I had seen them with this afternoon. You could see it in the way they handled them, stroking the glistening feathers, cradling the little, rock-solid bodies in their big hands as if they had been handling a baby—or a woman. I had learned from Smith and Daniel's book something of the sexual symbolism of the cocks and cockfighting, that in Greek folklore the cock had symbolized the sun, sex, and resurrection. I could now readily believe this, having seen the birds and their owners talking obsessively about them, quietly and gently brooding over them. I was also willing to entertain a comparison between this sport that so often ended in death and the concentration camps of the large-scale chicken farmers. And what, in truth, was the difference if cruelty to the creatures was the essential issue? Whatever else it was, cockfighting involved a great deal more than throwing two roosters and some money into a pit.

"When you get to the point of what's called the 'drag fight,'" Calvin Reese was saying, "—and this is one of the main things the Humane Society is death on, like it was the whole idea, you know—well, the drag fight's where breeding will show up: breeding for endurance, for heart, for gameness. That's what'll make a winner there.

"Why the drag fight? Well, you know, after twelve rounds of a championship [prize] fight they could use a ring only ten feet square. Well, it's the same with the cocks: they don't need the larger pit, so we put 'em off to the side in a smaller pit and let 'em fight it out. They're tired and can't move around that much." When a bird took three consecutive short counts and a long one without fighting back, the fight was declared over. Usually, Reese said, but not always, this meant the loser was either dead or dying. He saw nothing either cruel or unusual in this and warned me to reserve judgment until I had seen for myself the incredible gameness of the wounded birds struggling to the death in the drag pit. You could not, he claimed, truly understand cockfighting until you could understand this particular aspect of it.

183

Nor did the humane societies really understand what they were opposing, he said, citing in particular the animal protection groups in Great Britain who, so he claimed, had greatly abridged personal freedoms there. In the neighboring yard the breadwinner had just returned home with his ghetto blaster at full bore. A male voice sang of the joys of love to come, but Calvin Reese appeared not to notice the sudden and uproarious entertainment offered the entire street. He wanted to tell me about the meaning of personal freedom.

"We have a governor here now; to read the papers you'd think he was just trouble, wouldn't you? Do you know Evan Meacham? I do. I know him pretty well, and I can tell you he's a good man. Maybe talks a bit more than necessary—but who doesn't? And you know what's got him in the most trouble? He said that with the deficit this state already has he couldn't see giving the black people a holiday that would cost the state—oh, I don't know what figure he gave, but it was sizeable. And I'll tell you, I have to agree. Martin Luther King never did a thing for this country. Never fought a battle. A lot of trouble, that's what. And for saying this, he's got the newspapers on his ass. Ev-er-y day they just *hammer*.

"I know you're a writer and all that, but I'll tell you I have very mixed feelings about freedom of the press. They abuse their freedom. More people have been killed by the pen than the sword. What do you think?" We got out of the pickup into the rapidly cooling evening. "I'm stiff," Reese muttered, mostly to himself. He faced me again and shook his finger at me over the hood of the truck. "I've come to wonder if the best system isn't a dictator—if you could get a good one."

• • •

Avondale, the site of the Kemper Marley Tribute, lies southwest of Phoenix at the tag end of the Estrella Mountains. As we drove toward it morning fog was lifting off the mountaintops. In the uncertain, gray light Mexican workers were already in the fields of broccoli and cauliflower, huddled in hooded sweatshirts and wearing baseball caps against the later certainty of sun. We turned west along a dirt road, and then suddenly dead ahead loomed the giant statue of a gamecock perched atop an iron beam and beneath this, in bold letters, the legend COPPER STATE HOME OF CHAMPIONS. Beyond, I could see the parking lot, already half full. A metal barrel had been set up in it and filled with stove wood, and a group of men stood around it, their hands stretched toward its heat.

Inside the long, high arena were steeply sloped stands and concession booths. Signs warned against gambling and abusive language. The floor of the main pit was brightly lit and neatly chalked, and in its opposing corners stood ready the plastic water jugs the handlers would use to refresh their birds during the fights. The gathering crowd milled about, greeting one another, slapping backs, drinking coffee, smoking. Most were men, but a few wives had come along. There were no children. Concession booths offered souvenir jackets, caps, T-shirts, and oil-on-velvet paintings of cocks and cockers. A small group was gathered at the booth of a Filipino man selling "Slasher Knives Made from High-Pressure Steel." The steel itself, he told his listeners, was made from .50-caliber machine-gun cartridges. "These," he told us in a conversational tone, "are what the Hawaiian boys like to fight with." In the next booth a man offered to polish, clean, and sharpen gaffs on his electric whetstone for five dollars a pair. Do the cockers come to you after each fight? I asked. "The smart ones do," he said with a smile. "Of course, I highly recommend it."

Being introduced around the arena by Calvin Reese proved a mixed advantage. On the one hand, no strangers are ever permitted at these events, and the screening at the gate would have done full credit to the most vigilant of airport security forces, so without Reese's sponsorship I would have been barred. On the other hand, Reese's introduction usually ran something like, "This is Fred Turner. Fred doesn't know his ass from a green apple, but we're going to try to educate him a little." The people would smile then, but a bit quizzically. Why, their faces asked, is Calvin introducing us to this oaf? Then Calvin would say, "Fred's a free-lance writer, and … " But well before he could finish his explanation the curtain had been dropped, the smiles had vanished, and a hard light had entered the men's eyes. Reese could never explain enough, and so for the rest of that day and the next I roamed the arena a marked man, fixed by the inhospitable stares of those who knew what I was doing there. You could hardly blame them.

The Kemper Marley Tribute was a twelve-cock derby, which meant that each entrant pledged to fight twelve cocks; the man with the most winners took the pot. The master of ceremonies explained this over the PA system, standing in the brightly lit, freshly raked main pit, resplendent in his powder-blue tuxedo and ruffled shirt. When he had finished, a phonograph recording of "The Star Spangled Banner" roared into the chilly air, and the entire arena came to reverent attention, hats held over hearts, all eyes on the American flag that had been run up a short staff at one end of the building. Unlike the same ceremony at a college football or professional baseball game, here there was no talking, no surreptitious horseplay. When the anthem's last strain had crackled off into silence the crowd shuffled, then sat.

But not for long, for the announcer was now into his introduction of Kemper Marley. Marley was by then in his eighties, in himself the quintessential story of the modern American West. He had begun as a penniless cowboy and was now a man of immense wealth and power whose interests included liquor, cotton, cattle, sheep, real estate, and frozen food. Years before, Marley had been a target of reporter Don Bolles of the *Arizona Republic*, who was doing investigative work on the infiltration of organized crime into Arizona. On June 2, 1976, a bomb exploded in Bolles's car in a Phoenix parking lot, tearing the reporter to pieces, and whatever Bolles had developed on Kemper Marley went to the grave with him. Now Marley rose, kinglike, from his ringside seat, supporting himself with a blackthorn walking stick whose golden head was in the shape of a long-billed duck. As a wave of applause showered down on the old man, Calvin Reese reminded me of the Bolles case. "I don't care what you heard about that," he said. "They never turned up a damned thing. Don Bolles was a political hatchet man and a mean son-of-a-bitch!"

Around the edges of the pit the arcane system of wagering was now in process, cries and responses booming across the pit and running up through the stands, hand signals exchanged, quick consultations made. Meanwhile in the pit, two men cradling their feathered warriors faced each other from their respective score lines, one holding what I was told was a "roundhead," the other a "gray." At the referee's cry of "Pit!" the birds exploded from their handlers' hands, coming together in a clash of wings and bodies with the sound of a muffled pistol shot. Such was the force of their contact that they both recoiled from it, but hardly had they hit the ground before they had gathered themselves for another onslaught. This time the roundhead rose in the air above the trajectory of the gray and used this leverage to strike so effectively that it buried at least one of its gaffs in the gray's body. This was a "handle," which meant the handlers had to carefully disentangle the birds and return them to the score lines, from which they eyed each other with red malevolence. The gray appeared to me unhurt, but Calvin Reese assured me it had been, and the shouts around us in the stands confirmed this.

Again at the referee's "Pit!" the roundhead successfully repeated its previous tactic, although this time the birds did not get hung up. Instead they rolled across the dirt in a bewildering tangle of feathers, slashing and pecking at each other while their handlers hovered above them, the men's arms, held out tensely from their sides, oddly like wings themselves. Now the roundhead was atop the gray, and again it embedded a gaff: another handle and afterward another clashing contact, this one tellingly closer to the score line of the gray. Here the roundhead scored again and again without effective opposition.

Each time it was brought back to the score line, the gray's head drooped a bit lower. Yet, though clearly on the defensive since the second contact of the fight, it still showed remarkable stamina, continuing to join the battle just when the uninitiated observer would have thought it had nothing left to give, not even heart. But all its game responses met with the same result: the roundhead would fling it down, then plant a foot on the gray's neck and search with darting bill for an eye. At last it found one, and the dark fluid drooled along the partially opened beak of the gray and dropped heavily into the dirt. Now the cries of the wagerers subsided. The death was coming; it was only a matter of time. When the handler brought it back to the score line, you could see the gray's feet hanging stiffly while the man tried to blow some life back into the tattered and reddened body.

The pit was littered with smashed and torn gray feathers as the referee announced that the long (and final) count was coming. If the gray could not come off its line and show fight, the match was over. The count reached twenty, and the inevitable roundhead came for the gray again. The bird's beak dipped into the dirt as the roundhead struck once. The gray staggered up from its line, made a blind, undirected move, then fell on its side. Its body heaved once but not again. The cockers picked up their birds, shook hands, and one patted the other on the back as they exited.

187

In the stands there was movement as the losers walked their money over to the winners. Until this moment not so much as a handshake had formalized the wagers, yet no exchange at a race track's $100 window could have been more orderly. For these people, Calvin Reese said, a look and a sign across the seats constituted a more solemn agreement than any piece of paper ever could. Later near the concession booths, I spoke to a leathery little man about the remarkable decorum and probity of these exchanges between men betting hundreds of dollars. He looked at me squarely from beneath the dusty bill of a cap with a feed company logo on its panel and said, "There ain't a man here any less game or square than his birds."

• • •

When talking with a stranger, cockers like to use analogies that run from their sport to horse racing and boxing. There are, to be sure, pockets of the American population where racing is regarded as a shabby and criminally tinged business, and even larger pockets that are repulsed by what the late Red Smith used to call the "sweet science." Still, these sports enjoy regular newspaper and television coverage; I had noted this day, however, that whereas the Phoenix papers listed badminton matches in the sports pages' fine print, no mention was made of the Kemper Marley Tribute. This inequity was not the only difficulty I had with these analogies. But one strand of the cockfighting/horse racing analogy I did find valid: both sports are finally boring if you have no money invested in the outcomes. In an afternoon at the track you are initially compelled by the flash and spectacle of it all, those masses of splendid muscle whipping past, the color of the silks, the building roar of the crowd. But if you're not betting, the spectacle becomes repetitious sooner than you want to believe. So with cockfights, and as the day wore on and the water in the pit's plastic jugs took on the ruddy hue of apple cider I found myself losing interest. Mentally I pinched myself. Here was life versus death I was witnessing, and how often, I asked, is this contest so nakedly on display? I was willing to admit that my ignorance was a factor, that I simply did not know enough to remain interested by attending to the sport's finer points. And that same ignorance prevented me from entering the wagering, for I had worked at a track in my youth, and I had learned there that only a fool will bet on a contest he poorly comprehends. So I kept my money in my wallet and wandered over to the drag pits to witness life versus death in that severely restricted venue.

The regular wagerers, of course, routinely made the trip from the stands to the drag pits to see the outcomes of matches transferred there. Here there was no shouting, very little talk even, but instead a silent intensity at odds with the hubbub in the stands. In this arena, as Calvin Reese had said, both birds and spectators were tired.

Coming from the main pit a bird handled by one of the country's top cockers had had a distinct advantage. The bird handled by a Mexican kid had been on the defensive and had been badly mauled, yet the kid's bird hung on so long that at last the referee signaled them to the drag pit. Now the handlers faced each other in the small iron-barred enclosure, the top cocker, a pale man in a jumpsuit and with marcelled hair, the Mexican kid in a flannel shirt hanging out over his worn jeans. The kid's father coached him in a quiet, tense voice from just outside the railing: "Blow down his back, Jimmy! Pinch his wings! Keep his head up, Jimmy!" But as in the main pit, it looked like a losing battle. Jimmy's bird's responses became progressively enfeebled and ill directed until finally it would not attack at all but merely awaited the next charge of the bright-plumaged aggressor. Then suddenly it appeared miraculously to revive after a twenty-second rest period and flew at its assailant, striking both gaffs into the glossy chest. Down in the dust went the other and rolled on his side. The referee gave the count as the cockers retrieved their birds. The marcelled man's doughy face showed no emotion at this unlooked-for turn. He stroked his bird's legs firmly and evenly, while a few feet away the kid's father hoarsely exclaimed, "That's the way, Jimmy! That's it! See, he's coming back for you!" But Jimmy's dark eyes looked sad as he wiped his nose on his flannel sleeve. He looked as if he didn't share his father's optimistic assessment of the situation.

He was right. His cock's fight had been spent in that last Pyrrhic charge. Again and again the bird was rolled in the dust by the first peck of its adversary. Now one eye was gone, and its head was pecked to raw, hanging shreds. The kid's ministrations took on a terminal fervor; his father stopped his coaching. Jimmy blew his breath into the dying creature's slackly opened mouth, inserted his thumb there to give the cock something to clamp down on. In the other corner the top cocker confidently stroked his bird, smoothing its feathers, holding the bird lightly at the throat with thumb and forefinger. Though clearly tired and hurt, the cock's eyes snapped savagely at its opponent. Twice the kid's bird beat the long count by showing some fight, summoned up from what ultimate cache of rage or instinct I could not imagine. But again it failed three successive ten-counts, and now the long count was upon him.

"Long count coming," the referee intoned. Jimmy furiously stroked and blew, tried to tease some life back into the huddle of feathers he held in his hand. But when he set the bird on the center score line, it just lay there. "Winner!" said the referee. Jimmy looked over his shoulder at his father and shook his head once slightly.

● ● ●

On the derby's second day I witnessed a swift kill in the main pit. After the birds had been billed (introduced to each other), there had been but a single handle when the gray cock had flown at its orange-and-black opponent and struck it such a deft, decisive blow that it knocked the other against the wooden board of the pit's side where it lay kicking senselessly, flopping from side to side, unable to right itself. Then the three ten-counts, between which the mortally stricken bird's handler took trips to the water jug, bathed the bird's head, and dabbed at it with a sponge. But at the final, long count it just lay on the line, its beak dipping convulsively into the dirt. Its handler, a Hispanic with a small gray moustache, sunglasses, and an old Dodgers cap, picked his bird up by the feet and left the pit. I followed him down the dimly lit hall beneath the stands to where the cockers housed their birds in wooden cages. When I had overtaken him I asked whether I might talk with him. "Sure," he said evenly, continuing to walk, the cock now cradled in his arm with its head hanging limply. Could he tell right away, I asked, that his bird had taken a mortal hit? You couldn't always tell, he answered over his shoulder as we moved along the corridor to Room 93, which he and his partner had reserved for the derby. But on this occasion he could: "When you see those pin feathers fly, you know he's been hurt bad."

His partner opened the door from within, received the bird, and while I talked with the man in the Dodgers cap he removed the gaffs from the cock's legs, the slow blood dripping from the dressing table onto the cement floor. From the two tiers of wooden cages I could hear the rustle of the team's remaining birds. The handler was telling me that his father and older brother had been at this game for a long time but that until fairly recently he himself had been only marginally involved. "But," he said, "I got tired of doing body and fender work. That's dangerous work, breathing all that stuff all day. Anyway, I'm into it now. I raised fifty birds, and I found out that's just too many. Too much work, plus I don't have that much space. Got a half-acre. You need more than that for fifty birds, because the less space you got, the more you get diseases that spread.

"There's guys here that have really *huge* operations. I mean, there's guys here who don't even do the training and the feeding for their birds—got guys who do that for 'em. And I'll tell you, it's a lot of work to raise these things the right way."

I wondered aloud if he was saying that the outcomes of these apparently equal matches might be predetermined in part by economics. "Say I'm rich enough," I supposed, "to have a big country spread, choice feed, trainers, and so on. Does that mean that you can't really compete with me, that eight times out of ten my birds will beat yours?"

"No, not really. Because in a derby I just might not fight you. It's the weights, it's the luck of the draw who you happen to fight. Now, it just so happens that so far I've drawn tough competitors. *Tough*. So, I've lost. Next time, who knows?" He shrugged.

I said I'd read somewhere that cockfighting was the only sport that couldn't be fixed, the only fair contest left in America. Did he believe that? Well, he wasn't willing to speak about sports he didn't intimately know. "But we know a fight can be fixed, and a race; and the Patriots, they say, were all coked up when they played the Bears in the Super Bowl." He spread wide his arms as a way of saying, This is the way things are. "If I've got the right bird, I'll beat yours, I don't care who you are."

The naked bulb just above his cap threw down a shroud of shadow over his face, and the eyes behind the shades were utterly impenetrable. His partner had left the cubicle, and the cocker stood now, at ease, waiting patiently for my next question. From somewhere down the hall a cock sounded its testy challenge, and all along the hall it was sporadically taken up.

"Is that bird dead?" I asked, nodding at the cock I had so lately seen in the glare of the pit. It lay now on the floor beneath the dressing table, a little blot of blood darkening under it and seeping dully into the cement.

"No," he said, glancing briefly at the cock. "Not yet. I was just waiting for you to finish and go away so I could pull his head off and end his suffering."

Buying the West—and Selling It: Two Versions

In a regional version of the nationally popular *Megatrends*, a Western-states think tank reported in 1989 that the West was in the process of shedding its cowboys-and-Indians image. "We've changed," said the think tank's president, "from the Marlboro man, rugged-guy-on-a-horse image, to a more urbane, Mark Harmon, fishing-on-public-lands type thing." The claim strikes me as just as spurious as many that are made in *Megatrends*, though there is no doubt that in places like Boulder or Aspen poseurs aplenty can be found who wish to convey sartorially the impression that they are much more at home hiking the high lonesome than riding the dusty range looking at the ass end of a cow. But it will be a very long time before this newer image (supposing its intellectual reality) supplants the older one, and even if this should eventually occur in the West itself, it will never, I think, change the image of the West in other regions of the country—or in Europe, which appears wedded for-ever to cowboys and Indians. From these outlying regions of America and from Europe as well, people still visit the American West because they believe in the realities of cowboys and Indians; they believe, too, in the possibility of encountering some whisper or vestige of those great, bygone days.

To some forever unascertainable extent, this undying image owes something to the work of two Anglos from the hardwood forests of the Northeast. James Willard Schultz (1859–1947) was born in upstate New York, and Will James (1892–1942) in a provincial Quebec town. Both were drawn to the West because of Westerns they had read in childhood and because of what their imaginations had built out of that reading. Both ended up in Montana: Schultz lived among the Blackfeet and shared with them the last moments of their horse-and-buffalo glory; James punched cows and trapped wild horses on the fringes of the Blackfeet's old domain up near the Canadian border. Subsequently both men fash-ioned prolific literary careers based on their youthful experiences. Schultz wrote more than forty books, while James wrote twenty-four in a career of less than twenty years. In their times, both men enjoyed considerable popularity; James was at one point in the early 1930s about as well known a "cowboy" as Tom Mix. And both left behind classic books of the West: Schultz's *My Life as an Indian* (1907) and James's *Lone Cowboy* (1930).

Here, then, are two men who for better or worse fully bought the image of the Old Wild West and then successfully retailed it to several generations of American readers. If those readers were caught up in the dramas of *My Life as an Indian* and *Lone Cowboy*, so the authors of these books were themselves in imaginative and emotional thrall to that so perishable world they had once and fleetingly been privileged to experience.

I
INDIAN

July 1877, and the Missouri River steamer *Benton* had at last arrived at Fort Benton, Montana Territory. It was barely a year since the Sioux and the Cheyennes had spoiled the nation's centennial celebration by rubbing out Custer and a majority of the Seventh Cavalry on the Greasy Grass some two hundred miles south in the same territory, and the memory of this impossible reversal of the historical tide was still fresh and raw throughout the West. White hegemony had popularly been supposed firmly established there, but Little Big Horn proved the tribes were still unruly and untamed. Indeed, on their upriver crawl the passengers of the *Benton* had seen near the mouth of the Musselshell River the ritually mutilated remains of three white men, lying among the still-smoldering wreckage of their skiff.

At the fort and its dependent town, however, there reigned for the moment the kind of loosely lashed control to which the inhabitants, red and white, were accustomed. When the steamer announced its approach with whistle and smoke, Fort Benton bellowed back with cannon, ran up its flags, assembled its important personages down at the levee, and prepared a jolly welcome for the steamer carrying long-awaited supplies of bacon, flour, sugar, tobacco, and alcohol. In the forefront of the crowd stood the two traders who had bought out the American Fur Company, handsomely gotten-up men in suits and cravats, and ranged behind them were their employees—clerks, carpenters, bull whackers, mule skinners. There were also some independent traders there, and trappers and hunters in buckskin and moccasins with kit-fox caps and powder-and-ball six-shooters stuck in their sashes. Other interested parties included Keno Bill, who ran the saloon and gambling hall and the local madam and her girls. Behind the whites were some Blackfeet Indians—young men who had responded to the whistle and ridden down to see the show, Indian women in one way or another attached to white men here, and Indian beggars and alcoholics of the sort the Cheyennes contemptuously referred to as "hang-about-the-forts people." Beyond the adobe fort, the little town, and the camps of the traders, trappers, and hunters scattered out along the flats, was an encampment of several hundred lodges of the Pikuni Blackfeet who had been gathering here for days in anticipation of the steamer's arrival. Under the barrage of sound from the steamer's whistle, the fort's cannon, and the whoops of the welcoming whites the Pikuni ponies milled restlessly on the flats, and the camp dogs howled.

Among the *Benton*'s passengers who trundled down the gangplank that day was a young man a month short of his eighteenth birthday who had shipped from St. Louis where his uncle managed the Planter's Hotel, then famed throughout the whole region as the haunt of Western veterans, rivermen, drummers, and assorted sporting types who knew where the action was. The uncle had supplied the young man with letters of introduction to the principal traders here, and now James Willard Shults (he would later change the spelling) presented these and was ushered into Fort Benton society in the hearty and unceremonious Western way.

He was a somewhat curious fellow, this young Schultz: prominent nose, soft mouth, receding chin, and yet with something bold, defiant even, in his brown eyes. He was, to be sure, an innocent, a pilgrim, a greenhorn. In these late days of the Old West more and more of these unlearned newcomers were to be encountered out here where they seemed to have no business being: Eastern sportsmen, for instance, who had been assured that, Little Big Horn or no, the menace of the tribes was a thing of the past and the hunting was still fabulous; photographers lugging their huge, clumsy contraptions into the wilds, compelled to record with the new technology the same stupendous natural phenomena that had earlier inspired Catlin, Miller, Bodmer, and Bierstadt; touring European nobility; increasing streams of immigrant settlers who had been sold on the idea that the West was not a "Great Desert" but a garden instead; and the first of the land speculators and timber walkers whose hard eyes had appraised other regions and now were bent on assessing these new Western realities. Young Schultz was none of these. From St. Louis, where he was spending his summer with his uncle following graduation from high school, he had written his mother for money to go up the Missouri to hunt buffalo. Here, it seemed, was another of the lad's vagaries—but from the first there had been more to it than that.

From his childhood in the upstate New York town of Boonville he had been rebellious, irreverent, drawn to hunting, guns, the deep woods. Much later, he would write that the

> love of wild life and adventure was born in me, yet I must have inherited it from some remote ancestor, for all my near ones were staid, devout people. How I hated the amenities and con-ventions of society; from my earliest youth I was happy only when out in the great forest which lay to the north of my home, far beyond the sound of church and school bell, and the whistle of locomotives.

His father, Philander Shults, was indeed a staid, prosperous produce merchant, but he understood and sympathized with his son's outdoor inclinations and arranged for him to be taken on outings into the Adirondacks. Already in this portion of America civilization had so overwhelmed and surrounded the wilderness that the few remnant patches of wild lands could come at last to be regarded in a new and favorable perspective, as places of recreational as well as economic value, and Philander Shults evidently saw the Adirondacks as a good place for the training of a fractious son. But then the father died when "Willie" was ten, and it is possible to surmise from the biographical information we have that the boy suffered thereafter from the lack of a firm and understanding masculine presence in his household. He got into scrapes at Sunday school and grade school and was eventually packed off to Peekskill Military Academy on the Hudson, where it was thought the martial routines would be just the thing for him. Not so. Schultz proved an indifferent cadet, happier off campus than on, and certainly no candidate for West Point, which is what his guardians hoped for him. On his last day at Peekskill he fired off the campus cannon, shattering not only the nearby windows but also any lingering hopes that he might one day take his place in the Long Gray Line. It was probably with a mutual sense of relief that Schultz left Boonville late in the spring of '77 for St. Louis.

But if Schultz had been an indifferent student in his schools, he was nonetheless an apt learner in other, nonacademic ways, and out in St. Louis he quickly caught the excitement still emanating from the West. In those despised school years he had read the Lewis and Clark journals, Catlin, Parker, Frémont, and others, and their words and images had thrilled him as nothing else did. Now at the Planter's Hotel he came into contact with those who had themselves actually seen what the early explorers told of. But along with that excitement Schultz caught something else as well, and this was the sound of doom, of the end of the old ways. As early as the 1830s Catlin had predicted that the tribes, the buffalo, "and every living thing else" were doomed "to fall before the destroying hands of mighty man." Presumably he meant the mighty white man, but in any case, his was one voice in an incrementally swelling chorus singing of the swift destruction of the Old West. The young man heard that chorus, and it set him afire to get out there before the whole grand show should vanish as if by a showman's sleight of hand.

In those days Fort Benton was the head of navigation for the upper Missouri. The trip out from St. Louis was some 2,300 snag-and-sandbar-filled miles and took forty-four days if all went well. In the case of the steamer *Far West*, from which Schultz transferred (and which, incidentally, brought down the news of the Custer disaster), and the *Benton*, no major mishaps occurred, though the boats did have to be "grasshoppered" over numerous mudbanks. During these tedious stretches Schultz could console himself by looking out on the very scenes painted by Catlin and Bodmer: the weirdly eroded buttes and castles along the river; the breaks that gave suddenly long vistas into the hinterlands; antelopes, wolves, grizzly bears, and, always, the buffalo—standing in motionless clumps on the hills, moving to water along the flats, swimming the river, stranded on shelving bits of sand beneath the bluffs, drowned and decomposing on shallow bars. At the sight of such shaggy plenitude Schultz's heart leapt up. So it was a lie, then! The buffalo could not be endangered by the siege of the hunters: there were still far too many of them left to

197

suggest any threat to this ponderous, animate basis of Plains life.

The wilder and more gamy the river scenes on the *Benton*'s upriver progress, the more Schultz yearned to get ashore to hunt and explore. He pestered the captain with his requests—until the ship came upon that smoldering scene at the mouth of the Musselshell, after which Schultz found he was able to keep his tongue behind his teeth. And then, at last, the arrival at Fort Benton, and Schultz stepped out onto the land of his dreams—flags, cannon, Indians, whores, and all. "For me," he was to write many years later, "life really began that day in 1877 when I jumped from the deck of the steamer *Benton* to the levee at Ft. Benton."

His guide into this new life was one of the assembled there on the levee that July day: Joseph Kipp, a mixed-blood trader ten years Schultz's senior. Kipp—Raven Quiver to the Blackfeet—had been born to this life. His mother was Sahkwi Ahki, "Earth Woman," daughter of the Mandan chief Mahtotopa, "Four Bears," of whom Catlin had so much to say and whose full-length portrait he painted. Kipp's father, James, was Canadian by birth and one of the most famous of the early traders in the upper Missouri country. He had moved among the tribes there for more than forty years, had several Indian wives, numerous children, and retired, scalp intact, around 1860. Both Catlin and Prince Maximilian of Wied, the German naturalist-explorer, encountered this singular man and left accounts of his resourcefulness. As far as Schultz was concerned, had he scoured the whole of the Plains region he could not have come upon another man more uniquely qualified to introduce him to the strange and intricate realities of this half-white/half-red life than James Kipp's son. Others would befriend Schultz as well: the white trader the Pikunis called Sorrel Horse, and Sorrel Horse's Indian wife; old Hugh Monroe, who in more than a half-century as scout, interpreter, trader, and squaw man had experienced almost every aspect of Plains life and was now in his final incarnation as a mighty liar; and one of Monroe's many grandchildren, William Jackson. But first and last, Schultz's fortunes were linked with those of Joe Kipp; together they would see the decline and fall of the Blackfeet nation, and with that the end of something.

• • •

The Pikunis, with whom Schultz would have his firmest familiarity, were part of the three confederated tribes that made up the Blackfeet nation along with the Kainahs (Bloods), the Siksikas (Blackfeet), and the Piegans. The nation claimed as theirs a stretch of territory from the North Saskatchewan River in Canada to the Yellowstone River in the south, from the Rockies in the west to just east of the Bear Paw Mountains. Population figures for them before 1900 are conjecture, but, though several times decimated by smallpox, at their height they might have been as many as ten thousand of the fiercest horseback nomads west of the Sioux. Enemies, red or white, were as necessary to them as the buffalo, and with a joyous abandon they fought the whites, the Crows, Assiniboines, Gros Ventres, Kutenais, Crees, and Snakes (Shoshonis).

It wasn't always so, for the Blackfeet, like the Sioux and Cheyennes, were migrants into the Plains, having come out of the Alberta woodlands around Lesser Slave Lake. There they had been hunters on foot, trappers, fishermen, gatherers of wild rice and berries; their faithful animal servant then had been the dog, not the horse. Thus when, around the turn of the nineteenth century, they came out onto the vast openness of the Plains, they found themselves at a critical disadvantage: there were the great herds of buffalo, but the Blackfeet hunters were too slow afoot to give effective chase and too poorly armed to kill safely when they were lucky enough to ambush or trap one of the beasts. They were like the Stone Age peoples of long-ago Europe, swarming about the ankles of a mammoth, hacking and spearing until at last it toppled and there was meat for the camps. The oldest Blackfeet traditions speak of this as a time when more of the people than the prey died in the hunting of the buffalo.

But by the time Catlin and Maximilian of Wied encountered them in the early 1830s, the Blackfeet had achieved a kind of mastery over their adopted environment. Thanks to the whites they had acquired the horse and the gun and now ranged with a lordly freedom through their territory, following the game, fighting their tribal neighbors, assaulting the few whites who trespassed on Blackfeet lands. True, their mastery was precarious, subject to occasionally severe seasonal problems, to the numbers and movements of the game, and to the accidents of a nomadic hunting existence, but on the whole they lived well. The Northern Cheyenne mixed-blood George Bent could have been speaking of the

Blackfeet as well as of his own people when he observed that the acquisition of the horse, together with the apparently endless supply of buffalo,
made the Cheyenne "one of the proudest and most independent men
that ever lived."

Mounted, the Blackfeet (and the other Plains tribes) could chase the
buffalo and other game, while the horse made the hunter less vulnerable
to the sudden, unpredictable attacks of his prey. The gun, of course, permitted the Blackfeet hunters to shoot from a safer distance, to shoot
from concealment, and to shoot with more lethal effect, although even
at the end of the 1870s Schultz said some Pikuni hunters still preferred
the bow and arrow for running buffalo. Armed either way, one man
could now do the work of many, and the meat could be transported
much greater distances back to the camps.

Now began the process of cultural elaboration that by the time of
Schultz's sojourn among the Blackfeet had made the Plains tribes into
the generic "Indian" and forever stamped these riders and raiders on the
national consciousness. Warfare, which before the Plains period had not
been central to their daily life, became for the Blackfeet a colorful, intricate, and dangerous game. Early Blackfeet myths say that before the horse
there was no warfare and that such "combat" as there was with neighboring tribes was purely symbolic and involved no actual killing. Perhaps
this is only a vague, confused memory of the more humble days when
the Blackfeet were a woodlands people on foot. In any case, by the time
we have reliable records of them in the 1830s the Blackfeet had become
devoted to what may justly be termed here the "arts" of war. Honor
came to the man whose skills on horseback and with arms made him a
feared raider against the Crows or the Assiniboines. But, though often
enough these raids against neighbors ended in death, the main thing was
not to kill so much as to conspicuously display your courage in battle. You
took with you on the warpath your most gorgeous finery, and, circumstances permitting, you donned it—beads, fringe, necklaces, paint—
before riding into battle. You took with you also your coup stick, a small,
harmless, decorated thing with which you struck an opponent, contemptuously refraining from killing him. To strike with the coup stick and
then to ride safely out of the melee, this was the height of honor—and
in the hierarchy of honor, the man who struck the first blow with the
coup stick was higher up than the man who merely killed.

Nor did the raids have any real, practical objective, for these men fought not for territory, or captives, or usable material gain. They fought to avenge a death; or they went on the warpath to steal the enemy's horses, mounts they did not really need, since they were almost always oversupplied. But mostly they fought for the pure hell of it. And it was this "motiveless" daring maybe above all that recommended the Blackfeet and the other Plains tribes to the American imagination—and still does, for in the careless, windswept freedom of the Plains raiders the rest of America may have seen something that had been lost in the New World experience as America developed: some sense that this was meant to be a place of *play* more than of drudgery, a place where the curse of sweaty-brow-equals-bread might have been lightened at last. Surely, the older settlements along the Eastern seaboard had proved places of toil and sweat. Maybe the freedom to play at life was the sovereign virtue of the West and the horse-and-buffalo nomads who roamed its spaces.

Certainly it was the playful, non-goal-oriented aspects of Blackfeet life that proved the deepest attraction for Schultz, then and forever in flight from the world of white responsibilities he had been groomed for in New York. He came to love the pace of their life, which, like that of many nomadic peoples, alternated between the sudden danger, the thrill of combat, the chase, and longer periods of relative inactivity when the camps were quiet and the people sucked the sweet marrow of life in their divinely appointed place: the backbone-of-the-world (the Rockies) standing steeply to the west, "blue-sided, sharp-peaked, snow-capped," as Schultz wrote; the smaller, softer buttes to the east; and all before them the wide brown plains on which, perhaps now just out of sight, the buffalo grazed—"our real food," as the Blackfeet referred to them.

In these placid periods between battle and running the buffalo, the women were always busy in the camps—gathering wood and water, cooking, fleshing hides, mending moccasins. But for the men, these were truly times of ease, times to lie back on the willow-frame couches in their lodges, smoke, talk, tell the old stories. Perhaps there might be a little gambling with the bones or with the hoop and wheel, perhaps a horse race. But there was no urgent sense of tomorrow, and still less of laying up riches or working at some program of individual improvement. The people never saw themselves as "getting somewhere," because in the mythic long-ago they had arrived where they were supposed to be. Here was their place, and they were supremely content within it, a contentment reflected in that playfulness and pace of life the young Schultz so fully responded to.

After some days of smoke, dreams, the peaceful passage of the sun over their lodges to its home beyond the mountains, then it would be time to run the buffalo again. Or it would be a good time to go horse stealing against the Assiniboines. Or to war to avenge a cowardly deed by the Snakes. Suddenly, the leisurely routine was violently altered. The outriders had spotted a herd of buffalo, and out went the hunters on their trained horses. When they returned, the camps were red with fresh meat and feasts were given. Or a group of men would make their elaborate preparations for the warpath, tie up their horses' tails, and then be gone many days, returning, perhaps, with fresh enemy scalps or a herd of captured horses. After such an excursion the people would know that sooner or later it would be their turn to be raided. Then they would be the ones angry over the theft of prized horses. They would mourn a death, stripping their clothes, cutting their hair, scarifying arms, fingers, legs. And so it would go on; so it had gone on since the days when Na'pi (Old Man), the Blackfeet Creator, had shaped the world.

From that first summer until 1903, when circumstances forced him into exile from the Blackfeet and Montana, Schultz tasted almost every aspect of this life. And he tasted so deeply of it that ever afterward all else seemed stale and juiceless, as if he had gone early to that shadowy, substanceless world of the departed the Blackfeet called the Sand Hills.

He went on the warpath with a group of Pikunis against the Assiniboines, taking part with the rest of the warriors in the obligatory preparatory rituals: bathing with them in the sweat lodge, smoking the pipe, invoking the Sun, Old Man, and Mother Earth for protection and guidance. Of his prayer to these "heathen" deities, Schultz recalled that he prayed "with a right good will" and that no one in the sweat lodge thought this white man anything but sincere. "I wanted to know these people," he wrote of this episode, "to know them thoroughly; and I considered that the only way to do so was for a time to live their life in every particular in order to win their confidence." Thus armed with his spiritual protections and his Henry rifle, Schultz went off against an Assiniboine camp thought to be somewhere near the mouth of the Milk River. As it happened, the party surprised some Crees going homeward from a successful raid on the Crows, and the Pikunis returned to their camp with nine enemy scalps and more than sixty horses. Later, one of the war party told him that his rifle fire had been responsible for at least one of the dead Crees. Now, said the man, you have honor in the camp, and you can take a woman. Later, Schultz did so.

But before he took his own woman in the approved Blackfeet fashion, Schultz had other typical Blackfeet adventures: he helped a young man named Wolverine steal a woman from a neighboring tribe; he ate boiled dog with the Gros Ventres and buffalo tongue in the lodges of his adopted people. Then, about 1879, he made a further commitment to Pikuni tribal life when he married a relative of Joe Kipp's Pikuni wife. Nat-ah'-ki, "Fine Shield Woman," was about fifteen, a marriage-able age in Blackfeet culture. By Schultz's account it was from the first an unusually happy marriage, the more so as it became evident to Nat-ah'-ki that Schultz's commitment to her was a real one, not the casual, callous arrangement too many white frontiersmen then preferred: the "squaw" utilized for sexual and domestic convenience, then flung aside like a worn pouch when the white man wanted to move on. In Schultz's case he even took the unusual step of having the marriage formalized by an itinerant white preacher, a gesture that meant more to Nat-ah'-ki than to Schultz since he had long before renounced Christianity. Until Nat-ah'-ki died in 1902, apparently of a heart ailment, her white man remained faithful to her, and his continuing love and grief are unmis-takable in *My Life as an Indian*, a book he evidently thought of as a memorial to her. "Ah, me!" he wrote there. "Roll them back, you ruth-less harvester of the years. Give me back my Nat-ah'-ki and my youth. Return us to our lodge and the wide, brown buffalo plains."

• • •

Always there was the buffalo. In *My Life as an Indian* Schultz left per-haps the most vivid first-hand descriptions in our language of the thrill, the danger, and the mechanics of buffalo hunting, for he himself had ridden alongside the long-haired hunters, cutting his horse into the dust-clouded, thundering midst of a stampeded herd, sighting some fat cow just behind the shoulder, then squeezing off a shot. Then to see the plain "over which they passed become dotted with the dead, with great animals standing head down, swaying, staggering, as the life blood flowed from mouth and nostrils, finally crashing over on the ground, a limp and lifeless heap. Ah! that was a sight!" On such a run, he claimed, the best hunters might kill as many as twenty or even more buffalo, though he adds that the average was "not more than three." After such a hunt "the main camp was a sanguinary sight. There were string after string of pack horses loaded down with meat and hides, and some of the hunters even slung a hide or two or a lot of meat across their saddles and perched themselves on top of that. There was blood everywhere; on the horses, along the trail, on the clothing, and even on the faces of the hunters."

Matters, clearly, had greatly changed since the not-distant days when the unhorsed people had stalked a buffalo like Stone Age hunters would a mammoth. Here was killing on an unprecedented scale and far in excess of what could be consumed by the camps themselves—even taking into account the tribes' well-documented ability to utilize virtually every inch of a buffalo carcass: horns, meat, hooves, hide, organs. Here we are confronted with the evidence of something foreign at work within Plains tribal culture and speedily consuming it like a cancer. And none knew better what that invasive thing was than the grieving man who wrote *My Life as an Indian* in 1905–6. For Schultz had not simply lived among the Blackfeet: with Joe Kipp he had been a trader among them, which is to say, alas, that he had become a traitor to the very life he loved. What had begun along the East and West Coasts more than two hundred years previous had by the 1870s reached the Plains: the disastrous trade nexus that bound the tribes to the whites in an entanglement as fatal as syphilis or smallpox. And in this Schultz and Kipp were knowing participants.

The main push of the process began with the expansion of white population in the East in the second half of the eighteenth century and the subsequent movement westward of those advance agents of white civilization, the hunter and the trapper. As long as these adventurers were working only for themselves, their numbers and ecological effects were insignificant; they lived much like the hunting tribes on whose territories they poached and were lucky if they escaped getting killed. Very few got rich. But when the traders moved out into the new lands in the wake of those few first-goers, the situation was altered. Whether the traders worked for themselves or in concert with fur companies, they initiated the process that eventuated in the exhaustion of game supplies and the destabilization of intertribal arrangements.

Typically, the trader would establish his post beyond the farthest reach of settlement, yet not so far that resupply was impossible. There he would make it known that he would supply the local natives' hunting gear and certain domestic items in exchange for the furs the natives took in hunting and trapping. If any whites were working the area, he would trade with them in the same way. The effects of this arrangement on the landscapes and cultures of the hunting tribes were revolutionary and devastating, for the trade in furs smashed the ancient balance, both between a given tribe and its land and between neighboring tribes. Before the white traders, the red hunters had taken only what game they could use themselves (and sometimes they even had trouble supplying their own needs) or what pelts they could use in barter with other tribes. Now, though, they had a market for more pelts than they could use or trade to other tribes; at the same time, they were being supplied with revolutionary technology that insured both greater kills and greater returns: metal traps, poison, guns, powder, bullet molds. Nor were these new items of the hunt all the inducement the traders had to offer. Dozens of domestic items, too, had the cumulative effect of easing some of the daily burden of the woodlands hunting life: woolen blankets and capes; steel knives; metal cookware; needles and thread; and a bewildering, gaudy panoply of gewgaws like glass beads, mirrors, vermillion, and assorted jewelry. New items, these, foreign luxuries, yet too soon to become urgent necessities that eroded old ways and encouraged a dependency on the traders. Now the tribes closest to the traders were better equipped, better armed, than those farther away and so had distinct advantages in both hunting and warfare when they decided to poach on their neighbors' lands—as eventually they would when their own became depleted of game. There is good evidence that the Sioux, the Cheyennes, and the Blackfeet were all forced out onto the Plains by those gun-wielding tribes who regularly traded with the whites.

These innovations alone would have been enough to sap the cultural vigor of the tribes, but of course there was more, for alcohol was in the trade too, firewater, and it quickly became the main, indispensable lubricant of red/white exchanges. Originally introduced as a ceremonial libation to open business proceedings and encourage goodwill, alcohol—

rum, brandy, whiskey—speedily became a mutual necessity. Those few traders scrupulous enough to eschew its use, seeing so clearly its devastating consequences, quickly found their scrupulosity a crippling business disadvantage, for the tribes would simply refuse to deal with them and would take their business to men who saw nothing wrong with throwing in several belts of viciously doctored rotgut, some of it almost lethally high in alcohol content. By the 1820s, when the trade nexus had invaded the Midwest from the East, what had begun as a preliminary social custom had degenerated into a cynical practice in which the traders routinely began negotiations by getting their customers hopelessly drunk, then bought all their furs for a couple of kegs: John Tanner, a white captured by Indians in 1789 and who lived with the Ottawa and Ojibwa for thirty years in the upper Midwest, testified to the utterly debauching effects of the whiskey trade among those tribes. After a trading drunk, he said, the Indians would wake impoverished, craving a hair of the dog that had bitten them, and the only people to whom they could turn for "help" were the traders, who were good enough to supply them—on credit—with the necessities for another season.

Under these conditions, it did not take long for a given territory to be hunted out, forcing the resident tribes to move into the lands of their neighbors. In their wake followed the traders, and behind them the first of the white settlers. Sometimes it was the traders who first moved on, foreseeing in their dwindling take of pelts the imminent exhaustion of game in the new lands. What became then of their customers, left behind in a depleted landscape, was none of their concern. They were businessmen, not philanthropists. As Duncan M'Gillivray of the North West Company put it, there were only two classes of Indian tribes as far as the company was concerned: "those who have furs and those who have none."

By the time Prince Maximilian of Wied and his artist, Karl Bodmer, reached the upper Missouri country in 1830, the trade nexus was well established there, and the American Fur Company's man at Fort McKenzie, James Kipp, followed the SOP by using whiskey liberally in his business dealings. On August 11, 1833, the prince made this note in his field journal:

The [Blackfeet] Indians came [in the afternoon] with a small cask and everything serviceable they owned and gave everything to get their favourite drink. Many came singing and dancing and offered their wives and daughters in exchange for whiskey. Others brought horses, beavers, and other skins, and we saw indescribable scenes. The young as well as the old got something to drink, and even very small children here and there could neither stand nor walk.

No surprise, then, that Kipp's son, Joe, should have continued the practice, though he surely knew the consequences for the Blackfeet. And no surprise, either, that Joe's pupil and partner, Schultz, should simply assume that this was the way things were. So there were occasionally ugly scenes in the trading room at Fort Conrad when a drunken customer threatened mortal violence: a hazard of the trade. So sometimes an otherwise valued Pikuni friend or even relative would become a mortal enemy when in his cups: the next day he would likely come and make his apologies, this still-proud and independent man. So once in a while on a winter's morning the trader might get a start when he unbolted the trading room door and a stiffly frozen Indian man, propped there by some wag, fell into his arms: Western humor. (Schultz himself once lugged back to the fort some frozen wolf carcasses he'd poisoned for their pelts and stood these things up around Sorrel Horse's cabin. "They were an odd and interesting sight," he said, "standing there, heads and tails up, as if guarding the place; but one day there came a chinook wind and they soon toppled over and were skinned.") There would always be buffalo, Blackfeet, and whiskey enough to get the animals delivered through the natives. The beaver in which Joe Kipp's father had dealt had pretty much given out by the end of the 1840s, but when Schultz arrived in '77 there seemed to all concerned no dearth of buffalo. Business boomed right along.

Little more than two years later, however, Kipp and Schultz heard the first unsettling rumor that the buffalo were not to be found at all in the north country around Great Slave Lake. The herds had evidently drifted southeast, but everybody, the traders included, believed this must be a temporary thing. The Blackfeet, who, in response to the whites' demands for buffalo robes and tongues, had steadily increased their kill, believed the Nez Percés or some other northwestern tribe had found a way to decoy the herds to the other side of the mountains. Perhaps a war party would have to be sent to chastise the thieves and return the herds to their rightful owners. But in the winter following the rumor (1879–80), the talk of the camps was all of the disappearance of the buffalo, and Schultz recalled that there was an unusual amount of gambling among the men, some of it with violent and tragic results.

The next spring another blow fell when the Pikunis were informed by a heavily armed detachment of U.S. cavalry that an "agency" had been established for them on Badger Creek, just east of what is now Glacier National Park, and that much of the southerly portion of their old domain was no longer theirs. The people were at first dumbfounded, then angry. They knew the terms of the treaty sworn to by representatives of the Great Father at the mouth of the Judith River many years before. This land was theirs, and they would have it. But Joe Kipp, who was present at the confrontation, explained to them that the southerly portion of their lands had been opened to settlement (population pressures again) and that it would be folly to attempt resistance to the army. It is a measure of how much the Blackfeet had come within the whites' sphere of influence that these once-feared warriors did not resist but agreed to move their camps northward to the agency. Kipp told the heads of the three confederated tribes that he and Schultz would establish a trading post at Carroll just above the juncture of the Missouri and the Musselshell, where large herds of buffalo were still reported. Business could go on as before. To Schultz, however, Kipp confided that he now knew it was all over, that the West as he, Kipp, had known it was finished. Maybe another winter of trading for hides, at the most two, and then they would all have to find another way to live.

And what a winter that was! Joined now by an army of superbly armed white hide-hunters, the tribes went on an orgy of slaughter. The firm of Kipp and Schultz took in over four thousand robes, for which a Boston outfit paid them a handsome $29,000 and change.

As for the Blackfeet, they were now on their game-bereft agency and still wondering what had happened to them. Some had recourse to myth. In the long-ago, so one of their sacred narratives told them, the buffalo and the antelope had disappeared, and the people had prayed to Old Man to save them: "Oh, Old Man, help us now, or we shall die. The buffalo and the deer are gone. Uselessly we kindle our morning fires." So Old Man, accompanied by a young chief, set out on a long journey that brought them to the lodge of the man who hid the buffalo. Transforming themselves into a dog and a stick, they set free the herds and saved the people. Perhaps it was that way now. But Old Man seemed not to answer the Blackfeet prayers. Others among the tribes blamed the whites, saying that they had found some means of caching the herds—as in a way they had. Bewildered and broken, the Blackfeet drifted into the first of their starving winters, referred to thereafter in the tribal chronology as the "Winter of Death." Nat-ah'-ki and Schultz did what they could for family and friends, but conditions in that terrible winter of 1882–83 were so extreme that their efforts were equivalent to attempting to dry up a thunderstorm with an ink blotter. Schultz tried to publicize conditions at the agency in a letter to a New York newspaper, but it was never printed. He also wrote George Bird Grinnell, the influential editor of *Forest and Stream*, who told Schultz to prepare a full report that could be taken to Washington. Schultz did so, but before remedial action was taken at the agency fully a fourth of the Pikunis died of malnutrition or related illnesses. Schultz, Nat-ah'-ki, and their infant son (born in 1882) could continue in comparative comfort on Nat-ah'-ki's agency allotment, and Schultz could begin to fashion a new career as a guide to wealthy sportsmen who wanted to hunt the St. Mary Lakes region on the agency's western edge. But even so, there was no blinking the fact of those many deaths of relatives and friends or of the terribly altered lives of those who survived without hope or pride, without the buffalo.

• • •

Nor was Schultz himself to be exempt from the manifold consequences of that process in which he had played a late and minor part. True, he had some money and the means to earn more, and he had the freedom his skin color conferred. But up in what was now a white man's country he was a "squaw man," and he had to suffer all the indignities an uncomprehending and unforgiving white populace could dish out. Then, following Nat-ah'-ki's death in 1902, and after a brush with the law caused him to flee Montana for California, he had to suffer in exile

the growing realization that, with Kipp and the others, he had helped
bring to an end the freedoms of the horse-and-buffalo days. It must
have been partly an act of expiation, then, as well as one in memory of
his dead wife, that set him in 1905 to the writing of what became his
classic book. In those pages he admitted (for the first time?) that the
whiskey trade had been wrong. "I make no excuse," he wrote, "for the
whiskey trade. It was wrong, all wrong, and none realized it better than
we who were dispensing the stuff." But then this: "There was but one
redeeming feature about it: The trade was at a time when it did not
deprive [the Blackfeet] of the necessities of life; there was always more
meat, more fur to be had for the killing of it."

As we are now permitted to know, there never was such a time—
not then for the Blackfeet, not now for us with our more various but still
finite resources. If Schultz never realized this in the long, shadowed Sand
Hill years that stretched before him after he finished his one great book,
perhaps at least he sensed in writing down his memories something of
the profound, mysterious connections between love and death. That,
he said in *My Life as an Indian*, had been the curious thing about the
Blackfeet: they had actually appeared to love the buffalo they killed. He
called this paradoxical, as, to be sure, it was, if by paradoxical we mean a
seeming contradiction that masks a truth. Yet somewhere within this
paradox the haunted man may have seen some reflection of himself,
drawn to the Old Wild West, compelled there to participate in its
destruction.

> Wide, brown plains, distant, slender, flat-topped buttes ...
> odour of sage and smoke of camp fire; thunder of ten thousand
> buffalo hoofs over the hard, dry ground; longdrawn, melan-
> choly howl of wolves breaking the silence of the night, how I
> loved you all!

II
COWBOY

In a pine grove on a country road south of Reno, Nevada, sits an empty
log cabin fronted by sagging corrals that keep nothing in but the luxuriant

grasses of the Washoe Valley. The neighboring houses are mostly new, attractive, and expensive, so that the cabin and corrals appear anachronisms suffered to survive into the gentrified present. A few years ago the cabin was the headquarters of an ecology camp and before that the clubhouse of a dude ranch for divorcées recently run through Reno's splitting mill. But in the cabin's main room a tarnished bronze plaque above the fireplace tells you that this was once the home of Will James, the cowboy artist and writer, who lived here with his wife, Alice, from 1923 to 1927. It was here, the plaque says, that James wrote *Smoky*, the book that made him beloved by both children and their elders in a way unknown since Mark Twain. Flanking the plaque are a studio portrait of James—handsome, hawk-faced beneath a creamy Stetson—and a candid shot of Will and Alice taken on the steps outside just after they had moved here: he was thirty-one and unknown, and she but sixteen. On another wall behind a shattered frame are two water-damaged James drawings of broncos plunging and sunfishing, trying to buck their riders. It isn't much of a shrine to a man as famous in his time as Will Rogers or Tom Mix, one of America's most popular authors and an artist whose work once excited favorable comparisons with that of Frederic Remington and Charles M. Russell, Daumier and Delacroix.

More than fifty years have passed since James's death in the make-believe town of Hollywood, far from the Montana cow country he so loved, and most of the twenty-four books he wrote are now out of print. But copies of them in public libraries testify with their well-thumbed pages, scattered with the tracks of legions of readers, to the high regard in which he once was held, and here and there on full-page illustrations you can see the heavy indentations where some child has tried to trace with a blunt pencil James's cowboys and horses. Two of his books, *Smoky* and *Lone Cowboy*, are enduring contributions to American letters, a large achievement for any author, and the more remarkable considering how late he began writing and how little he had read of any literature save the Western pulps of his time. As for his artistic achievements, James has been credited by one authority on Western American art as having sparked the revival of interest in this school, one that continues into the present day. As in his writing, the appeal of his art was remarkably broad, drawing unqualified praise from cowboys and sophisticated collectors, entertainers and politicians—like the late Secretary of

211

Commerce under Ronald Reagan, Malcolm Baldridge, whose
Washington office featured a large James drawing. The 1985–86 touring
exhibition of his work—the first since his death in 1942—heralded a
more general reawakening to the singular, indisputable genius of the
man who appeared on the public stage out of nowhere in the mid-1920s.
Suddenly, without the foreground of literary or artistic apprenticeship,
there he was, like the lone cowboy of Western legend who drifts into
town trailing only dust and mystery.

• • •

Will James was not his given name, only the last in a series of pseudonyms.
He was born Joseph-Ernest-Nephtali Dufault, June 6, 1892, in the small
Quebec town of St. Nazaire d'Acton. His parents and siblings called
him Ernest, and his surviving brother, Auguste, recalled that Ernest
knew "how to draw as soon as he could hold a pencil." He had perfect
coordination, Auguste Dufault said, and "his mind could photograph
any thing, action, or movement, and that photograph was the model on
which he would draw." It was a trait that others who knew him as Will
James often remarked on with astonishment. Ross Santee, for instance,
himself a noted cowboy artist, said there never were any preliminaries to
James's drawings. "Bill always seemed to have the picture as a whole in
his mind," Santee said. He would make a "line or two at the top of the
page, a few at the bottom. I couldn't make heads or tails as I watched,
until suddenly a horse came to life and exploded right off the paper."

At age four the boy spent hours absorbed in the forms and habits of
the farm animals of his rural neighborhood. Auguste Dufault recalled
him staring at horses, cows, and dogs, capturing in his mind's camera-
eye their movements, expressions, the workings of their muscles, and
there on the kitchen floor, lying on his belly, he would draw them on
large pieces of wrapping paper. Ernest's shopkeeper parents were certain
they had a prodigy. A year later, when little Ernest began making soap
drawings on the bar mirrors of the hotel his father had purchased in St.
Hyacinthe, they were even more certain, for these drawings were so
remarkably accomplished they became one of the hotel's chief attractions.
At the end of his life, living at a dude ranch outside of Los Angeles and
broken in mind, heart, and body, James would occasionally decorate the

212

bar mirrors at the Green Spot in Victorville with soap drawings, in a ghostly reprise of those early days in St. Hyacinthe when his precocious draftsmanship had delighted patrons and parents alike.

From the first the subject of the drawings was American cowboy life: James was never any good at drawing anything else, as if the circuitry of his brain, arm, and hand were set up only to depict this single, narrow aspect of life. As a kid, of course, he had never actually seen a cowboy, a mustang, or a longhorn, but he had seen pictures of these marvels, and he had read some French translations of Western adventures. Before he had finished grammar school he knew precisely what he wanted to do with his life: he wanted to go west and become, as his brother put it with appropriate dramatic simplicity, "a rider." To Ernest Dufault, as to millions of other boys on the North American continent, there was something magical and heroic in the image of the lone man and his horse out there in a huge, untamed landscape. But Ernest Dufault's imaginative and emotional commitment to this image persisted beyond boyhood to become his *raison d'être*, and he never gave it up. Years later in his largely fictional autobiography, *Lone Cowboy*, he was to describe the feeling of profound contentment that could come only to the rider of the Old West. "When I hit out that spring," he wrote, "asetting on top of a good feeling pony, the morning sun ashining on fresh green sod, trees budding and millions of birds asinging everywhere, there was no room in my chest for anything excepting what was all around, under, above, and ahead of me." Somehow the slight French-Canadian kid already knew this years in advance of any actual Western experiences, and with an ingenious persistence he now set about achieving for himself something of this longed-for reality.

To earn his freedom from the mundane realities of home, he quit school after the eighth grade and went to work as a bellhop in a Montreal hotel. Out of his meager weekly pay envelope he squirreled away a few dollars to buy a second-hand pistol, an item, he knew, essential to the rider's gear. Accompanied by the admiring Auguste, he spent his spare hours at an abandoned quarry at the city's edge, where he practiced target shooting and quick draws. Meanwhile he laid siege to his parents for permission to go west. Finally in 1907, when he was fifteen, they wearily consented. The boy knew nothing of riding or stock tending, nor did he speak English. He had only ten dollars, a bag of cookies, and his beckoning, radiant dream.

Lone Cowboy is not a trustworthy guide to the facts of the early years of its author, and yet used with caution it tells us a good deal about the hard apprenticeship to cowboy life the boy served, first in the western Canadian provinces of Saskatchewan and Alberta, then in Montana, Wyoming, Nevada, Idaho, and California. Through the eyes of the young protagonist, "Will James," we can sense Ernest Dufault's primitive wonder at the salty talk of the cowboys, the life of the bunkhouse with its mingled odors of wet wool, leather, and wood smoke. We experience his fascination with the tack of a saddle shop, his simple and enduring delight at the actions of well-trained cow ponies. But also we get a vivid sense of just how hard an apprenticeship this really was, beginning as it did with the most menial, unheroic chores of the camp: washing pots and skillets, cutting and hauling wood, peeling potatoes. Gradually the boy was given jobs more in keeping with his ambitions: a string of gentle horses to ride, then some wrangling and night-herding. We can well believe the writer when he says in *Lone Cowboy* that he got many a "kick in the rear" for being in the way and that the hands used to tease him by saying, "We'd better kill him, he'll never be a cowboy." What gave them pleasure, James writes, "is that I was so sensitive to what they said." But, he adds, "them boys knowed what they was doing. They didn't see nothing soft about me and they noticed that if I did buck off I wouldn't get hurt easy, and there was no whining."

By about 1910 Ernest Dufault was no longer being told by foremen that he had better give it up and go back to daddy. He had served his apprenticeship and was in truth now what he had always wanted to be: a rider. And those who remembered him from these years said he was a good one, too. But he did go back to Montreal and to his family in 1910, retreating from an incident that must forever remain vague in detail.

Based on what James said much later to friends and on his account of the incident in *Lone Cowboy*, a guess is that while still in the western provinces he got into a barroom argument with a sheepherder. Suddenly the man flashed a knife, and James felt its blade cleaving down his cheek. He leapt clear of his attacker, drew his pistol, and shot and wounded the herder, then fled to his boardinghouse room where he was subsequently arrested and jailed. What happened thereafter is even murkier. In *Lone Cowboy* he says that his shot had merely grazed the herder, who later that same evening was shot again and badly wounded by the bartender. When the whole incident became known and the herder recovered, James was released. However, on at least three different occasions in later years James muttered a story about having burned down a log jail and escaped, and in view of his behavior on his return to his parents' home it is possible this was the case. He suddenly turned up in Montreal but stayed only long enough to tell them he was going across the border and that thereafter they should address him as "C. W. Jackson." Some months later he was "Clint Jackson," then "W. R. James."

He was using the name "Will R. James" in the fall of 1914 when he was arrested in western Utah on a charge of having stolen cattle in eastern Nevada and shipped them to Denver for sale there. The charge was true. James and a partner had been working on the Riordan Ranch in Nye County, Nevada, but as fall came on they decided to drift south with the birds. On their way the two came across a small bunch of strays off the Swallow Brothers Ranch at Shoshone and decided to drive them to Oasis, Utah, and from there ship them to Denver. At Oasis, James's partner boarded the train with the cattle; James was to wait there for word of success. But the day following, while he dozed beneath a barber's soothing lather, James overheard a conversation that told him too plainly that the theft had been detected and that suspicion had already settled on him. He was arrested before he could get out of town, subsequently decided to plead guilty, and was given a twelve-to-fifteen-month stretch in the Nevada State Prison at Carson City. The file card accompanying his mug shot gave his name as "Will R. James," his birthplace as "Montana," and his occupation as "rider." It noted, too, a long scar running from his right cheekbone down toward his mouth, and a close scrutiny of the mug shot shows what appears to be such a scar, evidence, apparently, of that barroom encounter with the sheepherder.

"Now I know what a mustang feels like when corralled," he told a visitor to the prison. But he relieved some of the monotony of the daily round by sketching and telling the guards stories to go along with the sketches. He got to be a favorite with them and was allowed to work with the prison remuda. He was behind bars and fenced off the range, but he was still a rider. When it came time to apply for parole he sent the board a three-frame drawing in support of his petition. The frame captioned "Past" showed James settling a loop over a steer's horns;

"Present" depicted him deep in thought in his prison cell; "Future" showed him gotten up in what he imagined were artist's togs and at work on a painting of a horseman. Additional text read, "Have had ample time for serious thought and it is my ambition to follow up on my art. Will James." He was granted parole in 1916.

All along this winding trail he had in a way been following up on his art, and in the same desultory fashion he continued to do so over the next four years. There have always been cowboys who for their own amusement and that of their partners have drawn the scenes of their daily life or who have made up songs and poems about rangeland vicissitudes, so in that respect James was not altogether unusual. What made him stand out in the memories of those who rode with him was how talented he was and how persistent, even compulsive, he seemed with his sketching. At odd moments in the bunkhouse, in the flickering light of campfires where he used charcoal sticks, in boardinghouse rooms with smudgy pencils, he sketched horses and their riders, cattle, Western wildlife. He drew on scraps of paper, on postcards, around the margins of pages ripped from catalogs, on the panels of boot boxes, even on cigarette papers. Once, up in Calgary, James and a bunch of the boys were making the local rodeo circuit in a Model T, and James decorated its fenders, hood, and sides with cowboys and bucking broncos. A foreman in Tonopah, Nevada, said he had to fire James because James spent more time drawing pictures of the stock than working with it. Some of his work was crude, to be sure, but all of it was alive, authentic right down to the last detail of the cowboy's rigging, and the boys liked that. They saved the sketches, packing them along in their war bags, mailing them home for safekeeping. One hand who trapped wild horses with James in Idaho in 1911 said he'd noticed James around the camp drawing "pictures of horses, women, cowmen, and animals. I picked up some of the drawings I liked and saved them. ... When we moved camp, I gathered up some more of them. ... kept the sketches in my bed, next to the tarpaulin. I mailed a few of the drawings to my mother to keep for me."

Several times between the parole in 1916 and 1919 James made feints in the direction of a serious art career, once going for advice to Charles M. Russell at Great Falls, Montana. As James later told it, Russell ignored him for many minutes while he brooded over a painting he was working on. Then he glanced quickly at the unknown cowpuncher's sheaf of sketches and muttered that maybe James should scatter them around in saloons where there might be buyers. It was not the encouragement James had hoped for, especially from Russell, who had once been an unknown cowboy himself before hitting it big. James went away discouraged about getting into the art game but still in love with horses and the drifting life of the open range. That might have been all that ever came of this ambition had not the rough realities of that life finally caught up with him and forced a decision.

It was the summer of 1919, and James was hanging around Reno, sleeping in alfalfa fields and barns, whooping it up nights with two other young cowboys. One day the three decided to stage a bucking bronc exhibition for the locals in hopes of collecting a few dollars. In an afternoon practice session James was up on a horse called Happy. He stuck with him until Happy had done his worst and seemed about ready to quit. James was just hopping off when Happy started in again, and this time he succeeded in pitching his rider head first onto a railroad track. James suffered a severe concussion and multiple scalp lacerations, and he was to feel the effects of this injury the rest of his life.

He convalesced at the home of one of his bronc-riding pals, Fred Conradt, whose teen-aged sister, Alice, tended the handsome cowboy while the slow days passed in talk of his great days on the range, his artistic ambitions, his professed desire to settle down. Here was a contradiction, and even if James hadn't resolved it—and never really did—he had at least come to know that at twenty-seven he was getting to be an old man at cowboying and bronc riding. Incurable romantic as he was about the old range life, still he could not have missed knowing that many cowboys were stove-up old men at forty, their insides shot from the constant jouncing of riding, their knees and backs stiff from unhealed injuries, their teeth bad from tobacco and lack of care. "The rougher and more dangerous a game is," he observed later, "the younger a man is when he quits it. Mighty few bronc riders that's been at the game steady and hard are still at it when they're thirty years old. ... I'd had horses fall with me in every way. ... I'd been kicked and struck, rolled over on top of and dragged." The ride on Happy had been a warning, perhaps the only one he was meant to get, and now under the innocent urgings of the blue-eyed girl who believed in his star he determined at last to follow up on his art.

217

But four years later it seemed like a false trail. He was back just where he had been when he'd tried to forsake the range for the studio: penniless and unknown in Reno. He and Alice now were married. He had sold a few drawings to *Sunset* magazine and had gotten some favorable attention from Charles Dana Gibson, one of America's best-known illustrators and then editor of *Life*. He had also acquired a small but interesting group of enthusiasts for his work: the great Russell, Harold von Schmidt, and Maynard Dixon, protégé of Remington and in his own right a prominent artist of the Western school. But James had also had disastrous flings at art schools in San Francisco and at Yale, and despite Gibson's encouragement he had failed to sell *Life* any of his work. So here he was, back in the Reno area, living in the Washoe Valley cabin his in-laws had charitably built for Alice and him. He had a large bundle of unsold or rejected drawings and very few prospects. There were a few horses in his corrals, and he still loved to ride, but every morning his body told him he could no longer be a bronc buster or even a full-time range rider. He, too, was stove up and yet not an artist either.

Alice felt otherwise. Just as during his convalescence she had encouraged him in his artistic ambitions, so now she encouraged him to write about the range life he knew so well and to illustrate the stories. She had been encouraging him in this direction for over a year, recalling how captivating a storyteller he had been in the days of their courtship. James himself was resistant, telling her that if the magazines had rejected his art work, they would be doubly certain to contemptuously reject his writing. Then one day, in a mood of defiant desperation, he went out to the little studio in the pines behind the cabin and dashed off an illustrated story he called "Bucking Horses and Bucking-Horse Riders." Shooting right for the top, he sent it to *Scribner's* magazine, telling Alice as he did so that it was "too easy done to be any good." He was amazed when it was promptly accepted.

Once he had gotten over the shock of acceptance, James plunged into a spate of writing and illustrating that had a kind of frenzy to it, as if he had suddenly realized how much he had to give and how relatively late he was in getting to this work. Each morning he would leave the cabin and walk up the slope to the little studio, there to spend the day at his drawing board/desk, rolling a steady succession of Bull Durham cigarettes, and emerging only at dinnertime. He quickly sold another story to *Scribner's*, one to the *Saturday Evening Post*, and a three-part series to *Sunset*. By year's end Maxwell Perkins of *Scribner's* had written him to say that the publishing house would bring out James's collected stories as *Cowboys North and South*.

The book and those that fairly tumbled out after it—*The Drifting Cowboy* (1925), *Smoky* (1926), *Cowboy Country* (1927)—created a literary sensation. There was simply no one in America doing this kind of work, and it had the critics reaching for their superlatives. "A gorgeous and almost unbelievable book," the *New York Herald Tribune* called James's first collection. "Each of the fifty pictures ... is brilliant and as filled with violent action as an exploding dynamite stick." Against the "synthetic manufacturers of oat-operas," said another, James stood out "like the moon competing against a street light." Here, for the first time it seemed, the authentic American cowboy spoke. He spoke not of six-guns and shootouts, for generally James avoided this Wild West cliché, but of those daily routines of cowboy life that had always fascinated the author himself: the way the desert looked at dawn and sunset and how easy it was to get fooled out there by mirages; how it felt to get up of a late-fall morning on the high plains with snow on your blankets, your rope stiff as a cable, and the remuda skittish inside the rope corral; the smell of range coffee and biscuits heating in a skillet; and, most of all, the feel of a good pony under you. "You know in my writing," James wrote Maxwell Perkins, "I've stuck to what I believed in more than to what people might like—Zane Grey's had men with one lung come out in our country and show the cowboy's up in a couple month's time. Owen Wister done pretty near as bad and I would never want to follow up on such styles just because people might be disappointed."*

Readers were not disappointed, either by James's content or by his writing style, which seemed utterly authentic: it was not standard English, and it was all the better for that. "Good English is fine," James announced in the preface to his first collection, "but it don't git there." His lingo did. No matter that it was in truth a highly stylized rangeland lingua franca that never existed anywhere. He worked close to the

---

* Here and elsewhere, in quoting James from his letters, I follow his punctuation, usage, and spelling.

border between effect and excess but rarely strayed over it, and what he produced read the way cowboys *ought* to talk, just as Ring Lardner's style appeared to faithfully reproduce the talk of all baseball players.

As for story plots and other narrative devices, James professed to know nothing about them—and maybe in a formal sense he didn't. Yet, as Alice had early on seen, he was a natural storyteller who in some way both canny and uncanny knew how to keep a story pulsing along with just the right number of narrative pauses to let the reader catch his breath while savoring the look and feel of the country that James used as his setting. "I don't know nothin' about plots," he told an awed interviewer. "I just start out and write about what I know. Sometimes it works out like I planned, and sometimes it don't. There ain't no technique to it. People either write or they don't. I think it's sort of a gift—like singing bass or being able to twiddle your ears."

Like his writing style, his accompanying illustrations were highly stylized, his cowboys all built on a self-portrait: hawk-nosed, long-waisted, bowlegged. His horses were all mustangs, his cattle invariably longhorns, even though that breed had long since been superseded by beefier breeds. Replying to criticism of his cowboy type, James wrote that what he had done was "put all the cowboys I've seen and known along with myself in the same pot and all boiled down I got one character what covers over seventy-five percent of the range riders, far as that goes all of us makes the same mistake if you'd call it such. You can tell a Russell, Remington, Leigh, Wyeth or Dixon far as you can see 'em they all got one character same as I got mine—it's just how they see the cowboy—it's why some are truer than others." By the end of the 1920s James's popularity had eclipsed that of both his great predecessors, Remington and Russell. The painter and sculptor Harry Jackson later spoke for many when he said that he had loved Remington and Russell all his life, but "one good black and white Will James drawing contains more timeless life-force than all their work rolled into one."

• • •

In 1926 James published *Smoky*, and by the year's end the book had raced through nine printings. By that time, too, its author was restless. Once he had told Alice that all he ever wanted was a log cabin and a

few horses in his corral. Now with money and celebrity he found he
needed more. He wanted a big spread up in what he claimed was his
birthplace, Montana, and just as years before he had laid siege to his
parents to let him go west, so now he besieged Scribner's to advance him
the funds to buy a ranch in the Pryor Hills outside Billings. In 1927 he
and Alice moved onto the Rocking R, with Alice's brother, Fred, as
foreman. But the dream ranch proved on experience to be something
else entirely: it proved to be the beginning point of a vertiginous downward spiral for the man who had dreamed it.

It would be tempting to say simply that, like so many celebrities of
his time and ours, James had too shallow a fund of personal culture to
handle his new and sudden status. That is what Alice James said after
he had destroyed their marriage and finally his very life. Unquestionably
this was a part of what became his problem; instant fame and the steady
roll of new money are hard for anyone to handle, and James had no
preparation whatever for these. After *Smoky* he was a full-blown celebrity,
in constant demand at rodeos, parades, horse shows, barbecues, Hollywood
parties. As Tom Mix said to Alice when she complained that she was
losing Bill, "He doesn't belong to you anymore, Alice. He belongs to the
public." But the causes of James's steep decline seem deeper, rooted indeed
in that very fixation on the Old West that had been his since early childhood and that had been the hidden heart of his immense success.

In fact, the Old West that James had come to love when he was little
Ernest Dufault up in Quebec was pretty much a thing of the past by the
time he arrived in the western provinces in 1907, and the longer he was
in the West, the more occasion he had to note the region's swift changes.
By the time he presented himself to the public as a cowboy artist, the
world he wrote of and drew was already in many ways more memory
than present fact: the open range had been fenced, the cowboy was
partly a farmer, the horse slightly anachronistic in parts of the West,
and the longhorn represented only by bleaching, splintering horns
nailed up over gates and fireplaces. James had to deny these changes,
and the more the West changed, the more his denial hardened into a
neurosis. He now found himself in an ironic box canyon, for a significant aspect of his books' appeal lay in the fact that he wrote about the
West as if the changes had never occurred, as if the reader himself
might climb on a gentle horse and have experiences substantially like

those he read of in James's pages: the West, James's books said, was still very much there and waiting.

Compounding James's growing sense of unease was the Canadian identity he concealed behind his public persona. Nobody who saw Will James in those years would have believed his real story—how he had made himself into the ideal cowboy people admired in the newspaper photos or rodeo judges' stands: Stetson hat, boots, correctly situated belt line, the tag from a sack of Bull Durham dangling from his shirt pocket. Not even his wife knew his real story—nor was she to know it until the day of his funeral, when his brother Auguste showed up at the Hollywood services. And James covered his tracks just as zealously at the other end of his trail. When he wrote back to Montreal, he always strictly insisted that Auguste burn his letters and keep the senior Dufaults in ignorance of their son's doings in the States. They never knew their son was a celebrity down there.

The Rocking R became his last defense against reality. He stocked it with longhorns imported from Mexico, allowed no improvements on its roads, and instructed Fred Conradt to do all the ranch work in the old-time way. In short, he attempted to create a kind of Williamsburg-on-the-range. "You ask," he had written Charles Scribner, Jr., after Scribner had loaned him the money to buy the ranch, "how much more land I'll need. Well, I only want what's close to me so no one can get near as progress creeps up. ... I want it as a cow country, cattle & ponies on the ridges and creek bottoms and when I set up on a knoll looking at my own little valley I want to see a rider once in a while and not a farmer hauling grain—you savvy what I mean." What Scribner's savvied was that their prized author was getting himself deep in hock and that in order to repay them he was committing himself to a killing writing schedule. Both Perkins and Charlie Scribner tried to warn him, but, unaware of James's real history and of how crucial a role the ranch played in that history, they could hardly understand the nature of the problem. James told them he needed the ranch for daily inspiration, and so he did. He could not tell them he also needed it because it formed a necessary part of a French-Canadian boy's rich fantasy.

And maybe as the thirties came on he was himself no longer certain of the distinction between that fantasy and reality. As a younger rider some of the boys used to call him Bullshit Bill behind his back. But, said

222

one of them, they refrained from criticizing him to his face because he "believed too much what he was saying for any of us to contradict him." Speaking of the fictional childhood James created for himself in *Lone Cowboy*, Ross Santee said it was the finest thing James ever wrote. "The fact that it was fiction," Santee said, "and Bill thought it was fact never made any difference to me. Bill didn't know the difference between fact and fiction." The present fact was that by the early years of the Depression decade James was far in debt to Scribner's, and yet he persisted in buying up adjacent parcels of land as they became available. Faced with these mounting debts and the parallel literary pressures, he sought relief and a further remove from reality in the bottle.

Like many cowboys whose work caused them to go a long time between drinks, James had for years been a binge drinker, a behavior pattern accepted in the West as an occupational hazard. Up on the Rocking R he began to drink while working, but kidded himself by invoking precedents: cowboys had always been hard drinkers, so there wasn't anything odd about this old cowpuncher hitting the bottle. Then, too, other artists and writers he knew mixed alcohol and work: Remington had kept a bottle at the ready in his studio, and Russell had been a hard drinker until his late years, when he had sworn off. "We all drank too much," Santee said of the cowboy artists of those years. In the beginning James tried to conceal his drinking from Alice and Fred, but when this was no longer possible he told Fred he needed the bottle for inspiration, that the pressures he labored under were so terrific he had to inspire himself artificially, else the ranch and all would go to ruin. Fred said he could understand that.

Some of the drunken stunts James now began to pull seemed harmless enough to outsiders, such as the time he veered suddenly away from a Manhattan rodeo parade, spurred his horse into a hotel lobby, and shot out the lights. Or the time in Hollywood when he held a press conference in his hotel room and informed the gaping reporters that, yes, he always did wear his boots and spurs to bed: they kept him from sliding out, he said. Or the time he manifested his dislike of city ways by building a campfire atop a Los Angeles hotel and cooking up a pot of good old range coffee there. And of course, the seriousness of the problem was for a time masked also by the convivial sorts who were happy to surround him, whether up on the ranch or in New York for the rodeos or in Hollywood where masquerading was the town's industry: Jim Hill, for instance, wastrel son of the old railroad robber baron, with whom James roared around the ranch's washboard roads in a big car, collecting caches of whiskey deposited by local bootleggers.

Inevitably, ugly patterns began to emerge. James would become violently abusive to Alice when drunk, he began to womanize flagrantly, and on several occasions he simply disappeared for weeks at a time, off on colossal benders from which he would eventually awaken without the least notion of where he had been or what he had been doing. By the time he was in Hollywood for the filming of *Smoky* in 1933, he was exhibiting the sure signs of brain damage. Victor Jory, who starred in the first film version of the book, later recalled how James would begin a conversation, nod off in mid-sentence, then several minutes later begin again on a wholly different subject. The film's producers had wanted the author to have a speaking part in the film—he was still remarkably photogenic. But after several days of coaching James, even setting up large-print cue cards for him, they sadly abandoned the idea. James was always too drunk to read the cards.

It was during the filming of *Smoky* that Alice finally gave up, determined to save herself at least. In their subsequent settlement James lost his beloved Rocking R and became once again a drifter, living with friends in Billings and at various dude ranches in southern California on the fringes of the movie world. There were numerous arrests for drunk driving, several hospitalizations, a numbed succession of women friends. Incredibly, in the insane welter of drunks, debts, the dissolution of a life, he kept the books and drawings coming, though by that point publishers used his early artwork in preference to the unsteady productions of his final years. Still, he averaged a book a year all through the 1930s. In the last year of his life he worked with a kind of doomed valor on what he believed would be the great American novel, the saga of three generations of cowboys, all of them named Bill, all of them refusing to acknowledge the realities of the contemporary West. "THE COWBOY WILL NEVER DIE," he wrote in capitals as the book's final sentence. This particular one did, though, on September 3, 1942.

In his will, after settlement of bills and debts, he left his estate to one "Ernest Dufault" of Ottawa, Canada. Doubtless he meant to have named his brother Auguste as his legatee. But in a symbolic way the mistake makes his point: he was his own unique invention—*sui generis*, of one's own kind—and America has not seen his like since.

Georgia O'Keeffe:
Her Conquest of Space

When my wife and I first came to Santa Fe in the mid-1970s we were given an introduction to the painters Bill and Julie James, he the grandson of the philosopher and psychologist William James. It was the beginning of a rewarding friendship, enhanced by the fact that in those days the Jameses were hosts to a large, informal salon that met frequently at their home on Old Santa Fe Trail. At the time, I don't think I quite appreciated what a distinguished group this really was or how fortunate we were to be included as marginal members of it. Eliot Porter was there with his wife, Aline, a painter. So were John Brinkerhoff Jackson, then the most prominent critic and historian of the national landscape, and Edward Hall, the noted anthropologist. The artist Agnes Sims and her companion, Mary Lou Aswell, were regulars. Aswell was the literary editor who had discovered Eudora Welty, and when Welty visited in the summers, she too came out to the Jameses'. I met the best-selling British novelist John Masters there several times. The next-door neighbors were the noted collectors and patrons of modern American art Gifford and Joann Phillips, and on New Year's Eve we repaired to their house for a champagne session.

This was a lively, intense group, brimming with ideas and opinions, and one of the things I found most stimulating about it was that the members knew their regional and local history. Almost all of them had come to New Mexico from elsewhere—though not recently—but they had taken the time to learn a lot about the beautiful, slightly exotic place they now called home. For me, being around them was the equivalent of getting an immersion course in Southwestern history—and a lot of great food and wine to go along with it. Worse things have happened.

The point of this brief autobiographical excursion is that in all those many gatherings I never recall so much as a mention of Georgia O'Keeffe.

There was plenty of talk, some of it quite spirited, about art, photography, books, film, politics. There was talk about the younger generation of Native American artists coming up—T. C. Cannon, Doug Hyde, Dan Namingha, Kevin Red Star. I recall a discussion of Haniel

Long's brilliant interlinear to the narrative of Cabeza de Vaca and whether this was a contribution to history or a meddling in it. I remember also a consideration of the Cinco Pintores and whether they had done lasting damage to art in Santa Fe with what someone called their "blue sky school of painting." But never any talk of Georgia O'Keeffe.

At the time this didn't strike me as peculiar. I was after all a newcomer and probably more callow than my years could account for, and so it was only after O'Keeffe had moved to a secluded home just a few hundred yards down the road from the Jameses' that I thought about it at all. By that point my wife and I were living directly across the road from Bill and Julie, and one evening when it was just the four of us at supper I asked them if they knew O'Keeffe at all or had seen her since she had become our neighbor. "We saw her—once," Bill said. "Years ago. It wasn't very pleasant." They'd been on some sort of outing north of town, Julie amplified, when they'd encountered an old friend who had O'Keeffe with her. The artist kept her distance, there under the shadow of a broad-brimmed hat, and when introduced to the Jameses had only nodded silently. As far as they knew nobody had seen anything of her since she'd moved into the house known as Sol y Sombra, though it was understood she was in very poor health. It was only then that I reflected, if briefly, on the silence surrounding the most famous artist in the region and one of the most famous in the entire country.

Memory is, of course, famously tricky, and it has been some years now since those salons at the Jameses'. So I called a few friends who had been part of all that to ask if my recollections were substantially accurate, and, if so, what that strange silence had meant.

"I think you are right about that," Jim Brennan told me. Jim had been a regular and a well-connected member of the Santa Fe art scene. "I don't recall Agi (Sims) or Mary Lou ever bringing up O'Keeffe. I don't think I even heard Eliot (Porter) talk about her, and of course, he knew her quite well. It may be we just didn't think of her as part of our world. She belonged to another world, somehow. In all those years I think I saw her only once."

Artist Sibyl Saam laughed lightly when I asked her about O'Keeffe. "Well," she said, "she wasn't exactly handing out directions to her house, was she? She had very strict rules about that sort of thing. I guess we thought of her as, oh, *formidable*."

Gifford and Joann Phillips knew virtually everybody in contemporary American art circles and had met O'Keeffe but twice and never in Santa Fe. Once was at the San Francisco Museum of Modern Art. "She was rehanging a show a friend of ours had just hung," Joann remembered (something for which O'Keeffe was famous). "Anyway, he introduced us and said, 'You know, Miss O'Keeffe, Mr. Phillips's uncle, Duncan Phillips, was one of your earliest collectors.' She said, 'Yes, I know. But he much preferred the boys. He liked (Arthur) Dove better.' Then she just turned away."

"She looked wonderful that day. She had on that Alexander Calder pin she often wore. She was a bit frosty with us, but she was very nice to our children, who were quite small at the time."

When I asked her about the wall of silence surrounding O'Keeffe, Joann paused to consider. Then she said, "I think there may have been something about the Juan Hamilton business that made people shy away a bit, but that wouldn't account for all of it. She wasn't really part of the Santa Fe culture scene, except for the Chamber Music Festival. She loved chamber music and was very generous to them. She wasn't part of the New York art scene, either. She'd come out here to get away from all that. She was really a woman apart."

And yet, if there was this wall of silence around Georgia O'Keeffe in those years, she was hardly neglected. She was instead a very visible presence in Santa Fe. There were, of course, all those posters of her art, for sale everywhere and hanging in framed versions in homes, shops, and restaurants. The skulls of horses and cows and antlered elk were starkly mounted on whitewashed walls in tribute to her work. At an art supply store on Canyon Road there hung a framed check O'Keeffe had written for a purchase; the owner had saved it as a sacred relic. Tourist brochures spoke of the city as part of O'Keeffe country, even if it wasn't.

I think all of this—the silence and the visual tributes—was one of O'Keeffe's extraordinary creations. Part of it probably was a consequence of a sort of notoriety, as Joann Phillips had suggested. There was what Joann had called the "Juan Hamilton business," the artist's late liaison with a much younger married man who became her intermediary with the wider world and whom she provided lavishly for in her will. There were those astonishing, beautifully erotic photographs Alfred Stieglitz took of her back in the New York days and that followed after her, even when her appearance had so dramatically changed and she'd become something of a severely garbed desert anchorite. And then there were those famously strict rules the artist successfully enforced about her contacts with the rest of the world: these were always to be exclusively on her chosen terms.

But beyond any of this, beyond the whiff of notoriety, the rumors, eccentricities, reclusiveness, caginess, there was something else at work here: the force of her *intent* was so great, her *will* to take creative possession of a particular place so powerful that through the long years of her struggle and achievement it created a special sort of space around her. Perhaps, even early on, she had known it would. Writing to novelist Jean Toomer in 1926, she looked down the winding road that would end in the red rock country of northern New Mexico and saw "aloneness—not because I wish it so but because there seems no other way." Like another famous American solitary, Thoreau, she had business to transact with nature, and it could only be done by one.

• • •

If you're trying to write about art, hanging around with practicing painters can save you from committing some fatuous mistakes to paper—though nobody can save you from all of them. For some years I had been wanting to make a pilgrimage to O'Keeffe country, to view the scenes of her unique conquest, and I thought it might be helpful to do so with my old friends Sam Scott and Eugene Newmann, both well-known painters and long-time residents of Santa Fe. Sam had run watercolor workshops out of Ghost Ranch for many years and knew the country intimately. As an inheritor of the influence of the abstract expressionists Gene had his carefully reasoned aesthetic attitude toward O'Keeffe and wasn't shy about articulating it. Here, so it seemed to me, was, potentially anyway, an almost perfect balance of background and insights. So, we set off from Santa Fe on a blustery, changeful March first, which seemed to us the first day of spring. The sky to the north looked dark, and it was clearly snowing in portions of the Jemez Mountains to the west. Sam thought the characteristic colors of O'Keeffe country might be changed by a snowfall, but we'd take our chances with that.

Like some others I'd asked about O'Keeffe, both men had had but a single sighting of her, Sam remembering the timbre of her voice, and Gene recalling he'd heard that voice raised in Santa Fe's Fine Arts Museum when O'Keeffe was berating someone for a promise that hadn't been fulfilled. On Española's main drag the throbbing of a low-rider's stereo system next to us at a light prompted talk of her somewhat uneasy relationship with the locals around Abiquiú, almost all of them Hispanic. She had carefully defined the terms of that relationship, too, had never learned Spanish, had essentially limited her interactions to practical matters. There she was, through the decades, planted in their midst, painting their lands, yet clearly determined to remain a "woman apart," as Joann Phillips had put it. Even so, there were incidents of her spontaneous generosity, both to individuals and the community, and so who could say what the balance sheet finally looked like—except that it bore her signature.

Past Española the roadside looked almost stunningly blighted by poverty under the now-bleak light and with winter's snows gone from the fields. The poverty would always have been here, and to judge from Farm Security Administration photographs might have been even more desperate when O'Keeffe came up here in the Depression years. But now there was an imperishability to much of the detritus of that poverty, and both Sam and Gene wondered aloud whether Ansel Adams could now find a frame for *Moonrise Over Hernández*, his famous 1941 photograph taken at the village we rolled past with its junked cars, rusted agricultural implements, its tatters of plastic.

Just short of Abiquiú we turned off Route 84 onto side roads heading toward El Rito, the naked country itself taking over now. We talked about what might have drawn O'Keeffe here in 1934, turning her back not only on New York but even on Taos where at least she might have had the support of its flourishing arts colony: to come here, alone, to this rugged landscape with its physical, psychological, and aesthetic demands. Was she looking for something at once specific and mysterious here? Or was she instead open to whatever she might encounter? Sam thought the latter. "You've gotta be *clear* when you come to this place—or any new place, really. And you don't want to sentimentalize it."

"But she did," Gene came back. He was a refugee from Nazi Europe, dried and toughened by boyhood in Colombia where he'd worked for his father in the cowhide business, and so maybe he'd

231

earned his cynicism—if that's what it was. He thought the central issue of O'Keeffe's work up here wasn't what she was looking for but what he termed her relationship to the visual reference, to the landscape forms she found here and utilized. He knew and admired her pre-Stieglitz work from Texas and South Carolina and thought that in it she'd seemed willing enough to leave the figurative references behind. But up here, he said, she'd pulled back from that edge. Sam disagreed. And I did, too, believing that what she'd found she had to do up here was to devise a strategy for taking on this powerhouse landscape, and that if there had been a retreat of sorts, it had been a strategic one that gave her a vantage point from which she might achieve some sort of parity with the landscape: stripping the bare-bones forms even further, down to their metaphysical essentials; making carefully calibrated rearrange-ments and simplifications; obliterating depth into an almost Oriental flatness: all this so that she could finally over time *dominate* a place she said was hers the first time she came into it.

And she'd had to learn the elements of this strategy by herself. Others had shown her their techniques, and through Alon Bement she'd learned of Arthur Dow's ideas on Oriental art. But nobody had taught her how to paint the way she found she had to out here. Even some of the techniques she'd so clearly mastered in her early years would have to be discarded or revised into accordance with these new realities. Here much seemed handed to you—immense sky, fiery colors, fantastic shapes—but the gifts were partly illusory, fraught with dangers. The mountain in the distance seemed almost to paint itself for you, she said—until you actually tried to do it.

Around a bend in the road, the Chama sparkling below us in a sud-den spurt of sunlight, we came upon a twisted old cottonwood. "There," Gene said, "that's an O'Keeffe tree, right there." Such is the nature of her dominance of this landscape that we looked at it in silence a moment, even wondering whether it might actually be one of the cot-tonwoods O'Keeffe had painted in the 1950s. We parked and got out, startling into flight some Canada geese in the watery fields below the road, their long shadows low in takeoff over the fields' first and tenta-tive green blush. While Sam did a couple of pencil sketches and Gene flipped through some color scans of O'Keeffe's paintings, I stood under the snaky arms of the old tree, trying to imagine the artist right here, on her own, as she had for some time wanted to be, and probably just as scared by her own audacity as in her late years she'd claimed she always was. Yet, she said grimly, she'd always continued. It wasn't, I felt, a brag. The work was her proof, the validation of that courage that had allowed her to continue.

The tree made me think of another woman apart, Willa Cather, out on the naked plains of southernmost Nebraska where, if she could find in some sandy draw a scabby cottonwood like this one, could feel at least a momentary visual relief from the relentless monotony of grass and sky. Her story was the reverse image of O'Keeffe's: ripped out of her Virginia roots and stuck down into the soil of the Great West—which she left behind as soon as she was able. Thereafter, Cather created fictional variations on a central theme: the artistic soul stranded in Nowheresville and struggling there to find some means of self-expression. Out here, however, O'Keeffe found the barren land releasing energies and creative impulses that had been dormant in her New York years.

It was noon by now, and our spot above the river a beauty, and we thought about opening a bottle of wine we'd packed along with our picnic supplies. We decided against it: possibly it would sharpen our response to the visual opportunities awaiting us, but then it might dull us as well. Hemingway, I told my friends, claimed that the art of looking was enhanced by hunger, and so we went on, following the sign for the Dar Al-Islam Foundation up the red, rutted road with the sagebrush spilling away on either side, scrubby, tough, irregular. Then, suddenly, we were at one of O'Keeffe's favorite spots, one she called the White Place, and here the spoken surmises of three garrulous men surrendered to the bizarre, blanched luminescence of this place of mud and ash, mounded up in minarets as if it had been the playground of the children of the Powers. We sat in silence before it, each of us, I thought, both awed by the look of the place itself and also mentally making the comparisons between it and O'Keeffe's renderings of it. The March wind drove the clouds quickly overhead, radically changing the color values from moment to moment. Sam wanted to try a watercolor, and while he did so I took some notes. After Sam had finished and we'd turned back down the road I had the distinct feeling of my friends' silent assent to the nobility of their fellow artist's effort here. They knew, as I could not, the intimate nature of that effort, the solitary engagement between artist and landscape—Jacob and the angel—knew what it took, knew of the daily taking of risks. Her New Mexican style was like walking out on a rocky ledge, I thought, with no room for misstep: either she would establish dominion or be defeated and the paintings would be botches in which viewers wouldn't even be able to sense what she'd dared. And there are some works like this, I think, but not too many. And whatever your ultimate judgment of O'Keeffe's work might be, there could be no caviling with the profound sincerity of her engagement here, the danger in it. For her, this had been no playground.

Coming back down the road we had a fine, panoramic view of the mountains to the west, a deep, bruise blue under their cloud cover and veined with snow. Rising out of their midst was the truncated top of Pedernal which O'Keeffe, perhaps not quite playfully, had once said God had promised to her if she remained faithful to her task of painting it often enough.

Then the picnic on the road to O'Keeffe's house beyond Ghost Ranch, looking off to the cliffs she considered part of her backyard. We had the wine now, a sturdy Côtes du Rhône, and hard-cooked eggs, salami-and-cheese sandwiches, and from Gene a South American dessert of *cotijo* cheese and *membrillo* (guava paste). When we'd finished we drove slowly past O'Keeffe's house, mostly hidden behind a high fence, and as we did I felt it again: that invisible, inviolable space O'Keeffe had created around her and that I'd first dimly sensed at the salons on Old Santa Fe Trail more than twenty years earlier. The space was to her artistic advantage, she clearly believed, but its personal costs might eventually have proved heavier than she'd calculated. She seems to have been a loner from early on, but it is one thing to be so in youth and another to remain one in the encroaching shadows of old age when even your great instrument, your vision, might begin to betray you. Maybe the late reaching out to Juan Hamilton reflected no more than O'Keeffe's weariness with the superb isolation she'd felt was necessary to her conquest.

Back on 84 we headed north to a spot in the red rock country that Sam wanted us to experience. The high, wind-driven drama of the day continued around us, the clouds flying overhead in quick masses, and off to the west, surrounded by sunlight, there was a dense snow shower like a theophany of the Old Testament God. When we came to the red

rocks—giant prows permeated with iron oxide the color of dried
blood—we parked in a turnaround, got out, and waited for traffic to
clear so that we could walk into the canyon opposite. With our wind-
whipped white hairs and slouching gait we might easily, I thought, have
been taken for a splinter sect of an Elderhostel outing.

Walking into the canyon, the gumbo mud sucked at our boots so
that each step became a heavier effort. All around us were ancient twists
of junipers as thick about as a man's waist. Here and there dead limbs
from them lay like bones against the red mud, recalling for us O'Keeffe's
1940 work *Stump in Red Hills*, and calling to mind also her intrepid,
solitary excursions through so much of this country, in the cold, wearing
sweep of the wind down from Pedernal, in the blaze of summer with
the sun striking off the rock faces and the bees swarming about her ears.
In this latter season, far away from her house, her only shelter from the
sun might be the oily shade underneath her car.

Now that we were within the canyon proper, Sam stopped. "I just
wanted you guys to see this," he said, turning around, "to *feel* it." We
were surrounded by the towering craggy reaches through which, high
up, there ran a rich green band of olivine so that the drama of the day
was matched by the permanent drama of the rocky colors and shapes.
"Here," so our situation seemed to be saying to us, "it is, *right here*." And
then the challenge would have been what to make of "right here" with
all its drama, both quotidian and ancient.

Our last stop in O'Keeffe country was Ghost Ranch. Behind the
center's buildings we walked a broad trail up into a box canyon where
we came at last to a dead cottonwood shedding branches and skin in
long, gray peels. "A Newmann form," Sam smiled, pointing out a
forked branch caught astraddle a larger limb. "A form trying to be a
form," Gene came back, and they both laughed. Through the years they
had traveled and sketched and painted over a sizeable stretch of earth
and probably knew each other's favorite shapes about as well as they did
their own. They would have understood therefore why O'Keeffe kept
circling back even in the last years to shapes she'd been working with as
long ago as those feverish nights in South Carolina when she'd drawn
by the hour, sitting on the bare floor of her flat.

On our way home we came to that bend of the Chama above
Abiquiú where O'Keeffe had painted the river, and we pulled onto the

narrow shoulder to have a quick look, Gene and Sam talking about John Sloan's 1927 painting *Chama Running Red* with its lone horseman approaching the river and the sentinel tree on the opposite bank. It was, they said, a very narrative painting whereas O'Keeffe's was almost defiantly non-narrative. "You know," Gene said then in a quiet way, "there must be very few artists who did what she did up here: to come in cold and make it your own. Pretty unusual, I'd say." As we went on we tried to come up with other examples. There was Cézanne in Provence, but then he hardly had come in cold—painting his Mont Sainte-Victoire over and over again as though he too thought it might have been promised him for this faith. Monet up in Giverny. But only two Americans came to mind: Homer up at Prout's Neck and Walter Ingliss Anderson down at Ocean Springs and Horn Island on the Gulf. But Homer often escaped to the tropics in winter, while Anderson is not of O'Keeffe's stature. And these were men, men who could go where they liked, whereas she could not, as she bitterly remarked in her New York years. And up here there was the additional problem of making entry into a resolutely patriarchal culture. Who else, we wondered in spring's fickle and quick-fading light, had done what she had here?

• • •

Who else, indeed, and how?

Establishing cultural context as a way of accounting for a work or an entire career is inherently a ham-handed effort that confesses a kind of failure as it avoids direct contact with the work it would explicate. What we really want to know about a work or career is simply stated: how the hell did she or he do it, anyway? Context can never really answer that query; the best it can do is to point out some of the materials the artist was handed by birth, background, training, and by what the Germans (who specialized in this sort of thing in the nineteenth century) called *zeitgeist*.

In attempting to account for O'Keeffe's singular achievement in the American West the ground of inquiry must begin with Sun Prairie, Wisconsin. For many Europeans and for American Westerners too this might be hard to accept, because Wisconsin is not Wyoming. Yet it is in Wisconsin's southern half that you begin to feel the gradual, gentle rolls

236

of the valley of the great river that divides America between East and West. And in places like Sun Prairie and Baraboo, Hillsboro and La Crosse you keep getting the ever-more-insistent sense that you're on the edge of something really big, until at last you find yourself rolling high across a bridge with the river far below—and maybe even hollering as you go, as I often have. Then on the other side, you're in the West and you can assent to the truth of the line written by a Chicago boy, Archibald MacLeish: "America is West and the wind blowing." O'Keeffe was brought up on that edge between the two halves of the country and heard about the land out there in the bedtime stories her mother read the children. She was raised with the wind in her face, the wind that had gathered force in its sweep across the immense grasslands. No one so deeply sensitive as she was to landscape could have failed to register all this at some imperishable depth that was at the same time potentially accessible. When she came up to New York from Texas in 1918 she was hungry and thirsty, too, for artistic and intellectual companionship, and for some years thereafter she found the city positively thrilling: you see that in her cityscapes. But she never got over the West. To her it was the real America.

In this she was deeply in what her friend William Carlos Williams would call "the American grain." And so were those earlier great voices of the American Renaissance whose brilliance was still shining on the modernist movement in 1918—Emerson, Thoreau, Hawthorne, Whitman. They all believed the true America lay somewhere toward the sunset, waiting to be claimed by artists courageous enough to travel beyond the Eastern seaboard with its ineradicable Old World influences. Emerson thought the outcome of the entire American experiment might depend on what was done out there. Thoreau claimed that whenever he went for a saunter his steps inevitably tended westward, toward the future. And Whitman, the great singer of New York, believed the West was where America's true songs would be expressed, its authentic images made. "Do you term that perpetual, pistareen, paste-pot work American art?" he rhetorically asked in *Democratic Vistas*. "I think I hear, echoed as from some mountain-top afar in the west, the scornful laugh of the Genius of these States."

Who can say definitively how much of this O'Keeffe absorbed? In her New York days she was evidently careful not to reveal too much to "the boys" about what she was thinking, what she might have been reading, what portions of the all-but-endless high-flown talk about modern American art, the Great American Novel, an American epic poem she actually listened to. Indeed, she was so secretive in this way that later on one member of the Stieglitz circle expressed surprise that she could actually read and write. (Still later, of course, as she set about the earnest work of building her legend, she was very careful to cover her tracks, making it appear she'd created herself out of sunlight, dust, and rock.) When she got tired of all that twaddle, she said, she simply left the table. But there is no doubt she knew her intellectual history, was keenly aware of the tenor of her times. And she knew, too, that the talk around Stieglitz provided a vital, counterveiling force to the riptide that was bearing some of America's brightest talents back to the Old World, especially to Paris. Later she would snidely say that the whole bunch—Dove, Marin, Hartley, Strand, Demuth—would have gone over in a moment had it been feasible for them. This wasn't fair. Yet Pound, Stein, Hemingway, Hopper, Malcolm Cowley, and Virgil Thomson had all gone, and the social critic Harold Stearns claimed that artists had to leave America or risk being stifled by the ineradicable strain of Puritanism in the native culture.

One voice of modernism she must have heard with especial clarity was that of Stieglitz's good friend, the doctor from across the river in New Jersey, William Carlos Williams. Stieglitz had loved Williams's book *In the American Grain*, and in calling his gallery An American Place, Stieglitz was acknowledging Williams's influence. The year previous, Williams, too, had tried the expatriate life but found himself unsuited for it. He was too American. Writing the critic Kenneth Burke near the end of his stay abroad, Williams said Paris would be a wonderful place to live and write if only he were French. But since he wasn't, "only America remains where at least I was born."

"Where at least I was born." That was the challenge, the problem for artists, writers, musicians from the beginnings here: being in this huge sprawl of a country that seemed bereft of accessible traditions or history—how to come in cold, as Gene Newmann had put it, and make it your own. Williams's decision had been to take on the severely local— Paterson, its mills and exhausted landscape—and hammer an epic out of it. Others were trying to take on New York and its soaring modernities, which the Europeans like Duchamp thought so rich in potential.

O'Keeffe was one of them. And still others began to make tentative forays into the imponderable spaces of the West, following the outsized blazes of Bodmer, Bierstadt, and Thomas Moran. Looking at the work of William Robinson Leigh, Walter Ufer, Hartley, and Marin you see just how imponderable those spaces really were for them.

Western spaces were also a problem for a woman born on the edge of the West. But she at least had grown up with Western grit in her teeth and had learned finally that this could be a kind of nourishment in disguise. In the west Texas dirt country in 1916 she often came home covered with the blowing dirt and later spoke of that as if it had been a blessing—as in truth it was for her. She wanted to feel that Western earth in all its sparseness, its mercilessness. Why else, you think, would she have taken those teaching posts way out there, so far from any other source of nurture and inspiration, except for the fact that however obscurely she understood that the West could be her mother lode? There was something about the sun in the West that drew her, something about the way it hit the naked land, burning deep into it, and in *Special No. 21* (1916) she got that in paint with shapes resembling molten boulders rumbling out of the canyon's clarified curves. *Special No. 21* is an earnest of what she would go on to do in northern New Mexico, even if in painting it she could not quite see that yet.

Between *Special No. 21* and her first summer in New Mexico lay thirteen years in New York and Lake George; fame and a certain notoriety; spiritual crises and medical ones. There were periods when she must have feared her work was done, that she had used up her allotted time and talent without ever quite hitting her mother lode. But always there would have been the memory of the West, its unrealized promise, even in the dark hours of 1933 when she was deep into her own, private depression. Even then she surely remembered that there was much more to America than skyscrapers and salons, summerhouses and mountain greenery. In coming to Taos in 1929 she felt a clear confirmation of what she'd always at some level known. Then, in the blaze of August 1934, like some *nueva conquistadora*, she entered into her true and final domain.

Tasunke Witko, Crazy Horse—and Still a Strange Man

At the junction of South Dakota 18 and BIA 27 on the Pine Ridge Reservation there stands a green metal sign to Tasunke Witko, Crazy Horse, the famed war chief of the Oglalas. At something like ten feet by six it's substantial and seems the more so surrounded by grasslands where there is nothing but sky and grazing cows. Westward are the *Paha Sapa*, the Black Hills, which the Lakotas call the Heart of Everything That Is and in the midst of which descendents of a Boston-born sculptor are blasting a gigantic monument to Crazy Horse out of a mountain face. A few miles up BIA 27 is the meander of Wounded Knee Creek where on December 29, 1890, U.S. soldiers caught Big Foot's Ghost Dancers and slaughtered them, thus writing the last words in the dark chronicle of America's Indian wars.

The sign gives Crazy Horse's dates as 1840–1877, the former perhaps conjectural, the latter definite. The text covers both of the sign's broad sides and provides the outlines of his career in the Plains wars of the 1860s and '70s when he led his people against the Crows, the Snakes, the soldiers. He owed his renown, the sign tells you, to the force of his personality, to his bravery in battle, and to his control over the "wildest warriors under his command." He was prominent at the famous Fetterman Fight in 1866; at the Wagon Box Fight the next year; at the Rosebud where the tribes fought General George Crook to a standstill in June 1876. A few days thereafter he was heroic at Little Bighorn where the Lakotas and Cheyennes rubbed out Custer and his portion of the Seventh Cavalry.

A surprising amount of textual space is devoted to the chief's burial spot, which the sign says is some fourteen miles to the northwest, between the forks of White Horse and Wounded Knee creeks. For the man who might be the Lakotas' greatest hero to be buried on the site of their final, tragic defeat seems like a convenient rearrangement of history, like Amos Bad Heart Bull's pictograph showing Crazy Horse killing Custer—which he surely did not. But the weight of available evidence suggests Crazy Horse indeed is buried at Wounded Knee. His parents had evidently brought his remains along on the trek north from Nebraska in 1878 when the Oglalas were being resettled at Pine Ridge. Nobody could have known that some twelve years later the place they chose for the burial would be etched in blood in the tribal memory.

When I asked Emma (Pinky) Clifford about this a change came over her face. Clifford is a descendent of Chief Iron Plum, a confederate of Crazy Horse's; a member of the Oglala tribal council; and owner of the general store in Manderson, a few miles west of the killing ground. I'd first met her in October 1990, when I was doing background work for a magazine story on the centennial ceremonies to be held two months later at Wounded Knee. Then on that bitter, bitter day with the windchill a couple dozen degrees below zero, I'd helped her haul hay for the horses of the Big Foot riders. From behind her store counter she recognized me as I entered and invited me to have lunch at a table near the produce bins. My question hung in the air until we had our plates before us. Later, it would seem obvious to me that she'd been considering what she wanted to say to this white outsider about the figure the Oglalas used to refer to as Our Strange Man. Her black eyes ranged the shelves of her store, then stopped, and she looked directly at me.

"Well," she said at last, "he's supposed to be buried up here. But he's wherever he needs to be." There was a declarative opaqueness to the statement that seemed to put up an invisible and unbreachable wall around Crazy Horse: I wasn't supposed to learn where he was buried nor even where Clifford thought he was buried. Just hours earlier I'd run into this same thing down at the tribal offices in Pine Ridge where Philip Underbaggage of the tribal council had arranged for me to interview members of Crazy Horse's *tiospaye* (extended family). Yet within minutes of meeting Dolores Mills and Gerald Big Crow it was clear neither had any intention of telling me anything. As Dolores Mills bluntly put it, "I know the things my mother told me and that my grandmother told her, but I'm not going to tell them to you." Pinky Clifford was more polite, but the wall was there.

"He's always been a mystery," she said now. "I have a deep, ingrained respect for him." She stopped there, and so I had to blunder ahead, asking if Crazy Horse was for some reason a more sensitive figure to discuss than Red Cloud or Spotted Tail or Gall or even the great

Sitting Bull? That was enough in the neutral zone for her to handle it easily, and she replied, "Oh, yes, I think so. It's because of who he was and what he stood for. He was a warrior for his people, and I think he saw a lot further than anyone else of his time in terms of how things were going to go, how we were going to be treated—and are still being treated." She looked up from her chicken drummies and rice. "Other than this, I have no comment."

Her husband happened into the store, and when he approached the table Clifford introduced us. He was friendly of manner and smiled broadly when Clifford told him I was a writer. But when she told him what I was doing here I felt the wall again. "Oh, Crazy Horse," he said distantly, turning away to inspect the bin of red onions.

But Pinky Clifford didn't want to turn me out bereft, and she gave me some names and numbers, beginning with the tribal vice president, Robert "Milo" Yellow Hair. "I'd start with him, and then work down that list in the order I gave you," she said. She followed me into the parking lot. "Wear your seat belt," she called after me. "It's important."

Milo Yellow Hair was friendly, too, and accessible. He'd been around in the white world and knew how to handle himself with the press. He'd done a PBS documentary called "The Spirit of Crazy Horse," but neither in that film, nor now in his office would he talk directly about the Strange Man himself. It was as if one hundred and twenty years after his death Crazy Horse was still so charged with *wakan* (sacred power) that he was too dangerous to handle in exchanges with the outside world.

How far back in time this condition goes may now be undiscoverable. Clearly, Crazy Horse was a highly charged figure when he surrendered to the United States forces at Camp Robinson, Nebraska, in the spring of 1877, and he remained so during the few months of life he had left. Half a century later when the early scholar in Lakota history George E. Hyde was doing fieldwork he found the chief regarded as a kind of "Sioux Christ." What, Hyde wondered somewhat peevishly, "is it all about?"

What indeed? During my few days in Lakota country one fall I came to sense the unvoiced presence of an oral tradition of Crazy Horse running like an underground river beneath the documented facts— strong, dark, and deep—that I was not meant to tap. Above it like the dry washes of his country runs another version that is occasionally touched from beneath by the indigenous source. It seems unlikely to me that the two versions will ever be truly merged. When a good deal of firsthand information could have been gathered on Crazy Horse, the victors weren't interested; to them he was merely a troublemaker. And there are things his vanquished people have wished to keep to themselves. Still, for all the lacunae in his story—and partly because of them—he remains one of the most mysterious and intriguing figures in the national history, one who clung with a tragic tenacity to his lands and traditions.

• • •

He was born near the confluence of the Cheyenne River and Rapid Creek in what is now South Dakota. His father, who bore the name Crazy Horse before him, was a holy man of the Hunkpatila band of the Oglalas. His mother was a Brulé, a sister of the famed chief Spotted Tail. Because as a child his hair was wavy and light he was called Curly, and on those few occasions when whites chanced to see him with his people about the soldier forts they asked if he were a captive—ironic, since what he was captive to all his life were the deepest traditions of his people.

As these things go, the traditions of the western Lakota were actually fairly recent. It hadn't been that long ago that they'd been forced out of the woodlands of Minnesota by easterly tribes that had acquired European technology near the end of the seventeenth century. Moving steadily west, the people the whites came to call the Sioux encountered the vast herds of buffalo and acquired horses and some guns. By the time of Curly's birth they had become numerous and prosperous by Indian standards, ranging over a territory that included most of the Dakotas, northern Nebraska, eastern Wyoming, and a bit of southeastern Montana. If once they'd had to make way for more powerful neighbors in the upper Midwest, out here on the Great Plains they were lords and acted like it: superb horsemen and hunters, fierce and fearless warriors, arrogant in their unshakable assumption of cultural superiority:

clear the way
in a sacred manner
I come

the earth

is mine.

So run the words of a Lakota war song, and here was the heart of those traditions within which Curly grew up. If in later days others forgot, he never could.

In August 1854, an incident occurred that was to serve as the boy's rite of passage. Already he'd killed his first buffalo and stayed up on a newly caught mustang. He was called His Horse Looking or His-Horse-on-Sight when his people went to Fort Laramie that summer for the annuities due them as per the treaty they'd signed in 1851, guaranteeing whites safe passage through Lakota country on the Oregon Trail. While the Indians were camped near the fort one of them shot an emigrant's stray cow, and Lieutenant J. L. Grattan was dispatched to the camps to demand the surrender of the guilty brave. He took along two field artillery pieces and twenty-eight men. Grattan was green, hot-headed, and ill-served by an interpreter at least half drunk before he left the fort. Negotiations speedily deteriorated, someone fired a shot, and then the whites opened up with their artillery pieces, mortally wounding the Brulé chief Conquering Bear. The enraged Lakotas then slaughtered all of Grattan's command and beat the young lieutenant's head into jelly before fleeing northward, carrying the chief with them. He was to die a few days later.

The incident shocked His Horse Looking, for he saw firsthand the incredible insolence of the white interlopers and also how utterly impartial it was. Conquering Bear had been the Lakotas' preeminent peace chief and had been so recognized by the whites since the treaty of '51. Yet they'd shot him down even as he'd struggled to keep the peace. If the strategy of the peace faction he represented had merely resulted in his murder, then maybe that strategy was wrong and it was best to take a stand now and drive the whites back where they belonged. The boy could not have doubted his people's ability to do this, being so purely what he'd been brought up to be. And if indeed he did see further than others of his time, as Pinky Clifford said, then maybe even so early he saw that it wasn't just the road through Lakota country the whites wanted. They wanted all the country, every bit. Which was in fact so, for by 1854 the idea of a permanent Indian Country into which white settlement would never extend had yielded to the convenient belief in a Manifest Destiny. Permanent Indian Country was now understood by the whites to be an outmoded fiction, and had not the Civil War diverted their energies, they undoubtedly would have taken most of it a decade sooner than they did.

Leaving the dying chief with the others at an encampment on the Niobrara, His Horse Looking went off by himself to meditate on his people's troubles. This was not designed as a vision quest—though that's what it became—because he'd made no formal preparations and may not even have been looking for that sort of supernatural guidance. Nor was this itself surprising: devoted as he was to Lakota traditions, he was nevertheless already unorthodox in many ways, as if the light hair had been a mark put on him to signify a deeper strangeness. For the next three days he sat on a butte, thinking. To insure wakefulness, he wedged pebbles between his toes and put stones under him when he lay down. But nothing came to him in the slow hours, and in a mood of weary resignation he made ready to return to the camp. Then something did appear, out of another world. But when his father and Hump, the storied warrior who was the boy's mentor, at last found him, he told them nothing of what he'd seen, keeping the secret of his vision for three years. Then he told his father how he'd seen his horse approach him in a strange, billowing shape and how mounted on the horse was a man with long, unplaited brown hair that hung to his waist. Behind one ear he wore a smooth, brown pebble. Somehow it was clear the man took no scalps, yet he was very much a warrior, for a storm of arrows and bullets flew at him and he rode fearlessly through them. His face was painted with a lightning streak and his body with white hail spots, and above his head flew a red-backed hawk. As the rider came on people clutched at his arms, trying to hold him back, but still he rode toward his destiny. What that destiny was the vision didn't show him, but surely he rode toward something significant.

The holy man instantly recognized the vision for the powerful portent it was and set about helping his son put together the materials of his dream's medicine. He gave him his name as well, taking for himself the name Worm. As young Crazy Horse rose to prominence there were additions to the medicine, some of these devised by a specialist named Chips who fashioned for the warrior a special leather cape and another pebble to be worn on a thong. But what was essential in all this was that Crazy Horse become the mystic rider of the vision, that he be first in battle, leading charges into the hail of enemy fire, conducting himself so as to embody the indomitable spirit of his people. Behaving thus, he would render himself as invulnerable as the man who rode unscathed through arrows and bullets.

The young man accepted the challenge. He rode into battle far in advance of his braves, charging the enemy again and again, wearing his sacred paint and a red-backed hawk in his hair. In the course of his career he had many ponies shot from under him but was wounded only once. But He Dog, who rose to chieftaincy with him, told a white historian much later that one shouldn't confuse such bravery with recklessness. Crazy Horse wasn't reckless, he said. He made plans of attack and never wished to needlessly sacrifice the lives of the men he led. A reckless man wouldn't alight from his pony in the heat of battle to coolly aim and fire. Crazy Horse did that, He Dog remembered, one of the very few warriors who did.

• • •

Always he'd been quiet around the camp and in the lodge, content from boyhood to listen to his elders and learn what he could. The habit deepened in manhood when silence became his signature. He attended few councils and rarely spoke when he did. He didn't sing or dance or raise his voice with others in the ritual lamentations that followed death. In a culture that promoted a traditional kind of boasting about military accomplishments he was notably silent about his own. Twice he forgot he wasn't supposed to take scalps, but these were the only instances.

Except for the highly stylized ones in Bad Heart Bull's pictographic history of the Oglalas there are no images of him. The camera made the Plains wars and their leading Indian figures famous—Red Cloud, Sitting Bull, Satanta. But Crazy Horse was as illusive here as in other respects and was never captured by the white man's magic box, though rumors persist of photos said to be of him. For almost all of his life the whites had no opportunity to photograph him, because he was never near them except in battle. Not until the last few months at Camp Robinson was he among them in a non-hostile situation, and then he resolutely refused to let any of them take his picture, though offered what was for that time and place a substantial sum of money. What his motives here may have been is guesswork; some said he simply shared the Indians' belief that the camera box captured a person's spirit. Maybe. More likely is that he wanted as little to do as possible with white man things—thought he was quick enough to recognize the value of their weapons.

We do, however, have some idea of what he looked like in his maturity. He was about medium height for a Lakota male, slender, well-knit. There was nothing, in other words, prepossessing about his physique. But the face and especially the eyes—ah, *there* you looked a little way into the mystery. He was lighter in color than most of his people and lacked their distinctive high, prominent cheekbones. His face was narrow, the nose high and sharp. Years after his death one who'd known him remarked that nowadays no one on the reservation resembled him. Black Elk, who moved with the Crazy Horse people until the very end and was second cousin to the chief, told the white author John Neihardt that Crazy Horse's eyes "looked through things and he always seemed to be thinking hard about something." Maybe, Black Elk said, "he was always part way into that world of his vision." A strangeness of manner and the burning intensity of the eyes combined with his extraordinary bravery to make others afraid of him. "I was not afraid that he would hurt me," Black Elk explained, "I was just afraid." Everybody felt that way, he said, for the chief was a "queer man" who would go through the village without noticing people or saying anything.

He had plenty on his mind as he stalked unseeing through his village in these days of the late 1860s, because with the ending of the Civil War the whites once more turned their restless eyes westward to the lands that were to have been the tribes' forever, and not even the most distant and far-roaming of the nomads could doubt that matters were fundamentally different now. Before the 1850s when the white presence on the Great Plains was negligible the tribes had fought each other for favored hunting ground, for horses, but mostly for honor in a protracted and deadly ritual game. But no tribe out there—not even the invincibly arrogant Lakotas—ever thought of wiping out their neighbors and permanently seizing their territory. By the mid-1860s, though, the increasing white presence had changed everything, and some tribal leaders like

Red Cloud, Sitting Bull, Satanta, and Crazy Horse began to see that this was no game they were in: this was something new and strange and ominous, a war in which the enemy wasn't interested in honor but fought instead for obscure ends.

In response to the new conditions the Oglalas appointed Crazy Horse and He Dog chiefs; neither would have become so through heredity. Their official title translates to something like "owners of the tribe," but popularly such officials were known as "shirt-wearers" after the garment they wore as a badge of office. The position carried with it heavy social and moral responsibilities, for the shirt-wearers had to be above reproach not only in war but in the village.

Crazy Horse wore the shirt with distinction and added further to his military reputation on December 21, 1866, when he decoyed the detachment of Captain William J. Fetterman over Lodge Trail Ridge outside Fort Phil Kearney on the Bozeman Trail. Fetterman was a man like the late Lieutenant Grattan and had boasted that with but eighty good men he could ride through the entire Sioux nation. On this clear, cold day he had his eighty when he rode out against the Lakotas who for months had been harassing the whites all along the trail. As Crazy Horse and a small group hung back and taunted the soldiers, Captain Fetterman led his men into disaster just over the ridge where Hump and his forces sprang out of ambush and cut them all down within an hour. The post commander gave a vivid description of how the Lakotas left the bodies of the blue-coats: "Eyes torn out and laid on rocks; noses cut off; chins hewn off ... ; brains taken out and placed on rocks with other members of the body. ... " Tactically it was a brilliantly engineered victory by Crazy Horse and Hump at the same time that it was a shocking defeat for the whites.

The next summer he was back at Fort Phil Kearney with Hump, Red Cloud, and a mighty force of Lakotas. This time they attacked a party of woodcutters out from the fort, but there was a detachment of soldiers along, armed with new .50-caliber, breech-loading Springfields, and the Indians had to withdraw in the face of superior technology. Though the Lakotas actually lost the engagement, the so-called Wagon Box Fight demonstrated to the winners the tribe's determination to take a stand in the Powder River country, and this proved to be a major factor in the decision to hold the peace conference that resulted in the Treaty of Fort Laramie in 1868.

The treaty was about as tangled and disingenuous an item as the whites could make it, and even today historians and legal scholars have trouble understanding its meaning and intent. Certainly the Indians who knew anything about it didn't understand it. What the Lakotas did understand, though, was that the hated Bozeman Trail and its forts would be abandoned and that the people would have exclusive and undisturbed use of all of what is now South Dakota west of the Missouri, including the *Paha Sapa*, the Heart of Everything That Is. That this territory was now also technically a reservation was doubtless unimportant to them, because they had no concept of what a reservation was. Moreover, Article 16 of the treaty granted them undisturbed use of a huge swatch of unceded land in northeastern Wyoming and southeastern Montana—the beloved Powder River country—where they were free to roam and hunt as of old. So, Red Cloud had apparently beaten the *wasichus* (whites) back and in some triumph went in to Fort Laramie in November to touch the pen. But within months the treaty was effectively undone by General William Tecumseh Sherman, who'd signed it but who regarded the abandonment of the forts on the Bozemen Trail as a humiliation. Sherman directed his subordinate, Phil Sheridan, to issue a general order stating that in practice there was to be no unceded, off-reservation land and that an Indian off the reservation was a hostile Indian subject to military reprisal.

From the beginning, the northern Lakotas and the Cheyennes had not understood that the treaty had placed any restrictions on their traditional ways of living, and certainly Crazy Horse and his people recognized no new restrictions. The Strange Man never signed nor recognized the treaty's legitimacy. But in the wake of it he and some others began to harbor suspicions about Red Cloud and Spotted Tail who by 1870 were openly campaigning for peace with the *wasichus*. Spotted Tail had been a peace chief ever since he'd done time in the white man's iron house at Leavenworth as punishment for the Grattan incident. As for Red Cloud, he'd been given the Washington treatment in 1870, and he'd seen there and in New York the heretofore unimaginable extent and power of the white man's empire. He wasn't the same man when he came back from the East and took up permanent residency near Camp Robinson where he received his supplies of blankets, coffee, sugar, and bacon. Crazy Horse was having none of this, nor was Sitting Bull who said his people were fools to trade their land and freedom for the white man's seductive goods. The difference now was that the intransigence of these two cast them in the new role of outsiders among their own.

Beneath the emerging political split within the Oglalas was old, bad blood between Red Cloud's people and Crazy Horse's that went back to the 1840s and that had grown worse in the early 1860s when Crazy Horse was courting a niece of Red Cloud's, Black Buffalo Woman. Then while Crazy Horse was off on a war party Black Buffalo Woman was married to No Water, also of Red Cloud's people, evidently at the chief's instigation. The matter simmered, and Crazy Horse, unmarried, never gave up his interest in Black Buffalo Woman, nor she in him. One day in 1870 when No Water was with the delegation meeting Red Cloud on the chief's return from the East, Crazy Horse took Black Buffalo Woman to his lodge. When No Water got word, he followed. He borrowed a pistol from someone in the village, came to Crazy Horse's lodge, and shot the chief as he sat by the fire, the ball striking him below the nose, then glancing along his upper jaw. Badly wounded, he fell into the fire, and No Water left the village, convinced he'd killed the great Crazy Horse.

In Oglala culture it was Black Buffalo Woman's right to have decided to move into the chief's lodge, and it was the husband who'd acted badly. But Crazy Horse was a shirt-wearer, and the affair and its ensuing repercussions significantly tarnished his name. When he recovered from his wound he sent Black Buffalo Woman back to her husband, but still the elders stripped him of shirt-wearer status. Some time after this he made a more conventional marriage, to Black Shawl of his own people, and by her had a daughter who died in early childhood. A rumor—one of many that cluster around him—says he also had a child by Black Buffalo Woman. If he did, the history and fate of this child may be part of the buried oral tradition.

So the split within the Oglalas yawned, and clearly Crazy Horse was not in a position to ask for Red Cloud's support or Spotted Tail's either as the whites squeezed the Lakotas ever tighter in the 1870s with spidering rail lines and the prospectors and emigrants who followed where the rails led. There were other holdouts, too—Sitting Bull, Gall, Two Moons of the Cheyennes—but the peace faction among the Plains tribes was growing, and it was now possible, as it hadn't been ten years earlier, for the military to identify the troublemakers. And there was now also a sort of third stream among the Lakotas: Indians who had come to understand what a reservation was and had conditionally accepted it, glad enough to take up residence there during the tough winter months, and who felt free to leave when the grass greened and they could ride northward to hunt and camp with those who resolutely stayed out.

Some of these warm weather warriors were with Crazy Horse in the late summer of '73 when he several times hit the party of whites surveying for the Northern Pacific in the Yellowstone Valley. The soldier escort was led by Lieutenant Colonel George Armstrong Custer of the Seventh Cavalry. In several sharp exchanges Custer was able to fend off Crazy Horse, and the surveying continued until the end of the season. It was the beginning of a running engagement between the Strange Man and the one the Indians called Long Hair that ended three summers later on the grassy knoll above the Little Bighorn when Long Hair went down with his men. Custer the man was never important to Crazy Horse, and he might not have been sure who the soldier chief was until after Little Bighorn. What was important were the deepening incursions of the whites into the heart of Lakota lands, incursions made the more troubling the following summer when Custer came prospecting again, this time into the *Paha Sapa*. And when the year after that Crazy Horse learned that Red Cloud and others down at the agencies had actually gotten to the point of discussing a dollar amount for the sale of the *Paha Sapa*, he must have seen as in a lightning flash how it all must go: how, soon, the Lakotas would be entirely surrounded by the whites and cut off from the authentic sources of their life. One does not sell the land on which the people walk, he said, and sent some warriors hurrying down to the negotiations at the Red Cloud agency. One of them frightened the commissioners witless by pushing into the midst of the talking, brandishing a Winchester and a fistful of cartridges, and threatening to kill them all. Other warriors on their horses began to circle behind as if to cut off retreat, but violence was averted, and when the chiefs and the commissioners couldn't agree on a price for the Black Hills, the latter gratefully retreated to Washington. There were some stubborn hostiles standing in the way of the sale, they reported to President Grant. Red Cloud, Spotted Tail, and their headmen understood the Indians must make way for railroads and settlements in the Black Hills, they said, and had accepted the inevitability of the reservation. What was clearly needed now was some means of convincing the hostiles of this.

Being who he was, a war must early have come to the president's mind as an efficient solution to the problem. He certainly had plenty of firepower available now and the requisite logistics in place. The number of hostiles involved couldn't be much more than three thousand, so he'd been assured, and when they'd been thoroughly thrashed, then the agency chiefs could be bullied into signing over the Black Hills. That would get the Western politicians off the presidential back, and the Hills could be thrown open to settlement and the exploitation of the gold Custer's prospecting party had said was there in such dazzling abundance. Grant also had in hand the instrument of pretext in Sherman's earlier ruling that a non-reservation Indian was a hostile one.

Accordingly, on December 6, 1875, Indian Commissioner E. P. Smith ordered that Indians roving in the north country surrender at the agencies by January 31, 1876, or be driven in by military force. The order was, of course, utterly cynical. Probably neither Crazy Horse's people nor Sitting Bull's even received it in time to comply, had they been so inclined. But then, they weren't supposed to comply, and the day after the deadline passed hostilities were formally declared in Washington.

The road to Little Bighorn and beyond, to Camp Robinson where matters were ended when Crazy Horse surrendered, began in the waning days of winter 1876. It was the view of General Crook that the best time to "hunt Indians" was in the worst weather, and so in the ever-unpredictable month of March on the Great Plains Crook went after the hostiles, on March 17 surprising a sizeable camp on the Powder River. At first, he thought he'd hit Crazy Horse, but it turned out the chief was camped a few miles away and these were the people of He Dog and Two Moons. Though surprised, the Indians fought staunchly back, and their human losses were light. Their material losses were heavy, though, in provisions, robes, blankets, and ponies (one hundred ten of which the soldiers shot), and the refugees fled to Crazy Horse in bitter weather. It was clear to all of them now, as it had been to him for some time, that this was to be a fight to the finish.

But the army's winter campaign hadn't been a success; the attack on the village on the Powder had hardly been decisive. Crazy Horse and

Sitting Bull remained very much at large, and now with the coming of better weather and their ponies strengthening daily on the new grasses it would be even harder for the army to catch up with them. Still, it must be done. So, a three-pronged offensive into the unceded country was organized with the goal of catching the hostiles and crushing the life out of them. One prong under Colonel John Gibbon moved south and then east from Fort Shaw, Montana Territory; another moved west to meet it from Fort Abraham Lincoln under General Alfred Terry and Custer; and then driving up from the appropriately named Fort Fetterman was Crook, whom the Indians called Bear Coat or Three Stars. But the army failed to reckon the Strange Man and Sitting Bull, and it failed also to understand the desperate mood of the tribes.

It had been an awful winter at the agencies. Along with the severe weather and a tardy spring there had been famine as the Indians' promised supplies arrived late or not at all, and deprived of their arms they'd been unable to hunt for themselves. Then too the stench of last fall's negotiations for the sale of the *Paha Sapa* hung in the air like a rotting carcass. Many who'd settled for agency existence were now having second thoughts, while those who'd moved seasonally between the agencies and the north country were finding new reasons to ride northward to the patriot chiefs. His father told him during this spring, young Black Elk remembered, that the family would be "going back to Crazy Horse and that we were going to have to fight from then on because there was no other way to keep our country. He said Red Cloud was a cheap man and wanted to sell the Black Hills to the *wasichus*; that Spotted Tail and the other chiefs were cheap men too, and that the Hang-Around-the Fort people (agency Indians) were all cheap and would stand up for the *wasichus*." Many other families had come to a similar conclusion, and by the end of May—what the Lakotas called the Moon When the Ponies Shed—their defections from the agencies had greatly increased the villages of the hostiles in the north. What the precise numbers were in June 1876 is still a matter of intense scholarly debate. Whatever the number, the important point is this: it was well in excess of what the army figured.

Nor had the army been able to calculate the power of Sitting Bull and the one so few bluecoats had ever knowingly seen, Crazy Horse. After Crook's attack on the Powder River village the holdout Oglalas had met in council and conferred on Crazy Horse an authority greater than any of the shirt-wearers (who now effectively ceased to exist), naming him supreme chief in both civil and military matters. The move was unprecedented and indicated both the Lakotas' desperation and their belief that only the Strange Man was equal to the crisis enveloping them. Then they sent riders south to the agencies with this news and with calls for everyone to rally to him and save the nation. For their part, the Hunkpapas had earlier conferred a similar title on Sitting Bull.

During the first week in June the Hunkpapa chief organized a sun dance on the Rosebud in the course of which he had as a vision of soldiers riding upside down into the Indians' camp. He interpreted this as a prophecy of a great Indian victory, though he and Crazy Horse had agreed the people should avoid the soldiers if they could. But they couldn't, and on June 17 Three Stars attacked them on the Rosebud. In a daylong seesaw fight Crazy Horse forced Three Stars to retreat toward his base camp. Crazy Horse's old tactic of decoying the soldiers didn't work this time, but another stratagem did: he sent his warriors in successive waves against the bluecoats, attacking them again and yet again from several directions with a discipline and relentlessness the soldiers were unaccustomed to from Indian warriors. Near dusk the soldiers turned back south, and the Indians were in a mood of grim invincibility. Then they moved on to the Little Bighorn. Crook claimed victory, but he kept his forces six weeks down at his base camp and was never again a factor in the punitive campaign.

Custer was as rash as Crook was cautious, and so it was he who found the huge gathering of villages along the Little Bighorn on June 25. The Indians had long known of his whereabouts; they simply didn't imagine anyone would dare to attack them. But just as the army hadn't reckoned with the gathered forces they now faced, so the Lakotas and Cheyennes didn't understand the sandy-haired man who saw this perilous situation as a magnificent opportunity to deal a deathblow to tribal resistance on the Plains. Despite the dire warnings of his seasoned scouts who had never before seen such dangerous signs, Custer divided his forces and then rode down to a greater glory in defeat than he could ever have achieved in triumph.

For Crazy Horse the hot, still morning of the battle was ominous. Ordinarily completely collected in the fiercest fight, now, poised on the cusp of his final and greatest victory, he was uneasy. Well before Custer sent Major Marcus Reno to attack the southern end of the encampment Crazy Horse was mounted and moving through the village circles. Then, abruptly, he dismounted at his lodge and came out with his medicine bag. Moistening a hand, he dipped it into maroon pigment and made handprints on his pony. Then he painted an arrow and bloody scalp on its neck. But he still wasn't gotten up for war when the first bullets from Reno's charge shredded the cottonwood leaves and ripped through the lodges. Now he made haste to put on the elaborate paraphernalia of his vision. Later, some would remember that his young men had become impatient with how long it took him to arrive down at the action against Reno's salient. He Dog said he teased the Strange Man about it, telling him, Too bad you missed the fight. But the chief was now himself again in his protective paint and laughed, pointing through the trees at Custer's detachment, above them on the high ridge in the sun. There was still plenty of honor to be gained, he said.

At this point in the battle the outcome still seemed much in doubt. The Hunkpapa circle Reno had struck was in some disarray though the great Gall would shortly stiffen and rally his men, and the appearance of the charging bluecoats in their midst might have made some suddenly doubt Sitting Bull's victorious vision. But as Black Elk remembered it, what changed things among the villages was the cry that now went up into air blackened with gunpowder and dust, "Crazy Horse is coming!" And there was the chief, in his painted hail spots, kicking his pony through the waters of the river and up through the grasses toward that ridge along which Custer rode in the high summer sun.

For many years after that it was believed that the chief had led his men north of the ridge and parallel to it, so that at the decisive moment he could swarm up behind Custer and cut off any hope of escape. In recent years, though, as a phalanx of historians, military specialists, and archeologists have gone over the battlefield foot by foot, it has come to seem that Crazy Horse's late arrival at the Reno fight and the short duration of the entire engagement would have made impossible that sort of time-consuming encirclement. Nobody on the Indian side that day knew precisely what happened. In the swirling mass of men and horses and the heavy pall of smoke and dust nobody saw much more than what was immediately around him. And of course there was no one left from Custer's detachment to tell the story. But it appears that Crazy Horse and his men went directly up and over the ridge and down its eastern slope before wheeling about and charging back over it again. White Bull, who was with the chief, later said Crazy Horse challenged him to ride back through the soldiers on the ridgetop and that they both did so. He Dog said that charge split Custer's detachment in two. The southern portion fought to the end where they were, while the northern portion, which included Long Hair, gradually retreated to a high knoll where they made a last stand.

From Reno's charge a few minutes after three in the afternoon to when the last trooper went down on the knoll was probably less than two hours, and then it was all over but the death lamentations and the scalp dances, both of which Crazy Horse customarily avoided. What he did that night in the wild villages whites may never know, nor what his thoughts were. The Hunkpapa Iron Hawk no doubt spoke for many of those celebrating when he said, "These *wasichus* wanted it, and they came to get it, and we gave it to them," but others surely knew also that the *wasichus* would keep on coming and that the Indians wouldn't be able to give it to them as they had this day on the Little Bighorn. They couldn't keep so large a force together for more than a few days at a time: there simply wasn't enough food available for the people or forage for the ponies. And the determination of the soldiers became evident only a few hours later when in the afternoon of the twenty-sixth more bluecoats were sighted as the tribes began pulling out. It was Terry's column, which shortly would discover what the Indians had left behind in the blazing grasses of the battlefield.

If he thought the whipping the tribes had given the whites might convince the army to leave the Lakotas their sacred hills and the Powder River country, Crazy Horse learned otherwise by late fall. The whites were viciously vindictive. Down on the agencies the loss at Little Bighorn prompted them to replace civilian with military authority, and when this was done the military presented the chiefs with a brutally simple ultimatum: sign over the Black Hills and unceded territory or starve. Nor was this all. The chiefs were also told they'd have to move from their present agencies east to the Missouri so that the military could save on shipping rations to a people now utterly deprived of their means to feed and clothe themselves. By the end of October the chiefs had signed while their disarmed, unhorsed braves looked on helplessly.

And then the soldiers came for Crazy Horse and Sitting Bull and the remnant Cheyennes.

In late November Three Stars hit Dull Knife's Cheyennes in the Bighorn Mountains, destroying their village and driving the refugees to Crazy Horse on the Tongue River. The chief had little enough himself at this point, but he shared what he had and kept moving. Maybe if he could hold out until spring. ... But in December with his wife seriously ill and his people suffering intensely he sent nine peace-talkers to General Miles at Fort Keogh under a flag of truce. When they neared the fort the whites' Crow mercenaries opened up on them and killed five. So apparently there could be no negotiations: it would be unconditional surrender or death.

The Strange Man now seemed even stranger to those left around him. He hardly ever stayed in camp, Black Elk said, but spent his days out alone in the cold, huddled with his thoughts. Once, Black Elk's father came upon him like that. "Uncle," Crazy Horse said to him, "you have noticed me the way I act. But do not worry; there are caves and holes for me to live in, and out here the spirits may help me. I am making plans for the good of my people."

In January Miles found the camp and attacked it, the Indians at last swinging their empty rifles like clubs in the hand-to-hand fighting and then managing to slip away to the Little Bighorn River, country that once had been home but that now was bitter and dangerous. By this point they were eating their ponies. And by this point too agency Indians were coming out to try to talk the chief into surrendering. When he looked into the pinched faces of his people he could see it was only he who kept them out. Spotted Tail with a delegation of two hundred came out in February and apparently told his nephew there was the possibility of an agency of his own somewhere in the Powder River country; also that they could go on a buffalo hunt in the fall. He carried with him some supplies for Crazy Horse's people. When Spotted Tail returned to his agency in April he told officials that Crazy Horse and the few other scattered bands of hostiles would be following as quickly as their winter-poor ponies would enable them.

In mid-April they began to straggle in at almost the same time that Sitting Bull was crossing to a safe haven in Grandmother's Land, Canada. First came Crazy Horse's confederate chiefs, then some small groups who'd moved with him almost until the last. And then the chief and his half-starved village. Some miles out Red Cloud, now reduced to the role of gofer for the white man, met Crazy Horse and distributed some sorely needed supplies. Then Red Cloud and Lieutenant William Philo Clark led the way in to the agency. A few less than nine hundred people and two thousand shaggy, gaunt ponies, they plodded in, a hunted, haunted procession two mile long while their own people and curious whites lined the way to surrender. Even so, they made a show of it. As they came up to Camp Robinson the chiefs lifted their voices in a peace song that was taken up by the warriors and then by the women. Hearing it but not understanding it, one white officer exclaimed, "By God, this is a triumphal march, not a surrender!"

Of course, the main attraction for the officer as well as for the other whites would have been the Strange Man himself, who by this point must have assumed for them almost mythical dimensions. Now they found him real enough, though even in defeat he had a presence like no other. Lieutenant John G. Bourke was surprised to find him so young, not over thirty, he guessed. He was about five-eight, Bourke wrote, lithe and sinewy and with a scar on his face (the Black Buffalo Woman/No Water affair). The expression on that face, the young lieutenant noted, was one of "quiet dignity, but morose, dogged, tenacious, and melancholy."

• • •

South Dakota 40 West takes you off the Pine Ridge Reservation into the *Paha Sapa* for which the chief fought until there was nothing left to fight with, not even will. I raced along it under a gunmetal sky, my mind on that cloud of questions that wrapped the Strange Man in mystery, questions I wasn't going to get any answers to. Half an hour before, back at the tribal offices at Pine Ridge, I'd been talking with Dale Looks Twice, trying to get answers to some of those questions, trying to tap into that subterranean river of tribal tradition I felt was there. Looks Twice had offered to help me with members of the Crazy Horse *tiospaye* and had just telephoned down the hall to Philip Underbaggage. They spoke briefly in Lakota while I waited, and when Looks Twice hung up and faced me again I saw the look I was coming slowly to know, the one that put up the wall around the Strange Man.

"The, ah, family," he began, then stopped and started up again. "The family says that because of the monument and the beer, they don't want to talk about him." The reference to the monument I got: the descendents of the Boston-born sculptor charge admission to the site, but the family and the tribe got none of the proceeds. I hadn't, however, until that moment known that there was a Crazy Horse beer. I was wondering whether to tell Looks Twice that there was also a Crazy Horse Saloon in Paris where a doorman once told me Crazy Horse was an Apache who'd scalped General Custer. I never got the chance, for at that moment a burly man wheeled into the office and confronted me at point-blank range.

"You're gonna have to leave the office," he said, standing over me. "I'm gonna give you twenty minutes to get off the reservation. If you don't, I'll put you in jail." He looked down at my notebook. "I ought to take that from you," he said, jabbing a forefinger at its offending pages. I could see he was thinking about doing just that and started to protest as Looks Twice hurried past him and down the hall. The burly man told me he was the tribal sergeant-at-arms, in full authority on these premises.

I stood up and started to speak, but he cut me off again. "If you speak his name again, I'll put you in jail. You can't say *anything* about him!" I had seen the tank at Pine Ridge and had no interest in spending any time with the fearfully battered drunks sure to be in its cells, so I left the offices with Lyman Red Cloud on my heels. Passing quickly by Underbaggage's office, I saw it crowded with dark-faced people among whom were Dolores Mills and Gerald Big Crow.

The only way to get off the reservation in the twenty minutes Red Cloud had given me would be to head due south through Whiteclay, that vale of terminal sorrow where at all hours the drinkers lie or lean at impossible angles outside the bars. But though Red Cloud had watched me get into my car, I doubted he'd follow me out of town and so I'd taken this longer route, through the beautiful, treeless grasslands that ran in waves westward into the dark woods of the hills. There I turned south through Custer State Park where buffalo, massive, almost black, grazed the hock-high grasses.

What had just happened back there? Had the Crazy Horse *tiospaye* asked the tribal authorities to throw me off? Had Underbaggage really set me up, and not with interviews? Surely, since the 1930s when whites began asking questions about Crazy Horse many others had been on errands like mine. And if it was the monument that had made matters explosive, why now? Korczak Ziolkowski had begun blasting away in 1948, partly at the behest of some Lakotas who wanted their great patriot memorialized like those white versions at nearby Mount Rushmore.

Or could it be that I'd played a small, unwitting part in the continued working out of the historic antagonism between Crazy Horse's people and Red Cloud's? The tribal offices, I knew, were the seat of power for the Red Cloud folk, and now as I retraced the way Crazy Horse had taken to Camp Robinson I was forced to rehearse in my mind the old story that Red Cloud and his people had actively conspired to bring about the imprisonment and death of Crazy Horse once the chief had come in.

The heroic holdout's arrival at Red Cloud's agency couldn't have been a cause for rejoicing for Red Cloud or for Spotted Tail who had his own agency to the north and east. These defeated, humiliated leaders were understandably jealous of what little power they had left and not eager to share it with the newcomer. Nor could they fail to see almost from the first day that Crazy Horse inspired a watchful respect in the whites who began to defer to him more and more as spring turned to summer. Snakes of rumors began then to crawl through the agencies. If Crazy Horse were allowed to go on the promised fall buffalo hunt with guns and horses and his headmen, some Indians told the whites, he would surely jump the reservation and head for the old north country. And if he did that, others would follow his lead and the army would be obliged to begin the whole arduous, hazardous business all over again. He was totally unreconstructed, it was being said, and was only biding him time, proof of which was his refusal to go to Washington to meet with the Great Father. The agent at Red Cloud, listening to these rumors, described Crazy Horse as sullen and morose and told superiors the chief's behavior "has rendered him unpopular with the leading men of his band who have drawn off from him."

Toward the end of August Lieutenant Clark called a conference at the Red Cloud agency. Crook had ordered him to recruit some Lakotas to aid the army in its pursuit of some Nez Perces under Chief Joseph who'd fled the military in a desperate bid for freedom. The army was stretched thin this summer with Apache troubles and labor strikes in Chicago and westward. Red recruits would be welcome, and there was no doubt these Sioux could fight. Crazy Horse attended along with Touch the Clouds, the seven-foot Miniconjou chief, and several other comrades from the old days. Louis Bordeaux and Frank Grouard were there to interpret. At first the chief refused to help. Perhaps he thought Crook's real target was Sitting Bull, not Joseph. He said he didn't understand the whites: they'd harried him for months to come in to the agency and lay down his arms and he'd done so. Now they asked him to tie up his pony's tail once more and go back on the warpath. There was more talking, and finally Crazy Horse said he'd go against the Nez Perces under certain conditions, among them that he wanted to take along some families close to him and do some hunting. If these conditions were met, he concluded, then he and his men would ride north and fight alongside the whites until not a single Nez Perce was left. Yet when Grouard (who knew the chief and feared him) finished interpreting this Clark had the impression that the chief had said the Lakotas would fight until no whites were left. Bordeaux caught the mistake and accused Grouard of twisting the chief's meaning. Angry words were exchanged all around, and Crazy Horse and his men walked out. Clark was convinced the chief intended to go on the warpath against the whites and informed his superiors who sent the beleaguered Crook hurrying back to Camp Robinson.

Once there the general heard more ominous rumors about Crazy Horse who was said to be dangerously excited. On September 2, Crook called a council on White Clay Creek, asking all the principal chiefs to attend, but as he made his way there he was intercepted by a Lakota named Woman's Dress who told him that when Crazy Horse shook the general's hand that would be the signal for his men to attack and slaughter the whites to a man. Crook hesitated, then turned back to Camp Robinson and went into secret parlay with his officers and friendly chiefs. The chiefs argued for arresting Crazy Horse and killing him, but Crook drew back from an involvement in a murder plot. He agreed, though, that the chief must be arrested before he could ignite both agencies. He gave the order, then left, perhaps thinking the problem might be solved if it should happen that Crazy Horse was killed while resisting arrest.

So now for the final time they came for the Strange Man, eight companies of bluecoats and a large retinue of Oglalas led by Red Cloud. Some days earlier he'd left Red Cloud's agency, feeling watched and unwelcome there, and with his rapidly failing wife had sought shelter with his kinsman, Spotted Tail. But that chief gave him a very public dressing down, telling him *he* was chief of his agency and that if his nephew wished to stay there, he'd have to be obedient. So, there was no place for him among his own, and he belonged to the bluecoats who brought him to Camp Robinson on September 5. If this was a triumphal march like that other, it must have had an unmistakable funeral pomp to it. As he was about to enter the camp grounds, He Dog, his trusted friend from the old, free days, rode up alongside and looked into the chief's sharp face, now even sharper with tension, telling him to be careful, that he was about to enter a dangerous place. But of course, there was little Crazy Horse could do to be careful. Like the mystic rider of his youthful vision he was utterly alone with danger all around him, and this time he was without his protecting medicine—the small, smooth pebble, the red-backed hawk, the hail spots and lightning.

In my rental car I cleared the town of Crawford, Nebraska, and came myself to the camp grounds of what's now Fort Robinson State Park, a neat array of brick and frame buildings spaced about an oval. But I didn't see them; I saw instead the chief in his red blanket, looking small and terribly alone as he rode through a large crowd of Lakotas who'd gathered to see what would happen. On the procession went to the adjutant's office, and I followed. I stood in the raw gloom of the day at the dangerous place He Dog had spoken of, before me a weathered replica of the office and forty steps away another building just like it. I had the place to myself, the tourist season being well over, but it felt crowded with the vanished forms of the black-haired, blanketed crowd, jostling, pushing to catch a glimpse of the Strange Man.

The chief and his guards went into the office, and the guards were curtly told they must take him down the line to the jail where he was to be held until under the cover of night he could be slipped out and hustled to the railroad. From there he was to be shipped to Fort Marion, Florida, or the Dry Tortugas where, surrounded by sea, there could be no warpath left to take. During the brief conversation the chief stood silent, tense but uncomprehending.

Black Elk was there that day in the crowd that waited outside the adjutant's office, but the backs of the others blocked his view. He could tell now, though, from the excited buzz about him that they'd brought the chief out and were moving him toward that other building. Then, he remembered, "I heard a loud cry in our own language, and it said, 'Don't touch me! I am Crazy Horse!' And suddenly something went through all the people there like a big wind that strikes many trees at once." What he hadn't seen was that Crazy Horse himself had suddenly, finally, seen what had been awaiting him—the white man's iron house. I followed his vanished footsteps through the dead grasses to the jail. I found it locked but looked through its barred windows to more bars inside. There could be no doubt now. Here was Death.

He stopped at the threshold, setting his feet, but they kept pushing him, as they had been doing for so long, and he cried out, whirling against them and drawing a knife from the folds of the red blanket. Little Big Man, who'd ridden with him to the end of the warpath, struggled with him, whether to aid the whites or to protect the chief from certain harm none ever really knew. But now he held the chief's arms (the vision again), and Private William Gentles lunged at Crazy Horse with his bayonet, running it through his back with such force it almost came out his stomach. The chief fell to the ground in agony, and some later claimed that Red Cloud himself then yelled out to the soldiers to shoot him where he lay. But they didn't, and as post surgeon V. T. McGillycuddy quickly ascertained, they didn't have to. "I found Crazy Horse on his back," he wrote, "grinding his teeth and frothing at the mouth, blood trickling from a bayonet wound above the hip, and the pulse weak and missing beats, and I saw that he was done for. ..."

The marble marker outside the guard house positively glared at me under the relentless light, its simple legend telling the curious that on this spot the chief was killed. Actually, he lingered until the morning hours, watched over in the adjutant's office by McGillycuddy, Touch the Clouds, and old Worm.

Did he in those dark, ebbing hours give a long, rambling speech, as some have said, loquacious at the end as he hadn't been in life? Did he sing his death's song in a weak and wavering voice? Did he bid farewell to his chieftaincy, saying to Touch the Clouds, "Tell the people it is no use to depend on me any more"? Or something else, some last utterance or gesture that has never gotten into the white man's print? Perhaps they know these things and many others as well up at Manderson and around Wounded Knee where the tattered ritual cloths and ribbons wave in the wind that rushes over the Ghost Dancers' common grave. Maybe they know too where the chief lies buried. As for myself, standing there on the spot of his mortal wounding, I realized I was glad not to know. "It does not matter where his body lies," old Black Elk told John Neihardt, "for it is grass; but where his spirit is, it will be good to be."

Winter Counts

I

Not long after we had blundered into these shores the question arose as to how long it would take to assimilate the new lands and their natives. To be sure, there was something remarkably arrogant in this—kind of like a kid taking his first bite of a pie as big as a house and wondering if there will be enough—since by the close of the first century of exploration, we had hardly so much as a map to show us accurately the extent and contours of the newfound land, whether it was shaped like the nipple of Paradise, as Columbus believed; or whether it hooked somehow onto the fabled Far East. Nor had we any idea of how many natives there might be awaiting our discovery within the continent's shadowy and unimagined interior. A tiny expeditionary force from the Old World, we were confined to reservations of white civilization on the coasts, trying there to survive starvation, mutinies, and the attacks of those natives we had so far dispossessed. Even so, it is possible to discern in the early Spanish, French, and English documents a shared assumption that one day all of America would be ours. And that meant we had a problem: what would we do with these natives and all this land?

The natives' point of view was precisely the opposite: what would they do with these whites? Some believed the invaders would eventually just go away. In the prophecies of some Southwestern tribes, for example, the white man was fated to disappear at last, ghostly, evanescent, like those who had once wandered through their lands, vanishing in a shimmer of heat and dust: the Coronado expedition, this was styled in European historiography.

Three centuries later it was apparently the whites who had known better after all, having in the intervening years so successfully imposed themselves on America that they had overspread it, however thinly, and owned title to all but a few scraps where the natives existed on sufferance. In 1890 the census bureau reported the disappearance of that line between white civilization and wilderness that from the beginning had really defined what America was, and as the final act in this process there was the opening to white settlement in this same year of eleven million acres of the Great Sioux Reservation in South Dakota.

The Sioux cession was equally significant as fact and symbol. More than the Iroquois, more than the stubborn Seminoles or the far-flung, elusive Navajos, the Sioux were to white Americans marplots and troublemakers whose lands lay squarely in the westward path of progress. In 1862, the Santee Sioux had arisen in Minnesota and effectively cleared the state of white inhabitants. Four years later on the Bozeman Trail in Wyoming, the western Sioux had wiped out Captain Fetterman and his entire eighty-man command. Two years after that the government agreed at Ft. Laramie to abandon the Bozeman Trail and its forts and to "give" the Sioux all of South Dakota west of the Missouri for their exclusive use, plus hunting rights in southeastern Montana—a humiliating capitulation as many whites saw it. And then there had been the Custer disaster that spoiled the nation's centennial celebration.

That did it. Howls went up in Congress and almost everywhere else for vindictive punishment of the Sioux, and hardly had the dust from the Little Bighorn settled when commissioners backed by a huge armed force arrived on the Great Sioux Reservation to threaten and bribe the Sioux into giving up the Black Hills, their Montana hunting range, and about a third of the Great Sioux Reservation—all this in violation of the Ft. Laramie treaty which required consent of three-fourths of the adult Sioux males to make any changes in its provisions. In their successful resistance the Sioux had succeeded also in focusing the attention of a nation on them, and that nation was no longer in the mood for gradual measures. William Tecumseh Sherman, who had been placed in charge of the Plains campaigns, spoke for the majority when he said that the Indians would "all have to be killed or maintained as a species of pauper." By the time of the opening to white settlement of those eleven million acres of Sioux land Sherman's vision had been fulfilled everywhere in America and nowhere more fully than on the Sioux reservations where the once haughty Lakota (as they called themselves) were in truth a species of pauper, utterly dependent on the uncertain flow of their treaty annuities, bereft of the buffalo, forbidden their religious practices, their tribal and band structures destroyed, and even their remaining lands slated for dismemberment into individual allotments as per the provisions of the Dawes Severalty Act. As the Commissioner of Indian Affairs put it in July 1889, "The settled policy of the government is to break up the reservations, destroy tribal relations, settle Indians upon their own homesteads, incorporate them into the national life. ... The American Indian is to become the Indian American. ... " This was assimilation, late-nineteenth-century version, but it would not be too difficult to see it as a plan for cultural extermination.

That was certainly the way the Lakota saw it. They had suffered defeats in the past—in skirmishes with the Pawnees, the Crows—and they had suffered the harsh vicissitudes of nomadic life on the Great Plains—hunting mishaps, scarcity of game, winters so savage even the camp dogs were snowblinded and crows froze in flight and fell dead against the sides of the lodges. Yet their winter counts, the oral histories of the bands that reminded them of these things, told them also that they had survived and endured with honor. History was a source of hope and encouragement then. Now history seemed to be coming to an end under the rule of these implacable *wasichus* (whites) who, it would seem, would be satisfied with nothing less than the disappearance of the people:

1881 *Ṣịteʹg.leṡka ḳteʹpi*
Spotted Tail/they kill.
(Spotted-Tail, chief at Rosebud [Reservation], is killed.)

1882 *Cʹạcʹeġa ḳʹịʹla cʹịcaʹwạ icʹiʹḳte*
"Drum/he carries on his back (nickname)"/his son/a/
he kills himself.
(Drum-on-the-Back's son shoots himself.)

1884 *Tʹatʹạʹḳa Ska tʹawiʹ cu ḳiḳteʹ*
"Buffalo-Bull/White"/his wife/he kills his own.
(White-Bull killed his wife.)

1888 *Woʹpʹaḣta yubleʹcapi*
"Bundles"/they are opened and exposed.
([Reservation] policemen stop the traffic in "medicine.")

1889 *O´g.le Sa t´ạk´si´tku wạ ic´i´kte*
"Shirt/Red"/his younger sister/a/she hanged herself.
(Red Shirt's younger sister hanged herself.)

—Entries from the winter count of Ben Kindle of
the Oglala Sioux (trans. Martha Warren Beckwith)

Not surprisingly, deprived thus of their history and of hope, the
Lakotas caught the Ghost Dance fever that swept through so many
Western tribes in 1889–90, for the prophecy of the new religion said that
history was not at an end, that indeed the past was returning in the
spring of 1891. At that time the dead Indians would return along with
the buffalo, and the *wasichus* would choke to death on the land they had
been so greedy to possess. A new earth would roll over the old one the
wasichus had profaned, and history would recommence its round. A desperate hope, to be sure, as Sitting Bull acknowledged when he asked
what difference it made whether the new religion was true or not. We
have nothing else to hope for, he said.

1890 *Si T´ạ´ka kte´pi*
"Big/foot"/they kill.
(Big Foot and his band massacred at Wounded Knee.)

II

"When your life seems to be coming to an end, you'll try anything,"
Victor Douville said. We were sitting in the dimly lit trailer that houses
the Lakota Studies Department at Sinte Gleska (Spotted Tail) College
on the Rosebud reservation, talking of the upcoming ceremonies marking the centennial of the massacre of almost four hundred Lakotas by
United States soldiers at Wounded Knee. Douville was a fifty-year-old
Brulé who had taught Lakota Studies at the college since 1972. The
Ghost Dance, he judged, would eventually have died out without the
massacre because it was essentially too foreign to Lakota cultural princi-
ples. "But the way it happened was a tremendously traumatic thing

because so many people got killed there. So, after Wounded Knee the older people stopped trying to educate the children. Until that event they had been thinking they could hang on to the old ways. But when so many were killed, they came up hard against another reality and realized they would have to walk another road—and so would their children."

Was that, then, the lesson of Wounded Knee? He paused, looking across the barren room with its single light shining on his long black hair and full face. "Well," he said at length, "it's one lesson, but not the only one.

"There's another lesson, too, which is that you should never impose your values on other people, and certainly not by force. To some extent the dominant culture is still trying to do this, not by force, but by tremendous daily pressure. It's called 'assimilation.' But the more they try to force foreign ways on the Lakota people, the more they [the Lakotas] resist. Part of what you're looking at here—the poverty, the alcoholism—is the result of that resistance."

But for Douville (and for others, as I was later to learn) the ultimate lesson of Wounded Knee existed beneath the memory of those frozen and wind-warped corpses that lay clustered on the flats at the massacre site and those others scattered for miles along the ravine where the troopers had ridden the fleeing people down and murdered them. The Ghost Dance had been a false hope in that the old buffalo days were not going to magically return, "though there are a few who still think they will." But the old ways of thought, the old values that existed before the Ghost Dance could be recaptured, and they could be recaptured at centers such as Sinte Gleska. Since the 1970s, he said, "more and more people are beginning to trust their cultural instincts. I have to give AIM [the American Indian Movement] some credit for this: they raised people's consciousness. Now they're beginning to look back—not to the return of the buffalo and the ancestors like in the Ghost Dance—but to the old ways like generosity, sharing, and respect for elders and for the earth. This system isn't the way the dominant system works, but this system can work here, and people are beginning to see that. It worked in the past. It worked for hundreds and hundreds of years." People were beginning to turn to the tribal colleges and especially to their Lakota Studies departments to rediscover their traditional values, "and the more they find out who they are, the more they find out those traditional values can help them with their lives." Eventually, he predicted, what was going to happen was that "as more and more people get educated, they're going to bring these values into the political situation. The making of our decisions is going to be influenced more by our traditions instead of [by] the imposed system." This, he suggested, might be the real meaning of the much-discussed "self-determination," and for these reasons he was optimistic, "in spite of everything." The Ghost Dance, he said, had been a revitalistic movement like those that had galvanized the Iroquois and the Admiralty Islanders, but maybe the Lakota people were now in the midst of a different kind of movement, less defined, less dramatic, but no less real and perhaps with more lasting consequences.

The theme was reinforced by Elgin Bad Wound, president of Oglala Lakota College on the Pine Ridge reservation. "Read our catalog," said Bad Wound, reaching for a copy and doing this for me. "'To promote tribal identity, and thus enhance the chances for student success, tribal leaders envisioned a community-based post-secondary institution, grounded in tribal history and culture.'" He put the catalog aside, leaned back in his chair, and gestured toward the window, beyond which was a traditional brush-and-sapling enclosure where college ceremonies were often held. "The mission of this college is tribal self-determination. That's the main thing the tribes are struggling for: the right to be let alone and to manage their own affairs. The situation is simply this: in exchange for all this land (gesturing toward the America that stretched away from the boundaries of the reservation) and for peace, we expected certain services and money. This isn't a dole. Indians don't want to be wards. They want to be *Indians*, they want to be tribes, with their own values, their own agendas. Things are different now, sure, but we made those agreements between nations, and the federal government just hasn't lived up to its end of the agreement."

Granting that this same government had in fact created Oglala Lakota College, as well as the other tribal colleges under the provisions of the Tribal College Act of 1978, Bad Wound echoed the sentiments of Victor Douville and other Lakotas that the government's greatest single failure had been its long-standing, ill-considered, and wasteful policy of forced assimilation, a policy most significantly prosecuted through its educational system. You could not, he claimed, overestimate the profound damage done Indian youngsters by white-oriented curricula taught by white faculty. I got a succinct assessment of this damage in a subsequent talk with Dale Looks Twice, program director for the Lakota language radio station, KILI: "All the BIA schools did was teach assimilation," Looks Twice said, "and you can't imagine how discouraging it is when you're Indian to be taught year after year to be a good little non-Indian." Elgin Bad Wound said white-oriented, white-administered education was a "daily disparagement of tribal beliefs. And not just disparagement: there was a total *absence* of tribal culture in the schools, and that's just as bad. You had the story of America as 'The Pioneers Moving West,' and off in the shadows were the savages. But in many cases there weren't any Indians at all. We didn't exist. Which was the whole point."

Calvin Jumping Bull of the college's Lakota Studies Department was, like Bad Wound, a product of the BIA educational system, though of the pre–World War II generation. "Those schools," he said, "were run on a military kind of model. Actually, they were more like prisons than schools. In high school we were allowed to go home once a month. But some of the kids didn't get to go home from September to May unless their parents came for them. And in many cases the parents *couldn't* come for them. You were strictly regimented from 6:00 A.M. till you went to bed at 9:15." But for him, the more significant fact was that the schools were completely devoted to the goal of assimilation. "There was nothing native. No dancing, no language, no history. I remember there was one guy from Oklahoma who came to work in the library. He wasn't Lakota, but at least he got together some guys to form a little dance group. I think he was the first guy to do anything like this, and this was something like 1951, so, as you can see, we've come a long ways."

Earlier in our conversation I had asked Jumping Bull about the lessons of Wounded Knee, but he had not responded. Now abruptly he returned to this, claiming an integral connection between Wounded Knee and the history of Indian education. Both the massacre and the subsequent educational history, he said, proceeded out of the same blind need to dominate. "This kind of tragedy shouldn't have happened in the first place. But the dominant society—once it gets the idea it *has* to be dominant—well, this is the kind of thing that *will* happen.

"First they thought, 'Well, we'll kill off the buffalo. That'll control 'em.' But that wasn't enough. So then they said, 'We'll divide and conquer,' and so they killed off our leaders: Crazy Horse, Sitting Bull,

Spotted Tail—all killed by their own people. And still that wasn't enough. So, they decided they'd have to kill off the religion, and so you have Wounded Knee. And even that wasn't the end of it, because you have this system of schooling. And so it's still the question: *Why?* Why does the dominant society have to be *so* dominant? Why can't we have our traditions, our ways? Why do we have to become 'civilized'?" He smiled broadly.

"America makes a lot of talk about freedom. Right now they're talking about freedom for Saudi Arabia. But here we haven't had much freedom. Did you know that for many years I had to get a pass to go off the reservation? It's a fact. And that's where Wounded Knee II comes in. There was a guy came down here, a Chicano, years ago who told us our reservation was really more like a concentration camp. We didn't want to hear that. Then those people [AIM] came along and focused attention on the facts of life here, on the ways the dominant society was still trying to control all aspects of our lives. They served their purpose in reminding us of this, and our purpose here [at Oglala Lakota College] is to remind our students of who they are. If we do a good job of that, they'll see what they can become."

III

November 29, 1990. By this day a hundred years ago events had locked into place here on the remnants of the Great Sioux Reservation. The fervor of the Ghost Dancers had been raised to new heights with the announcement by one of the Lakota prophets that the apocalypse had been moved nearer "since the whites are interfering so much … ." In response to fears of another Sioux uprising troops of Custer's old unit, the Seventh Cavalry, reinforced by an additional three thousand men, were on the reservations, and the first badly frightened Lakotas under Chief Big Foot had fled into the Badlands to escape punishment and to continue their dancing. Sitting Bull was under daily surveillance at his camp, and within a few days orders would secretly be issued for his arrest or execution, whichever should prove most expedient.

On this bright, windy day of high skies filled with mares' tails I accompanied Dale Looks Twice of KILI to interview Marie Not Help

Him, great-granddaughter of a survivor of Wounded Knee who had left eight family members on that field. On our way from Porcupine Butte (where Big Foot's people had been intercepted by the army and escorted to the killing ground at Wounded Knee) to Pine Ridge we passed through the site, and Looks Twice had me stop along the road running beneath the hill on which the troops' Hotchkiss guns once were poised. He pointed out the approximate positions of the various companies, Big Foot's tent, and the lodges of the people. "Over there," he said, pointing left, "is the ravine where the people tried to escape when the firing began." Five horses wearing the first shaggy coats of winter ambled in unsupervised freedom across the road and down into the ravine. Looks Twice watched them, then remarked, "We've been struggling and struggling to survive since Wounded Knee, and one thing I'm proud of is that we've never sold out to corporations that would tear up the reservation. Over on Wind River the Arapaho got a lot of money at first for mineral leases. Now they get maybe a hundred dollars [per person] a year, and where are they? We still have our land, and it's beautiful."

Outside Marie Not Help Him's trailer home a small delegation of Latter Day Saints worked the rutted streets, books and pamphlets in hand, collars up against the wind. Inside, I counted eight family members coming and going, folding laundry, cooking breakfast, eating it. But once Not Help Him settled into an easy chair and took Looks Twice's microphone in hand they all disappeared.

Then commenced the tragic litany, delivered in an incantatory way, leading inexorably Wounded Knee: the execution of Sitting Bull and the mutilation of his corpse; then the decision of Big Foot and his council to try to evade the troops and make it almost two hundred miles south to Red Cloud and his people at Pine Ridge. But now the old events, so often rehearsed in historiography, began to resonate with the character of life lived, the chronicle of the generations being extended here in yet another winter count, falling from the lips of the stout woman who almost absently held the microphone, out into the still air of a trailer parked close to the chapel to which the few and torn Wounded Knee survivors had been carted to live or die: the weather on that two-week flight so severe the breaths of the humans and horses instantly froze on the blankets of the women and children; the recitation of the names of Big Foot's scouts; their interception at Porcupine Butte and their forced

275

encampment at Wounded Knee. "All during the night the people could hear the ammunition wagons arriving. All during the night the military was interrogating the men, trying to find out which ones had been at Little Bighorn. They could hear the soldiers drinking and the sounds of orders being given. At one point some of the soldiers came over to Big Foot's tent and asked him to come out and fight."

In the morning, the order came for the men to produce their guns. "They wanted to see if they were Henrys or other guns that had been taken at Little Bighorn." Black Coyote, the man generally associated with the first shot, "was deaf and couldn't understand the orders. He held his gun up and said, 'I have never turned this gun against any man, but I have used it to feed my family. And now I must give it up?'" In the struggle that ensued, "the gun discharged, but our people say Black Coyote's finger was never on the trigger, that both his hands were on the stock."

On the third day after the massacre, there was the burial of the people in a trench atop the hill. "The soldiers jumped up and down on the bodies so they could fit more into the trench. Some of the people buried there were still alive. There was a young man, who was sixteen or seventeen. He was wounded and frozen, and as he lay there he cried out. But they just threw him in. There were some babies still alive who were thrown in there."

When she had finished her cheeks were shining with tears. Even Looks Twice, who has been collecting oral versions of the massacre for KILI sat stunned by the force and content of her narrative, his recorder spooling on in silence. "To the *wasichus*," Marie Not Help Him said at length, "all this happened a long time ago. To the Lakota people this is still with us. We are still in mourning. I can still remember my great-grandfather holding me on his lap. I can still hear his voice telling me this and how hard his heart pounded when he would tell about the deaths of his family. I can feel his breath on my forehead, how it smelled of sage. It always reminded me of things growing."

IV

Pinky Iron Plume Clifford wanted me to understand that the ceremonies today (December 28) and tomorrow were not a matter of a few months' planning but had been pointed toward for four ritual years. A mixed-blood Oglala who had been serving as treasurer of the Wounded Knee Centennial Commission, she was coordinating last-minute details from her store a couple of miles from the massacre site which even now the Big Foot Memorial riders were approaching at the end of their two-week pilgrimage. In making the observances stretch over the symbolic four-year period the commission had clearly wanted to impress the people with the cultural significance of the event. But as Clifford and I drove over to the site so that she could see to the delivery of hay for the riders' horses, she remarked that not all the people were interested, and that even some of those who were disagreed about what the event signified and how it ought to be observed. Some felt the period of ritual mourning should not be ended because the American government still had not apologized for the massacre and had recently merely expressed a formal regret. Others objected to the presence of the (white) media at the ceremonies. And there was great disagreement about what ought to happen subsequently at the site, some believing it ought to be incorporated into the National Park System, others feeling the tribe itself ought to develop it as a tourist attraction, and still others feeling that the land simply as it is constitutes the best memorial. Even the very earth of the site itself (to which we had now arrived) was disputed, a plat of it looking like a nightmare of white-dominated history: here within a relatively restricted area of the reservation are tribally owned lands; allotted lands; deeded lands of three distinct varieties; and sections whose ownership has for years been a matter of legal dispute. So, whatever was planned for the future of the site was certain to raise historical antagonisms developed over the past century and more.

Yet in a way metaphorical of Lakota culture's peculiar and tenacious struggle for cultural survival against very great odds, the ceremonies of the 28th and 29th were held—and impressively so—though even the weather seemed to conspire against them. On this day it was minus three degrees at noon and dropping, with a stiff wind out of the northeast. Still, a brave gathering of vehicles was already at the site and more were arriving by the minute. A sullen sun made the snowy hills a steely gray, and the few grasses that poked through were a sickly yellow. The wind sent wraiths of snow across the road and spinning upwards in small clouds from the earth. Exhaust from tail pipes whipped away as if shot from gun barrels. Most of the gatherers waited in their vehicles, but on the hill a few people wrapped in blankets or parkas stamped about near the mass grave, beating their arms against their bodies. Below in the road tribal police cars flashed their lights and TV and movie cameras were set up and facing east, awaiting the arrival of the riders.

They appeared at 1:30, coming over a hill a mile off, a string of swiftly moving gray dots in the blowing snow. As they came down the road they coalesced into a dense dun cloud of riders, horses, and breath, while above them fluttered feathered lances and wind-shredded flags. They swept down the highway and then into the site itself, the horses snorting and clotted with rime, and made a great prayer circle in the midst of which stood four medicine men, including Zack Bear Shield who lived behind the hill and had been ritually feeding the spirits of the dead for more than twenty years. When the circle had been closed at last, then the riders' high tremolo cry went up into the snow-swirled skies, and the medicine men began the prayers that would enclose and sanctify an event in the people's history. If white America had forgotten Wounded Knee, and if even many of the Lakotas themselves had succumbed to the long pressure to put it behind them as "history"—that dead thing—it was clear that there were many others who remembered and who had seized upon the event as a way of reminding the people of who they were, where they came from.

When the prayers were finished and the medicine men had left the circle, the riders took their horses down behind the hill into the portable corrals as word made its muffled way through the watchers that because of the intense cold the ceremonies would be continued at the Wounded Knee District School down the road in Manderson. Here there were to be the testimonies of the riders who had retraced the dodges of Big Foot's people a hundred years ago when the country had been full of soldiers hunting them.

In the barnlike, high-ceilinged gym more than fifty of the riders stood about in front of the stage, still in their heavy range wear, their faces haggard, cheeks and noses ravaged by frost, eyes glazed with distance, fatigue, and something else the non-participants would never quite know. More than an hour into their testimonies I could still smell the cold emanating from their blankets, parkas, hoods, and chaps as if it had been the spirit of the old event itself that had permeated these people during the two wintry weeks they had spent in the emptiness of the north country, which now they had brought inside, but which no amount of forced heating could alleviate. Wounded Knee I was almost palpably present inside the brightly painted cinder block walls, a brooding, bleak, unappeasable presence, and I think even the *wasichu* journalists, their cameras and recorders flashing and whirring, shivered a bit under it.

Wounded Knee II was present also. When Ben Nighthorse Campbell, congressman from Colorado, addressed the audience, he remarked on the tremendous difference he saw between this event and one held in 1976 to commemorate the centennial of the Little Bighorn. Then, he said, law enforcement officials had been so nervous there might be an "uprising" on the battlefield grounds that "there were almost more marshals than there were Indians," and when Campbell and some others had returned from the field to their cars, they had found the feds taking license plate numbers. Quite a change, he said, referring to the Wounded Knee ceremonies, and as he was drawing the comparison my eyes were on a big, striking-looking man sitting in the bleachers, his braids wrapped in fur. A small circle of emptiness surrounded him as though he possessed a sort of negative *wakan* (power). He appeared not to be listening to the congressman's remarks, but whatever Russell Means was thinking about at that moment, there could be no question that he and his organization had been the major reason for the anxiety of those lawmen at the Little Bighorn in 1976. Before AIM there had been no Indian "uprisings" since the Ghost Dance, and just as the Ghost Dance had aroused white fears wildly incongruous with the actual nature of the phenomenon itself, so AIM had conjured up in our time the ghost of the armed savage on the warpath, and Means had been transmogrified into the avatar of Sitting Bull. If there were federal law enforcement officials here, they were very much undercover, and even the tribal police hung discreetly about the edges of the gathering, mingling there in a guardedly friendly fashion. *No one*, it was clear, wanted Wounded Knee IV, and in the long and still-smoldering aftermath of the takeover of 1973 everyone remained vividly aware of the possibilities.

When I had been here in the summer of 1973, the smoke was still in the air and Pine Ridge was a stunned and very dangerous place. It no longer had that feel to it, and yet the month previous when I had talked with people in Rapid City, and on the Pine Ridge, Rosebud, and Cheyenne River reservations about the upcoming centenary observances, virtually all of them had brought up Wounded Knee II. The comment of Victor Douville was typical. AIM, he said, was really a thing of the past, especially on the Lakota reservations, "but they certainly made everyone aware of what the conditions were here, and they instilled pride in the younger people. In this they did well, and as a piece of political advertising, I'll have to say it [the takeover] was a master stroke." Pinky Clifford told me that in the planning of these ceremonies there had been a determined effort to keep them from becoming a political platform for any group, and to an extent that effort seemed to have been successful. And yet Wounded Knee II was surely a presence here, and if it was not as much so as the massacre itself, still the character of these ceremonies seemed powerfully conditioned by the events of 1973. It was not only the remarks of Ben Nighthorse Campbell that reminded you of this, nor those of some of the riders who expressed hostility to the *wasichus* who had perpetrated the massacre and their successors who persistently misrepresented it. It was also—and more essentially—that Means, Dennis Banks, Clyde Bellecourt, and the others of AIM had brought the idea of the redress of historic grievances to the reservations, and it was likely here to stay. Wounded Knee III had been planned as a spiritual event, but no one could keep Wounded Knee II out of it. Means might be sitting by himself in the bleachers, but he was there, and everyone knew it. When the testimonies of the riders had been concluded, I sat down next to him at the feast of boiled buffalo and tripe.

This was easy enough to manage because at the long portable table just as in the bleachers there was space around him. At first, he took no notice of me, being then at work on an earnest, fuzzy-haired liberal out from the East Coast to hawk his new Indian magazine. The young man had asked Means for a literary contribution, and now Means was stating his conditions in terms the young man was trying hard to digest. When Means had finished, the editor was looking at a potentially serious boil in his budget. Then it was my turn, Means asking the nature of my errand. When I mentioned the name of the magazine that had sent me here, Means repeated it twice, giving it a vicious twist, then spooned up a mouthful of tripe and appeared to contemplate his next remark. I could see the young man across the table regarding me with what I took as a mixture of commiseration and relief.

"Well," Means finally said, "I guess we should be grateful any time the lordly white man takes notice of us." He turned back to the editor, asking if he had seen *Dances With Wolves*, which had recently been playing in Rapid City to around-the-block lines. Another illustration, Means was saying, of the white man's generous attentions. "I guess we should be happy to be portrayed as colorful primitives, as savages." But even he could no longer sustain his ironic tone. "An *abomination*!" he broke out, and then went into a detailed inventory of the film's faults.*

That evening as I stood in the crowd exiting the gym I saw him again, holding up an AIM T-shirt that was for sale, regarding it speculatively as if he had never seen such an item before. Behind me, also waiting to exit, two white girls in their late teens voiced disappointment at the way things had turned out, for they had wanted to sleep overnight in the gym and evidently weren't going to. "I thought," said one, "this was gonna be, you know, a real powwow where we'd all get together, in our sleeping bags, you know, and just kind of mellow out."

V

A century ago, when the firing at Wounded Knee finally ceased and the soldiers had left the field to the dead, the wounded, and the dying, there had been a brief hush before a blizzard swooped in, blanketing the victims and warping the bodies into the attitudes of the last, winking rigors. December 29, 1990, brought that storm forcefully to mind: at 8:00 A.M. it was a minus twenty-one in Gordon, Nebraska, where I had spent the night. In another of Dale Looks Twice's interviews Claudia Iron Hawk had said it was from Gordon that the whiskey seller had come out to service the troops the night before the massacre. Others, including Mari Sandoz, say the man was from Rushville. But it was surely in Gordon that the troubles began that culminated in the takeover of Wounded Knee in 1973, for here the winter before a Lakota named Raymond Yellow Thunder had been found dead, grotesquely propped up inside a truck in a used car lot. The authorities' casual dismissal of the matter had brought Russell Means and more than a thousand AIM people down into Gordon in the movement's first real show of force.

---

* Means himself has since become an actor in films.

This was in the back of my mind as I rode in the wrecker that was haul-ing my utterly frozen rental car to the Co-Op garage on Main Street. Foremost in my mind, of course, was whether these friendly, obliging mechanics could get the car thawed in time for me to make the Wiping of the Tears ceremony at the grave site, scheduled to begin in about an hour. They had said they would do their best, and in the unhealthy air of the garage I could see they were: blowers, ether injections, the works. As they went about this task they never asked what I was doing in their country, and after one of them went out, then returned from a service call, I was glad they hadn't. I overheard him telling his partners about that call: "He said to me, 'Hey, you guys are pretty randy. Are you this way with everyone?' So, I says to him, 'No, only with Indians.'"

I knew something of Gordon's Indian attitude, and as I watched this same man diligently trying to get me on the road again, I had occa-sion to recall a comment of Belva Hollow Horn's when I had talked with her about the centenary ceremonies. All the bordering towns, she claimed, were so hostile to Indians it was difficult to so much as go into them for gas and groceries. "Gordon, Alliance, Rushville, Chadron—they look at you like you're from outer space. There's so much fear and ignorance." She doubted any whites from those towns would come up for the ceremonies. "Probably," she said, "it'll just be the Indians and the media with maybe a few politicians thrown in." She had followed this with a laugh, but it was a laugh as bitter as today's weather.

Probably there was a goodly measure of that fear and ignorance inside this garage where American white men were helping a stranger who looked like themselves, and standing uselessly around, my hands in my pockets, I could let my mind range back to another day I had spent in Gordon, a hot, still Fourth of July years before. On that day, in com-pany with Caroline Sandoz Pifer, one of Mari Sandoz's sisters, I had encountered a big Lakota man at this very garage who had told me of a powwow being held that day up on the reservation. Afterward, I reminded Mrs. Pifer that on a Fourth of July a century before Red Cloud and fif-teen hundred of his men had ridden into the nearby town of Chadron for the festivities, and that her father—alone among the whites—had gone up into their encampment to spend the day with them. "Goodness me!" Mrs. Pifer had exclaimed. "If fifteen hundred Sioux were to show up in Chadron now, they'd scare every white clear out of the country!"

An hour later, riding the empty roads north toward the ceremonies thirty miles distant, I had to wonder how much really had changed in the intervening century since the whites in this country had hollered for the military to stop the Ghost Dancers. And I was still mulling this over when I arrived at the massacre site to find the ceremonies just beginning. My mechanic friends in Gordon had indeed done their best.

The crowd at the grave site was much smaller than that which had greeted the returning Big Foot riders the day before. Mingling with the huddled group, I learned that some descendants of the victims had objected to the public nature of the occasion and so had arranged for the medicine men to conduct the end-of mourning ritual privately. Those who had elected to participate in this public version were now being escorted by the medicine men from the small Catholic church atop the hill to the trench the white gravediggers had hacked out of the frozen earth after the blizzard had cleared and into which their relations had been so unceremoniously dumped. Though some whites continue to dispute the Lakotas' oral version of the brutal details of the burial, photographic evidence shows too plainly the stripped and looted bodies stacked like cordwood at the trench and also the proudly posed figures of the gravediggers. Black, bent figures against the gray and white of the sky and snow, the descendants now moved singly to the trench, left ritual offerings, and departed slowly, their vehicles trundling down the hill in little clouds of exhaust and snow, taillights winking. Behind, on the hilltop, observers and media people hopped painfully about, waiting for deliverance. Means was there, fur-capped and mufflered to his flashing black eyes. "This is nothing to us," he said to no one in particular, referring to the weather. "We're used to this."

Inside the cab of a truck parked in front of the church an official spoke into a microphone looped through a partly opened window, announcing that again the ceremonies would be adjourned to the gym. He said there would be a recounting of the history of the event, followed by a reading of the names of those who had died here. The governor would be there to speak of reconciliation, though Senator Inouye would not be present, as had been advertised. And then, he said, there would be another feast to which all were welcome.

When the church doors were clapped closed and the last herd of cars and pickups had filed down onto the road to Manderson, there were left only a five-person French film crew and myself. The crew was debating its next move: there were other ceremonial events scheduled this afternoon at Kyle and Pine Ridge, and so which to cover? Inside the chain-link fence that guards the grave the plates of food left in offering to the spirits had already hardened like death itself, and the garlands of plastic flowers vibrated stiffly in the wind on their wire stems. The creek flats below that yesterday had been filled by the riders had been smoothed by the blowing snow. Beyond them lay the ravine, and beyond that the dark, naked forms of the trees along Wounded Knee Creek. It was simply too cold to stand there any longer, meditating on the Ghost Dancers, on the frozen body of Big Foot who, with his twisted, upraised hands, had seemed to be struggling to ask one final question. But I had that image for company late that evening as I headed through the bitter blackness of the Badlands, back toward Rapid City and American civilization.

Visions of the Pacific

I

A few months short of my forty-third birthday I finally saw the Pacific. Clearing the southerly jumble of San Francisco—Daly City, the airport, and all—my wife and I in our rented car curved west toward a still unseen coast. And suddenly, coming out from behind a high headland, there it lay, a grand glittering disc. Our view from above took in so much that I thought I could truly discern the beginnings of the globe's curve where sea met sky like the edge of a scimitar.

Flying west the day previous, I had been hoping to see the continent's end as I passed above the flat, rectilinear stretches of the midlands; the ever-bigger rivers choked in March with brown chunks of spring-loosened ice; the gradual rise of the land westward through snow-flecked tablelands and mesas; and then, at last, the mountains, high, white, solemn. I had hoped that light would last into California and show me with its sharpened, dying rays that golden sea. But somewhere in Nevada the last of the light went in an amethyst haze, leaving me still unfulfilled of that sight.

Oh, I had seen oceans before. Midwestern though I am by birth, I had for years known the American Atlantic. I had come to know, too, the hot green of the Gulf. Once I bobbed effortlessly in an Aegean swell as another sunset made Poseidon's temple at Soúnion radiant, and Byron's name, scratched into a column, grew black in final definition. A small fishing boat with red sails stood off, its men shaking their hands at me to warn of sharks.

But still I had no Pacific to me, and so my Americanness seemed privately incomplete. I was still back in the 1840s, before we had become a Pacific as well as an Atlantic nation. Now, in this very morning moment, I caught up with history.

Immediately my thoughts went to Steinbeck, whose *Red Pony* had defined California for me ever since I read it in late childhood. In

285

particular I thought of the old grandfather of "The Leader of the People," who tells the wondering boy Jody of a line of old men along the Pacific shore, hating the sea because it had stopped them, put a halt to that big, crawling beast that had purely followed instinct in going ever westward until there was no west left. If then I pondered the curiousness of this phenomenon—of men hating the Pacific because it stopped their restlessness, made them sink roots—I don't remember; all I remember is the image itself. I was young enough at the time to skip over the implications here and fasten on an actual line of black-clad old men along a shore that looked very much like my Lake Michigan's, their faces set, furious, reddened like the violent flesh tones in the illustrations to the volumes of *Book Trails*, my first significant books. Through subsequent years other California images had been superimposed—blondes, beach boys, the Rose Bowl—but beneath these there yet resided that primitive one of the old men and the sea. Especially the sea, implacable as Steinbeck had suggested it, inattentive to history and human strivings. And so, seeing it now, I saw again Grandfather and the black-and-red men, balked at its frothy verge.

But as the highway accommodatingly kept company with the shoreline, other images intruded. Like an archaeologist of memory, I now saw beyond Steinbeck to the California excavations of recent years, digs that went down, not for gold, but for bones, artifacts, ashes, that sedimentary speech that, enunciating an old mortality, announces our own. Here was a view of this land and sea that had nothing fundamentally to do with Steinbeck's story of the westering, however personally compelling this remained. Thousands of years before the long advance over the terrain I'd just flown across, men came up out of the Pacific in long rattan or reed crafts, oared, sailed, guided by their instincts too, but in this instance to go eastward toward the rising sun. Asians, Phoenicians, Polynesians in their turn came here on scarcely imaginable errands, the light ever before them, beckoning, the shadows behind them, arrowlike in their wakes.

Of their crafts no single bit survives. Perishable like the crews who manned them, they have disappeared, and we cannot anywhere dig so deep as to exhume a prow of ancient intention, discover forgotten design: no Sutton Hoo awaits us along these shores. But some stone anchors have been found, and a few fragmentary Chinese manuscripts exist to tell of that ancient reality, in light of which Steinbeck's old men ranged along the shore seem boys indeed.

Nor did even these musings take me far enough. For there were those on these Pacific shores who could have watched the gradual bobbing advance of the argonauts in their reed boats. Wanting to style ourselves "discoverers," first here and first surely to assess the meaning of here, of where here was, we refused to countenance the antiquity of the native presence in the New World. Black-clad and red with the mistakes of the Old World, we were for many years in an old enslavement to one version of history. We were stuck on the figure of twelve thousand years ago as the earliest date for humans in the New World: this was our flattened vision of history, beyond which it seemed imprudent and even dangerous to go, as if we too were sailors in Colón's crew, frightened by seas of wider speculation. Then we thought larger, thought twenty thousand—a barrier broken by carbon 14. Now an understanding of the phenomenon of racemization—the steady, inexorable breakdown of amino acids in bone—says seventy thousand, or more. In this yawning perspective the strange new expanse that greeted the restless eyes of the whites looks more like an old highway, long known in its tides and trades by dark precursors of whom the garrulous old Grandfather knew nothing.

But then, of course, Steinbeck wasn't writing a history text; he was writing a story about what it felt like to have made that perilous passage, to have come out of the last deserts, down out of the blue air of the Sierra, through the foothills, and into the broad and fecund green of the Sacramento and San Joaquin valleys, beyond which lay the end of the enterprise. And this is what the tale's Grandfather has in mind as well: not history, a dry recital of the facts of westering, but what it felt like to have done it. "I tell those old stories," he says to Jody, "but they're not what I want to tell. I only know how I want people to feel when I tell them."

In this sense, it makes no real difference what the history of California's Pacific is. The British historian Maitland was right when he observed that the essential matter of history was not what happened but what people thought and said about it. This is why the Pacific coast is littered with the name Balboa, for in the Western white imagination, anyway, the Pacific means Balboa, the discoverer.

287

So it was him I thought of last and longest as we continued southward toward destinations bearing names the Spaniards bestowed upon all this newness, the sun swinging out from the land, arcing westward over the waves toward Cipangu and Cathay, as bright with its old promise as when Balboa beheld it shining on the billowy green expanse he saw from a jungle hilltop.

II

Peter Martyr, that gossipy guy who hung around the royal court and talked with many involved in Spain's New World enterprises, said Balboa was a fencing master born on the Portuguese border at Jerez de los Caballos. He was tall and well knit, Martyr said, and possessed of a steady disposition. Martyr didn't say whether he had imagination, but events show plainly that he did—a fatal gift, in his case. He was one of that number pulled overseas by the wake of Colón's 1498 landfall at Paria, where the admiral finally encountered evidence—monkeys, deer, pearls—appearing to speak plainly of those Eastern kingdoms so long sought. And so when Colón returned with these exotic items, there was a rush. Gentlemen with neither training nor aptitude nor any understanding of the lands and stakes involved obtained licenses from the crown to go out and return rich. Don Roderigo de Bastidas, a wealthy notary from Triana, obtained such a license, his patent authorizing him to bring back precious metals and gems, slaves, mixed-breeds, monsters, serpents, spices, and drugs. Vasco Núñez de Balboa shipped with him and in 1501 saw the eastern portion of the Panamanian isthmus, before the ships, peppered by the borings of shipworms, turned back to the outpost of Haiti. Bastidas went back to Spain, apparently with enough riches and adventures to fill out the rest of life. Balboa, yet unfulfilled of either, stayed on.

For seven years we hear nothing of him. The island was a pestilential place now—dying Indian slaves, dying Spaniards, dwindling resources and prospects, the mines nearly dead, too. Occasional *entradas* into the island's heart resulted in no new treasure finds, no kingdoms, only the continued savaging of the natives. On Haiti now there was a line of haters along the once-golden shore, hating the land they stood on, hating the sea that divided them from home, from the Indies, from anywhere else but where they were.

In 1509, Alonso de Ojeda, a seasoned if cruel and imprudent conquistador, and Diego de Nicuesa got licenses to explore and colonize the lands from the north coast of present-day Colombia up through what are now Panama, Costa Rica, and Nicaragua. Ojeda went out from Haiti in November; Nicuesa following with reinforcements a few days later. Balboa, bored, sunk hopelessly in debt, gloomily watched them spread their sails for adventure. He had wished to go too, but a colonial law wisely prohibited debtors from leaving on such expeditions without having made settlement with their creditors, and Balboa could make no such arrangement. So, he was apparently doomed to wear out more time on Haiti.

A few days later, the lawyer Martín Fernando de Enciso, Ojeda's second in command, pulled out with more men and supplies. When the ship was well out to sea, Balboa, the absconding defalcator, suddenly emerged from a barrel where he had been stowed by a friend. Standing on the canting deck, blinking in the tropic light, the hero entered the history of the New World. He had with him only his sword and his fierce dog, Leoncillo. The lawyer was furious, fearing he would be held accountable for Balboa's debts. But there was nothing to be done now, and soon enough, as laws, customs, and most of civilization's stays fell apart, rotten, under the relentless pressure of the unfeatured jungles, there would be many in the company who would thank God that there had been nothing to do with Balboa but keep him.

From the first the expedition was a fatal bungle. At the future site of Cartagena, Ojeda foolishly provoked the wrath of the natives and so lost seventy men, including the famed pilot Juan de la Cosa: in an omen of the entire venture, a party searching for survivors of this clash came upon Cosa tied to a tree, his body aquiver with arrows, raving on toward a poisonous death—a destination plotted for him since first he shipped for the unknown with Colón in 1492. Ojeda himself was badly wounded as well, and survived only because he commanded his surgeon (under pain of death) to cauterize his wound with two red-hot iron plates.

In such a state, already battered and fearful, the company arrived on the eastern shore of the Gulf of Urabá, where the chastened Ojeda established a tiny outpost he called San Sebastián after that arrow-martyred saint whose protection he now devoutly sought. A few months later, Enciso yet to arrive with much-needed relief, and prospects at San Sebastián becoming bleaker by the day, Ojeda gave up and went back to Haiti, broken by his encounter with the wilderness of the New World. There he took holy orders and died a monk in the order of St. Francis.

A tough, limited man was left in charge of the wretched outpost, but, though limited, Francisco Pizarro had what it took to keep things together until the terrifically tardy Enciso finally arrived, running his ship into a shoal reef as he did so and busting it to flinders. Taking rapid survey of the condition of his command, the lawyer saw clearly that he was not equal to this: the country bristling with jungle and swamps, unknown more than a hundred paces beyond the festering clearing; the natives armed and filled with venom against the invaders; and the men themselves—what few were left—reduced to eating roots and palm buds, fearful, mutinous. "Let us," so an old chronicle quotes one of the crew, "leave these deadly shores, where the sea, the land, the heavens, and men repulse us." They would not be likely to take orders from a man of law. Only Balboa could fully function here.

Where others lapsed into sweaty sickness, their quilted stuffs stained with fever, or squatted in the bush, helpless in yellow disease; sat listless as demasted vessels or fell into hopeless plottings; Balboa alone, singular, saw into possibilities, saw beyond these sorry beginnings, the muddy little clearing with its leaky huts, pathetic mockup of Spain's hierarchical order. The man had an itch, and this hot wilderness, limitless in potential for him, inflamed it. He plunged to his work now, taking charge of the expedition, by common consent the ablest man among them.

He informed Enciso that he had been to the westward shore of the gulf and that there the natives did not use poisoned arrows. So the company loaded their remnant stores into two brigantines, crossed to the western shore (still westering), and there, under the leadership of the ex-stowaway, successfully attacked a native village. Pursuing its fleeing inhabitants upriver, the Spaniards stumbled across a cache of gold: anklets, coronets, bracelets in the amount of ten thousand *castellanos* (which Washington Irving later computed to be $53,259). The new outpost they established was christened Nuestra Señora de la Antigua del Darién in accordance with a vow of Enciso's; but everybody called it simply Darién. So began the white march to the Pacific.

Within a few months the strong man had eliminated the last of his local opposition, had deported the ineffectual Enciso, and had himself proclaimed *alcalde* (mayor) of Darién. Vision, it is said, is the sure knowledge of what to do next, and whatever may be said of the quality of Balboa's vision—ruthless, vainglorious—he had it: knew the proper proportions of conquest here, the conciliatory gestures, the obdurate cruelty, the divisive alliances that rendered inconsequential the numerical superiority of neighboring tribes. He was not a man of many words (they came haltingly to him when he had to engage in formal discourse, as his letters to Ferdinand show), but a force armed with a vision of something beyond where he now found himself, a future kingdom to conquer, a city to find and sack, and, above all, those golden gables of the Far East to claim. With a special certainty he began the penetration of the isthmus to what he may already have suspected, or at least hoped, lay on its southern side. And always, the savage Leoncillo ranged along with him, drawing an archer's pay for its work against native adversaries.

It was after he had bullied a chieftain named Comogre into an alliance that the way to the other side and its hidden sea was cleared. Comogre's son, aghast at the cupidity of the invaders, bitingly remarked that if gold was the stuff for which they had forsaken all—homes, families, country—there was another sea to the south, and beside it a kingdom of fabulous wealth with more gold than even such as they could ever use. The description of what would prove to be the Pacific and, in time, the kingdom of the Incas (though that would be Pizarro's story, not Balboa's) was greeted with unrestrained joy, some of the blackened adventurers even weeping at the prospect of such plunder.

Speedily the company returned to Darién, where Balboa set about preparing for the march south. They left on September 1, 1513, a party of 190 Spaniards and 800 Indians, their way smoothed at first by Balboa's previous intimidation of the nearer tribes. But as they went farther into the unknown they began to encounter those who had not heard of the invincibility of the whites and so opposed them—particularly warriors owing allegiance to one Quarequa who put up a fierce resistance, losing six hundred of their number. Of this, the last major engagement on the march to the Pacific, it was said that some of these warriors fought in the battle dress of women and "shared the same passion." These men were subsequently thrown to the dogs, led by Leoncillo, who

291

tore them to pieces under the watchful eyes of Christians acting under authority of the Laws of Burgos, which specified the execution of sodomites. Later, the Flemish engraver Theodore de Bry depicted this scene, Balboa, center, in elegant dress, coolly pointing out the intricacies of the operation while in the foreground the dogs rend and tear the almost naked bodies.

On the twenty-fifth of the month, Balboa was told by one of his guides that the sea could be glimpsed from a nearby summit. Accompanied only by the dog, as if no other was so fit to share the moment with him, he scaled the slope and stood at last, "Silent, upon a peak in Darien"— the poet's conflation of him with "stout Cortez" a brilliant mistake. Looking down through the dense tangle he saw it. Had he been atten- tive to the whole moment, as probably he was not, he might have heard behind him the heavy suspiration of his native bearers and his cursing comrades, toiling upward together. Many of the Europeans had shipped for no better reasons than had their leader, but probably none was so alive to the potential of this moment as the man who now stood, perhaps in pose, on the summit as the others struggled up around him, crying, "The sea! The sea!" And it is this moment, of course, that is commemorated in history and in those dozens of "Balboas" that dot California's shores.

Four days thereafter, having encountered local obstacles—pathless jungle, steep slopes, natives—the company arrived at the sea's edge about the hour of vespers, and Balboa, in helmet and breastplate, a drawn sword in one hand and the Spanish flag in the other, waded into the mild surge and took formal possession.

III

There can be a quality to a seaside morning that is like no other, soft, dreaming, circumambient. Waking up into it, you become aware that in sleep a sort of serene privacy has included you, and you are blessed for the day. At Santa Cruz, where we stopped on the Pacific, there was such a quality to this morning as I sat on the glassed-in porch of a seaside cot- tage, scratching words about Balboa across the rough fiber of notebook pages. The smoke of morning coffee lifted into the profoundly silent air, and at the end of the gently sloping street I could see morning standing out on the Pacific, pearly gray and touched with the faintest underblush of pink.

Like the old conquistador who had to endure an interval between his first view of the Pacific and his actual contact with it, I had yet to touch it. I had seen sunset flame out across its hushed waves, had seen it turn to ink as the first stars spangled, and now, still dry and sandless, I put down my pen and sauntered down to the sea.

Already a few young mothers with children had spread their gear on the small beach that lay behind a stone jetty, but the town's college kids, whose missions kept them abroad far into the night, were not yet in evidence. I cast off my sandals and stepped to the water's edge, where a small boy played with two toy boats—one a tug, the other a stately seagoing craft with canvas sails. Launching his caravel, he saw it quickly capsized by the merest wavelet, its sails suddenly sodden and lank. But the tug bobbed like a barrel, righting itself after each roll, its enamel paint brightened again and again. Wading past him then, I heard the brine's hiss about my knees, saw the green swell coming up about me. The clouds in the distance were like sails. I stretched my arms out over the water, taking my own sort of possession, thinking as I did so not only of that old and vain action, but also of the meanings of "possession," which include the act of possessing and also the state of being possessed: to be held, swept up, enrapt, as now I was by this sea. Musing there in this mild embrace—the boy, his boats, the beach, all held before me as I turned back—I wondered again what it was in "The Leader of the People" that had so taken me those many years ago: whether I had even so early responded to a hidden threnodic note in the fiction; whether at the time I first read it I sensed that it was really about the failure to real-ize paradise, the grand newness of everything here proving unequal to men's baseless dreams, the whole of the New World forfeit to the lust for the Ever Elsewhere. Or was this rather a superimposition of later thoughts, as the older man is compelled by his own tides to revise the boy he once was?

Whatever the case, that threnodic note is there for me now in Steinbeck's story. It stands out plainly. And if it is not the story's major theme, neither does it seem hidden, a minor strain.

In this context it seems arguable that threnody or the elegiac is the dominant tone of our literature. If the story of the formative white encounters with the New World is the story of tragic disillusionment, and the singular discoverers—Colón, Balboa, Cortés, Dalfinger, Raleigh, La Salle—tragic heroes flawed by their inability to become possessed by the lands they claimed, then it might seem now inevitable that our literature would somehow express this. To me, it does so.

Of course, there are literary monuments that clearly do not and are just as clearly in the American grain. Franklin's autobiography, Crèvecoeur, and the early Whitman come quickest to mind; Poe, Dickinson, James, Hemingway, do not seem in the American elegiac mode. Nor do the prominent writers (many of them ethnic) of the years since World War II, as if that event and its conclusion had sealed off the past and its themes forever. But then, think of how many of our great, seminal works and writers do express the elegiac mode, beginning with Governor Bradford's *Of Plymouth Plantation* and its celebrated description of New England's wall of winter woods, the soul of that bleak, featureless wilderness that seemed the very antithesis of human hope. Cooper's Leatherstocking stories; Hawthorne's tales and romances of innocence and paradise lost; Melville's South Sea romances; Emerson (that desperate optimist), calling two centuries after the fact of first encounter for Americans to develop an original relationship with their lands; Thoreau; the post–Civil War Whitman; Parkman; Twain's great idyll of a boy's escape back into the wild heart of New World nature—and the failure of that escape; *The Great Gatsby*; *In the American Grain*; *U.S.A.*; *The Grapes of Wrath*. Even in the years since World War II the elegiac mode has occasionally surfaced once again, and when it has, the result is often a work of a peculiar, haunting resonance: *Henderson the Rain King*, *At Play in the Fields of the Lord*, *Little Big Man*, much of Mailer, Roethke's "North American Sequence," even the film *Alice's Restaurant*. And all this is not to mention (more than passingly) the elegiac mode of some of the most arresting works of the Latin American literature of our time, as in Carlos Fuentes's *Terra Nostra*, Neruda, and Gabriel García Márquez.

There is something brooding, somber here: the memory of bright hopes dashed by first encounters with magnificent lands and seascapes, of a paradise poisoned by dreams saved from a fantastic pettiness only by their size and tragic consequences, of death and utter disappointment, of blighted seaboards and blasted rain forests, of entire native cultures, fragile as feathers, that disappeared. Traveling the jungles of

South America, passing the hopeless little outposts of civilization staffed by characters out of Conrad, Claude Lévi-Strauss wrote that "our adventurings into the heart of the New World have a lesson to teach us: that the New World was not ours to destroy, and yet we destroyed it; and that no other will be vouchsafed to us." That is the burden of our New World history and our literature, the beginnings of which are to be found in Seville, in the Archives of the Indies; in those bundles of manuscripts, the frozen, still-burning records of what was done here, of the ends of enterprise, of caciques and conquistadores, of the threatening wilderness that lay all around. Seizing Balboa's bundle, we think to lay hands on the story of a great discovery and find instead an all but unutterable blackness within. ...

IV

When first he heard of the Pacific, no less than when he first beheld it, the thought of the East's fabled treasure houses blazed in Balboa's head. So when he and his company arrived on the Pacific's shores and a native chieftain described the domesticated animal of the rumored kingdom somewhere over the water to the southeast, molding its likeness in the shore's wet clay, Balboa saw a dromedary, there being yet no way for him to imagine a llama. And at that moment, precursors to Steinbeck's old men, there came to be a line of men on the Pacific hating it because it stopped them.

And they would continue to hate it for the maddening weeks that stretched out, end to end, into months and even years. Ferdinand, although he had appointed Balboa *adelantado* (governor) of the "South Sea," had placed him under the command of a new provincial governor sent out in 1514, Pedro Arias de Avila (Pedrarias). Thus Balboa was rendered powerless to enact his vision of the new water as a highway eastward while the vicious old Pedrarias fumbled and stewed at his command post of Acla.

Pedrarias was in truth the very embodiment of that fierce negativity the Old World brought to its discovery of the New. The man carried a coffin with him on his travels, had it installed in his quarters. In a long career in foreign places, he spread death about him as though that coffin contained a fatal pestilence that he would loose first on Africans and now on Indians. No sooner had he established his command at Acla than he ordered such insanely cruel attacks on the natives of the isthmus that shortly the flimsy truces managed by Balboa were all undone, and it was hazardous for whites to travel anywhere beyond their outposts. Nor was life within these outstations much more bearable. At Acla and at Darién, ragged beggars crowded the lanes and squares. Unburied bodies sprawled swollen in ditches and in mass graves never closed because they were constantly in use. Hidalgos and men-at-arms hung about in irritable idleness, itching to go for gold. And the roads leading out of these places were lined with rows of severed native heads, gaping, shriveled, sightless on pike points, the work of Pedrarias's cousin, Gaspar de Morales, who imagined that such things might prove good and continuing examples to enemies.

At last the old man, sick, torn between his growing fear of the terrible place he had made this and the mounting evidence of wealth to be had from the lands of the South Seas, commanded Balboa to transport materials for brigantines overland from Acla to the sea and there construct the ships. He would sail those sweet waters to the Pearl Islands and perhaps from there to the empire of the great Khan himself: who could say how small a stretch of sea divided the Spaniards from their goal?

Balboa, competent as ever, even under so rash a commander, accomplished the transport of the materials (no small matter) and built the ships, though in the process most of his native laborers died. Alas, the shipworms had been at the new vessels the while, and on a trial voyage to the nearest of the Pearl Islands, their hulls like honeycombs, they sank into the opalescent waters: nails, screws, rigging, all lost. It all had to be done over, and Balboa did it, finishing in October 1518.

Why, then, does he linger down there for two months and more, the contract fulfilled, the ships apparently seaworthy? Why does he not return to his commander at Acla? Rumor comes up from the south shore, traveling those very paths Balboa had blazed, telling Pedrarias that his man is preparing to desert the poisoned outpost and sail for the East, leaving history and its consequences behind and heading prowlike into the ahistory of the future.

The wily old death-bringer accepts the rumor's truth, sends back a suave message to Balboa, politely requesting his return to Acla where they will discuss details of that South Sea voyage they are to make together. Meanwhile, he dispatches Francisco Pizarro and a heavily armed detail southward across the isthmus to intercept Balboa on his return journey or else apprehend him on the southern shore.

Now there is a fatal lapse in Balboa's thinking, the grand vision lacking a certain critical attention to detail. Or is it, as he would soon claim, that he is innocent of the traitorous charge, and meant no mutiny? Whatever the case, he turns back toward Acla, obedient to the summons—and is shortly met by Pizarro, that ruthless, one-dimensional figure, who takes him prisoner without ceremony.

Back they go, Balboa clanking in irons, away from the sea, the beach, fair breezes, waiting ships, away from light and vision, along paths already a bit overgrown as if in league with worms against all such paltry human designs: to the rotten little town with its huts, its sickness, its yet unhatched plots. And there in the village square Balboa's vision is summarily terminated. Along with his alleged coconspirators, whom Balboa had caused to see themselves wrapped in strange silks (doubtless the only genuine vision they had ever had), Balboa is executed. In the streaming tropic gloom, while the condemned beg for mercy, or swear their innocence and undying allegiance, calling on the Virgin, and even Pedrarias's executioner whimpers a bit in the fading light, the sudden enormity of his task weighing on him like Conscience itself, Balboa's head is toppled, weightless, from his shoulders, rolls briefly in the jungle mud, the eyes blinking once or twice like one who is startled. Inside a near hut, waiting for this end, Pedrarias nurses his unabated terrors and a running ulcer on his scrotum.

To the south, under patient skies and punctual, unrecking tides, the brigantines of Balboa swing emptily at anchor, their hulls still innocent of the deep waters of what one day will be known as Balboa's Pacific.

Western Americana
from Fulcrum Publishing

Land Circle
Writings Collected from the Land

Linda Hasselstrom
ISBN 1-55591-082-3, 5^{1}/$_{2}$ x 8^{1}/$_{2}$, 372 pages, HC $12.95

"This is one of the best books I have read"
—*John Murray,* The Bloomsbury Review

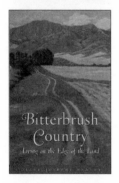

Bitterbrush Country
Living on the Edge of the Land

Diane Josephy Peavey
ISBN 1-55591-293-1, 5^{3}/$_{4}$ x 8^{3}/$_{4}$, 256 pages, HC $22.95

" ... Lucid and charming, full of the stillness and exuberance of the country ... "
—*Gretel Ehrlich, author of* The Solace of Open Spaces

Growing Up True
Lessons from a Western Boyhood

Craig S. Barnes
ISBN 1-55591-350-4, 5^{1}/$_{2}$ x 8, 248 pages, HC $22.95

"Simple yet beautiful." —5280 Magazine

Fulcrum Publishing
16100 Table Mountain Parkway, Suite 300, Golden, CO 80403
To order call 800-992-2908 or visit www.fulcrum-books.com
Also available at your local bookstore.